AFRICAN SAINTS

SAINTS, MARTYRS, AND HOLY PEOPLE FROM THE CONTINENT OF AFRICA

FREDERICK QUINN

A Crossroad Book
The Crossroad Publishing Company
New York

The Crossroad Publishing Company
481 Eighth Avenue, Suite 1550
New York, NY 10001

Printed in the United States of America

Library of Congress Cataloging-in-Publication Data

Quinn, Frederick.
   African saints : saints, martyrs, and holy people from the continent of Africa / by Frederick Quinn.
     p. cm.
   Includes bibliographical references.
   ISBN 0-8245-1971-X (alk. paper)
   1. Religious biography – Africa. I. Title.
BL2400 .Q56 2001
200'.92'26 – dc21

                                     2001006185

1 2 3 4 5 6 7 8 9 10   10 09 08 07 08 05 04 03 02

For
Nathan D. Baxter

"The saints of God speak the same language"
Awliyo Alla iyadda is af taqaan

— Somali proverb

CONTENTS

INTRODUCTION

From Greenland's icy mountains, From India's coral strand
Where Afric's sunny fountains Roll down their golden sand,
From many an ancient river, From many a palmy plain,
They call us to deliver Their lands from error's chain.[1]

Do you remember the map on the spread of Christianity in the Sunday school room of the church where you grew up? Where Christian lands were colored a triumphant red, framed with a strong black border? Outside were the less attractive, sandy-brown colored Islamic countries, and toward the north, dark blue spaces indicated where Huns and Goths lay in wait, ready to cause trouble.

Thick dotted lines led from Jerusalem along the Mediterranean coast to Rome. Jerusalem–Rome was the key connection, the map told us, the New York–Washington or Los Angeles–San Francisco axis of its time. Lesser trails frittered off northward to what became Russia and Northern Europe. At the map's lower extremity was North Africa, largely barren spaces with a few palm trees, camels, and oases. Cartographers then and now did not operate independently of the teachers, pastors, and scholars who told them what to include in the maps.

Sunday school handouts went with the maps of an earlier age, profiling missionaries who looked like stern sixth-grade math teachers or grim school principals. Postcards depicted White Fathers with long beards and pith helmets standing next to rickety bicycles after visiting the grateful inhabitants of thatched huts. (Those of us who owned bicycles wondered how missionaries made it through jungles on such frail two-wheelers.) Protestants in heavy black suits gestured to rows of attentive children who sat on wooden benches in churches whose features vaguely suggested a Methodist church back home. And always the missionaries triumphed; some shot lions, while others converted natives (the outward mark of conversion was wearing Western dress).

The spirit of the times was reflected in a popular French school text *l'Histoire de France* by Lavisse, which contained a section about "a school in Algeria." The book resembled the missionary news

1

then proliferating in Europe and America about Africa. In this case students read:

> Among the pupils, you see some dressed like you. Those are the little French. The others wear a white *burnous*. Those are the little Arabs. The teachers are French. They teach the little French and the little Arabs what you learn in school. The Arabs are good little students. They learn as much as the little French. They also do good homework. France wants the little Arabs to be as well instructed as the little French. That proves that our France is good and generous for the people who submit to her.[2]

A half-century later, a radical reorientation of Western perspectives about Africa is required. Church growth in Africa is astronomical. The continent's population may be 770 million persons, of whom 350 million are Christians, including 175 million Roman Catholics; there are 320 million Muslims. A century ago, the number of Christians might have been 4 million, increasing to 75 million by 1965.[3] Assume you are the mapmaker and leaflet editor today. How do you display the new African religious mosaic on a map? Territories inhabited primarily by Christians are scattered about the continent, as in southern Sudan or southern Chad. Islamic republics, like Mauritania, Libya, and Algeria, exist as well. Great urban centers display the range of Catholic, Protestant, and independent churches — mosques, cathedrals, prophets, faith healers, diviners, and herbalists all operating in the same neighborhoods.

Sunday school profiles today would include Mercy Amba Oduyoye, a leading Ghanaian woman theologian, in place of David Livingstone in shirt sleeves at the head of a team of oxen. Steve Biko, clubbed to death in a South African jail, would command the interest Albert Schweitzer once held. Blessed Cyprian Tansi, a Nigerian contemplative monk, would be better known than Cardinal Lavigerie, founder of the White Fathers. St. Josephine Bakhita, who went from a Sudanese slave market to sainthood in an Italian convent, and Desmond Tutu, a courageous opponent of apartheid in South Africa, would be featured. Figures of an earlier era attract attention as well, such as Simon Kimbangu and Dona Beatriz of the Congo, William Wade Harris of the Ivory Coast, the Martyrs of Uganda, Augustine, and the Desert Mothers and Fathers. The problem for the compiler of an anthology like this one is not finding names to include, but limiting their numbers.

Parenthetically, I have not limited the names included in this book only to Africans, but have added Europeans and Americans. Some, like Cardinal Lavigerie and David Livingstone, represent the approaches to mission of a vanished era. Others, like Henry Venn, never left England, yet exercised a major influence on mission policy and practice. Why include them? Because they made an important contribution to the advancement of the church in their time and in their way. What I have sought most of all was to present a variety of representative Christian figures, to which Muslim, Jewish, and traditional religious practitioners were added. Coming from all parts of Africa, they represent a faithful witness in trying circumstances. It would be easy to double their numbers, and this compilation and the sources suggested can open doors to the thoughtful reader wishing to probe the amazingly diverse range of spirituality in Africa.

•

It is a new Africa we are looking at, one in which most churches are self-governing, with their own distinct liturgies, music, and preaching styles. African voices are heard increasingly in the parliament of the world's religions. It is also an Africa where the intrinsic worth of many values, such as loyalty to an extended family and respect for creation, are affirmed. Negative practices, including female genital mutilation, the subjugation of women, the health and educational plight of children, political corruption, and the abysmal human rights records of many independent African governments are questions religious bodies must confront daily.

And there is the mixed heritage of Western missions to weigh. Of course they brought the Gospel, and with it literacy, medicine, agriculture, and other good works. But at a price. Often the transmission was a one-way affair, with little attention to indigenous beliefs, even though many of these beliefs were highly compatible with Christian ideas. For example, so-called ancestor worship is akin to the Christian notion of the Communion of Saints. In other instances, raising up native pastors and bishops was a slow task, not fully realized until after a century of missionary contact. The matter of relations with another great world religion, Islam, remains to be sorted out. Two fast-growing faith traditions, religions with deep mystical piety and strong African roots, are often on a collision course rather than making common cause. Need that be the case?

Another problem was the insensitivity of missionaries to indigenous Christian churches evolving around them. This resulted in the religious energies of Africans being turned toward the formation of over ten thousand independent churches, claiming over thirty-four million members. Such churches adopted names that were an amalgam of the names of established churches, vestments that blend different liturgical traditions in a colorful manner, the use of titles like "patriarch" and "prophet" for church leaders, and the centrality of ministers as healers, ecstatic prophets, interpreters of dreams, and charismatic leaders of local congregations. As is the case with such independent congregations anywhere, the question of succession looms large, promoting splits and syncretism of doctrine and practice.

•

Conventional wisdom tied the spread of Christianity in Africa to Western missionary-driven initiatives. But church growth was always the result of African Christians converting other Africans, and the exponential spread of the church in Africa came in the post-independence era, when a generation of missionaries either died out or went home. "African church history isn't the same as missionary history; missionaries hardly show up in it," Andrew Walls, formerly director of the University of Edinburgh's Center for the Study of Christianity in the Non-Western World, has observed.[4]

Its transmitters include freed slaves from America returning home to West Africa, where they moved, first along the coast, then inland in search of their home communities or places to settle. Often the slaves, in an era before recorded tapes and television, had memorized Scriptures told them by other Africans and hymns that they translated into local languages. A few carried symbols, such as crucifixes or rosaries, or a Bible for the handful who could read. Since diffusion of the Gospel was by independent agents, the result was often originality and freshness of biblical and doctrinal interpretation that might give heartburn to doctrinal strict constructionists.

To this ferment add the nineteenth-century arrival of missionaries who translated the Bible into local languages. "The really liberating thing the missionaries did was to let the Scripture loose," Walls remarked. "That was crucial. That did more to preserve, transform, and renew the culture than the best intentions of missionaries, which were often more destructive." The spread of literacy through bush schools, then high schools, colleges, and seminaries, and the sending of bright young Africans for advanced education in Europe and the United States were part of the missionary effort. What emerged were a literate class of catechists and evangelists and a generation of translators and government employees, some of whom became leaders in the African independence movement. Similar contributions were made through missionary initiatives in agriculture, technology, and medicine.

•

Any discussion of the spread of Christianity in Africa should include the role of black Americans in the nineteenth century's last two decades. Lacking white volunteers because of Africa's disease-ridden climates, many white churches sponsored black missionaries, who they believed could better adapt to the climate. More than a hundred black Americans thus served in Africa from 1877 to 1900, most of them in Liberia, Sierra Leone, and the Congo. Their names included major figures like Alexander Crummell and Edward Blyden. The theology and perceptions of Africa of this generation of black American missionaries differed little from their white American contemporaries. Expansionist, triumphal Western Christianity was in the air, the religious counterpart of Teddy Roosevelt's "Manifest Destiny." "Go ye, therefore, and teach all nations" was an often-heard injunction from the white churches; black missionaries added from the Old Testament, "Ethiopia shall soon stretch out her hand to God" (Ps. 68:31). Representative of late nineteenth-century African-American mission thought was this "Hymn of Sympathy and Prayer for Africa," written by Alexander P. Camphor, a black American Methodist pastor in Liberia:

> Far across the mighty ocean
> Is a land of palmy plains,
> But that land is not enlightened;
> It is one where darkness reigns.
> There the heathen in his blindness
> Knoweth not the blessed word,
> Nor of Jesus Christ, the Savior,
> Precious Lord, our only Lord.[5]

•

Both World Wars were galvanic events in the emergence of locally led African churches. During World War I the total number of colonial conscripts was over eight hundred thousand soldiers, noncombatants, and defense workers. The wars also meant a decrease in the number of Western missionaries and leadership roles passed to Africans. In this regard, the Roman Catholic Church planned carefully over a long period of time. Two imaginative popes, Benedict XV and

Pius XI, encouraged the emergence of African priests and bishops, clergy who were educated in languages, theology, and spirituality, and who studied in Rome or elsewhere in Europe. The first two African diocesan bishops were consecrated in 1939, the first African cardinal in Tanzania in 1960.

•

A word about definitions used in this book. By "saints," "martyrs," and "holy people" I have considerably extended the boundaries used by the Roman Curia to define such categories. A saint in the Roman tradition, as a point of departure, must be a Roman Catholic who led an exemplary life, is now in heaven, performed at least two certifiable miracles while on earth, and can be prayed to as an intercessor with God for those among the living and for souls in purgatory. Not many Africans have crossed that bar, especially in recent centuries. A wider net is cast in the Protestant tradition, basically that all believers are saints, and, while Protestants generously expropriate many traditional Roman Catholic saints, they also add persons who have led exemplary lives in their own right. By including "saints" and "holy people," I have broadened the categories to welcome figures such as Mary Slessor, Kimpa Vita (Dona Beatriz), Farid Esack, a South African Muslim writer, and Desmond Tutu, the living and the dead who, without question, represent people of religious courage and virtue.

I have not included prophets, seers, and ecstatic healers because I liked them and their spirituality, but because they are representative of religion in Africa, and their typologies are also to be found in other world religions, as well as in Western Christianity. As for martyrs, these are persons who suffered torture, persecution, and death for their faith. Christian human rights activists like Steve Biko belong here. "Holy people" include not only Catholics and Protestants, but Jews, such as Albie Sachs, South African Supreme Court judge and assassination target, and Muslims, like Imam Abdullah Haron, a popular South African Muslim cleric whom the South African police killed in 1969. Additionally, I have added examples from the sacred literature of Africa, including proverbs, prayers, and folk tales with moral or mystical content. The purpose is to show the diversity of African spirituality. This anthology is selective and illustrative, not definitive or comprehensive. Hopefully it can serve as both an individual devotional guide and in classes on African studies or comparative world religions.

•

When Christ, rejected by the religious authorities of his homeland, proclaimed the Israel of God to all the nations, he encouraged the spread of Christianity into Africa and elsewhere. A strong early Christian presence in Africa was a reality, although modern textbooks emphasize its spread toward Asia Minor, Greece, and Rome, thence North into Europe. Among the first evidences of a Christian presence in Africa was the flight of the Holy Family into Egypt to escape Herod's persecution. A generation later, the apostles Peter and Mark, in all likelihood fleeing the political-religious disturbances in Jerusalem, may have followed a similar route into Egypt. From there Peter possibly dispatched his First Epistle General to the Christian communities. By the end of the first century A.D., Christian communities flourished throughout Egypt with its vigorous commercial, cultural, philosophical, and religious life.

This is not the place to tell the history of the church in Africa, but to make a few observations.[6] The relationship between Africa and the spread of Christianity is far richer than is usually thought. Old Testament encounters began with the early migration of Abraham into Egypt (Gen. 12:10–21). Moses was educated as an Egyptian prince. The queen of Ethiopia is depicted as visiting King Solomon (1 Kings 10:1–13 and 2 Chron. 9:1–12), with whom she conceived a son, Menelik I, thus launching a royal line of kings each of whom was called "the Lion of Judah." Ethiopians claim than the Ark of the Covenant was spirited from the Jerusalem Temple to the Coptic church in Aksum.

New Testament ties with Africa are equally rich. The Flight into Egypt brought the Holy Family into Africa, as noted above, and it was an African, Simon of Cyrene, who was commanded to carry Jesus' cross (Mark 15:21–28 and Luke 23:26). Suggestions that St. Mark the Evangelist founded the see of Alexandria exist, as do accounts of his martyrdom in Egypt in 68 A.D. Perhaps the best-known biblical-African account is that of the high official from Ethiopia who encountered Philip on the Gaza-Jerusalem road. The eunuch, a court official of Queen Candace, had come to Jerusalem to worship and was returning home in his chariot, reading from the prophet Isaiah. Philip, prompted by the Holy Spirit, asked, "Do you understand what you are reading?" The Ethiopian replied, "How can I, unless someone guides me?" He selected a passage from Isaiah, after which "Philip proclaimed to him the good news about Jesus." The eunuch said, "Look, here is water! What is to prevent me from being baptized?" Next he commanded his chariot to be stopped, the eunuch and Philip entered the water, a baptism was performed, and "when they came up out of the water, the Spirit of the Lord snatched Philip away; the eunuch saw him no more and went on his way rejoicing" (Acts 8:26–40).

Unfortunately, the diffusion of Christianity was not conflict-free. The expansion of this bold faith with its radical claims contrasted dramatically with the religion and political system of the Romans, which resulted in violent persecutions and martyrdoms. The Emperor Diocletian (243–316) ordered that all churches be demolished, all sacred books burned, all Christians deprived of any legal rights, and all Christians not in official positions be reduced to slavery. The early Christian historian Eusebius described the setting:

> This was the nineteenth year of the reign of Diocletian in Dystrus (which the Romans call March), when the feast of the Savior's passion was near at hand, and royal edicts were published everywhere, commanding that the churches should be razed to the ground, the Scriptures destroyed by fire, those who held positions of honor degraded, and the household servants, if they persisted in the Christian profession, be deprived of their liberty. And such was the first decree against us. But issuing other decrees not long after, the Emperor commanded that all rulers of the churches in every place should first be put in prison and afterwards compelled by every device to offer sacrifice. (*Hist. Ecc.* viii 2)

For late third-century Christians in Egypt, the choices were thus martyrdom or flight. The human capacity for cruelty is boundless, and Eusebius describes Romans hanging naked Christian women by one foot, and men being tied between two young trees, so that when the branches were released and sprang back into place, their bodies were pulled apart. Although the numbers cannot be verified, Eusebius estimated that there were approximately sixty martyrdoms a day for five years under Diocletian, accounting for the deaths of a hundred thousand Christians in Egypt alone during this period. It is understandable that the Egyptian Church dates its liturgical calendar from the Era of the Martyrs, which begins in 284 A.D.

•

My interest in religions in Africa began in 1958 when, as a young American diplomat, I first attended services at the Anglican Church of St. Andrew in Tangiers, the British consulate church for the past century. The Lord's Prayer in Arabic was carved in a Moorish arch over the altar, and outside the cries and metallic pounding of Berber iron workers blended with the wheezy harmonium and small British expatriate choir inside singing a breathy "All Things Bright and Beautiful." Two church-sponsored medical missionaries worked in the middle of Morocco, and our small congregation supported them and received cheerful letters in return. I knew little about Muslims but read the Koran and H. A. R. Gibb's, *Mohammedanism*, the standard introductory work of that era. I also met an American who had converted to Islam and dressed in a *jellabah*, representing a major crossing of cultural boundaries. I wished a dialogue could take place between Christians and Muslims, but this was 1959 and I was told by missionaries and diplomats that that could happen only in low-visibility, controlled circumstances, since the two great faith traditions had nothing in common with one another and were in fact at war since the Crusades.

Port-au-Prince, Haiti, was my next assignment. I continued to learn French and was exposed to the amalgam of African and Caribbean practices that coalesced in what was called voodoo religion. From 1961 to 1963 I was stationed in Ouagadougou, Burkina Faso, and came to know both the Benedictine Monks and White Fathers there. The Benedictines, with their exquisite cultural sensibilities, drew on traditional African music in the liturgy and African art in the design of vestments and altar furnishings. I remember dawn arising over the pre-Sahara as worshipers gathered silently in a semicircle, sitting on carved wooden stools near the starkly simple altar. Its crucifix was an African Christ hung on the crossed blades of a lion hunter's spear, and outside the morning sounds of desert animals were a descant to the chanting of the psalms.

The White Fathers were God's special forces, heading by motor scooter and tiny *deux chevaux* French cars into the bush, where they lived in groups of three,[7] founding churches and schools, and advancing their brand of militant Christianity. Generous in their hospitality, they would hand me a "White Father's cocktail," a large French glass containing fermented local grain and lukewarm beer. We talked for hours about local religion and politics, and I learned of the life and works of their founder, Cardinal Lavigerie, the desert hermit monk, Charles de Foucauld, and the brilliant mission theorist, François Libermann. While in Ouagadougou I became friends with a young American anthropologist and Columbia University professor, Elliott Skinner, who introduced me to traditional Mossi religion, as we sat with trans-Saharan truck drivers in open-air restaurants near the town's main market.

Following two years in what was then Upper Volta, I was assigned to an academic year at the University of California at Los Angeles. James S. Coleman, a human and intellectual dynamo, was director of its African Studies program during the Golden Age of area studies in America. In addition to taking courses, I sat often on the floor of the UCLA graduate library, devouring books and journals on African history, religion, and anthropology. My studies were truncated by an eighteen-month midcourse assignment to Vietnam. This was during the height of the American buildup in Vietnam, and Lyndon B. Johnson in one of his imperial gestures decided each province needed an American Foreign Service advisor. The benefit for me was long evenings and weekends to pour over French historical works, from which a book, *The French Overseas Empire*, emerged.

A posting as public affairs officer in the American embassy in Yaounde, Cameroon, 1966–1968, returned me to Africa. Spare time was spent doing archival and oral interview research among the Beti, a rain forest acephalous society of perhaps half a million Bantu-speakers. This was an opportunity to understand not only traditional Beti religion and values, but to write about the encounter of the Beti with German and French Roman Catholic and Protestant missionaries as well. My late wife, a professional Africanist and student of Islam, and I came to know the Jesuit professors at the local seminary and Protestants at the Presbyterian Mission. After having completed master's degrees in African studies in 1966 and history in 1969, I returned to UCLA to complete a doctoral degree in history in 1970. The results were published in several scholarly journals and the research materials filed in a special collection at the Hoover Institution in Palo Alto, California.

During this time I participated in the Episcopal Diocese of Washington's program for the ordination of the nonstipendiary ministry for persons who would be ordained yet work at their regular jobs. I supervised the United States Information Agency's educational and cultural programs for Africa from 1978 to 1980 and later, as a chaplain and adviser to the dean of Washington National Cathedral, participated in interfaith programs welcoming other religions, for the Cathedral was consciously a "A House of Prayer for All People," as its processional banner stated. Then in April–May 2000 I spent two intensive months in Abuja, Nigeria, beginning research on this book.

•

I write from the perspective of a Christian priest who has lived among Jewish, Islamic, and indigenous religions. As such, I applaud these other faith traditions with which I have come in contact and find them equal to my own before God. If there is to be a relative ranking of faiths at some point in the eschaton, I am content to leave that task to the author and originator of all religions. Like others, I have had the choice of being inclusive or exclusive and have clearly opted for the former course. My reading of the Old Testament is that a central theme in it is the search for the Messiah, which Christians find in Jesus Christ. My reading of the New Testament is that Christ, rejected by the then-ruling segment of his co-religionists, opened the way of salvation to all people through the new Israel, the Israel of God. "The boundless universality of the divine son" is a phrase Andrew Walls used to describe Christ, and this is the God I see at work among the world's religions.

The church, having increasingly opened its doors to persons of color and its altars to women and those of same-sex orientation, now must demonstrate greater inclusiveness and cooperation with other faith traditions, including common worship and action with them. This is needed for living in a world whose most isolated corners are easily reachable by telephone and air travel. Should not the sharing of values follow the sharing of technologies and the discussion of beliefs that unite and divide us be as important as the traffic in compact discs and videotapes?

Yet any pluralist position about the world's religions will encounter objections. What about the restrictive Christ, cited in John 14:6: "I am the way, and the truth, and the life. No one comes to the Father except through me." And in Acts 4:12: "And there is salvation in no one else, for there is no other name under heaven given among men by which we must be saved."

As for the first quotation — "I am the way" — if considered in context it is a pastoral expression of consolation, not a statement of boundary setting. It appears in the Gospel of John as a response to a frightened Thomas. Jesus, having washed his disciples' feet on his last night on earth, has just told them he is going to a place where they cannot follow. He speaks of it as "a house of many rooms," where he will prepare a place for them. The message of this chapter of John is one of assurance and reassurance. Diana Eck, a Methodist and professor of comparative religions at Harvard University, has written, "And what did Thomas ask him? Did he ask, . . . 'Lord, when the Prophet Mohammed comes six hundred years from now, will he hear God's word?' No, on that night of uncomprehending uncertainty he asked, 'Lord, we do not know where you are going; how can we know the way?'

And Christ answered, 'I am the way.' . . . It was a pastoral answer, not a polemical one. It was an expression of comfort, not condemnation."[8]

As for the statement of Peter in Acts 4:12 about salvation — "There is salvation in no one else" — in Eck's view it represents Peter, alive with his post-Pentecostal surge of faith, making a series of bold statements not intended to be limiting of others, but reflecting the new-found power of God in his life and that of God's followers. Eventually, these statements provoked sharply differing responses. Such decrees are not eternal verities handed down by God, but statements about Christ reflecting the experiences of specific followers. They should not be understood as examples of biblical truth and Christian doctrine, but as individual expressions of trust and commitment by devoted followers in difficult settings. Such statements about absoluteness are in reality the public prayers and utterances of the faithful, addressed to friends, enemies, and ultimately to God. Of these texts, the English theologian Reinhold Bernhardt has written, "Anyone who tears them from their historical foundation, generalizes them, and uses them to condemn non-Christian religions is thus falsifying their original character."[9]

My conclusion is that by the second century the church was locked into bitter doctrinal battles, hammering out creeds, chasing heretics, and abandoning the expansive vision of the time when the church was young. In its place its Western leaders raised the bar as to what constitutes acceptability for membership. But two millennia later different circumstances allow us to revisit the issue. Why not leave the final judgment up to God about who makes it through the narrow gate? Few of us surely could claim the credentials to pass judgment, nor could the religious institutions of which we are a part do much better. Too many holy people, just and suffering servants, come from churches and faith traditions different from ours; I am content to walk the Way of the Cross with them rather than pass judgment on them.

There are obvious sinners, apostates, false prophets, and plain opportunists in Africa, but that can be said for the United States or any other country as well. Rather than use a time of dramatic change as one to draw inward, this new age, in which the shift of numbers in the wider church has moved from north to south, can be an opportunity for European and North American Christians to find common cause with other peoples. Andrew Walls concludes:

Never before has the church looked so much like the great multitude whom no man can number out of every nation and tribe and people and tongue. Never before, therefore, has there been so much potential for mutual enrichment and self-criticism, as God causes yet more light to break forth from his word.[10]

No more lucid summary of the pluralist position is available than in the old mission hymn, which Professor Eck cites, "There's a Wideness in God's Mercy," representing both a statement about the Israel of God and about the atoning Christ who walks in solidarity with the world's suffering:

> There's a wideness in God's mercy like the wideness of the sea;
> there's a kindness in his justice, which is more than liberty.
> There is welcome for the sinner, and more graces for the good;
> there is mercy with the Savior, there is healing in his blood.

> There is no place where earth's sorrows are more felt than up
>   in heaven;
> there is no place where earth's failings have such kindly
>   judgment given.
> There is plentiful redemption in the blood that has been shed;
> there is joy for all the members in the sorrows of the Head.

> For the love of God is broader than the measure of the mind;
> and the heart of the Eternal is most wonderfully kind.
> If our love were but more faithful, we should take him at his
>   word;
> and our life would be thanksgiving for the goodness of the
>   Lord.[11]

•

Conversations with Andrew F. Walls, formerly a missionary to Sierra Leone and professor emeritus of the Study of Christianity in the Non-Western World at the University of Edinburgh, were helpful as we shared a starkly Calvinistic dormitory but warm hospitality of the Pittsburgh Theological Seminary. Professor John O. Voll, professor of Islamic History at Georgetown University in Washington, D.C., suggested several leads to Islamic sources. Encounters with Desmond Tutu and Trevor Huddleston in South Africa and England gave me rich material, as did the friendship in Cameroon of Jean Zoa, Theodore Tsala, Englebert Mveng, and Bernard Fonlon. The White Fathers in Ouagadougou and the Benedictines and Jesuits in Yaounde were generous hosts. Professor Hilda Kuper of the African Studies Center, University of California at Los Angeles, introduced me to the professional study of the anthropology of African religions. I only wish that she were alive to see this response to her efforts.

Professor Herman Schwartz of the Washington College of Law, American University, and his wife, Mary, a psychotherapist, Howard and Matthew Greene, analysts of international educational and cultural issues, and Drs. Fred Hilkert and Susan Lazar, friends of many years, provided stimulating conversation on the subject matter of this book, often during periodic Cosmos Club lunches in a setting convivial to intellectual discourse across disciplines, as did Drs. Marianne Schuelein and Ralph Krause

It is a pleasure to acknowledge the expert assistance of the staff of the Virginia Theological Seminary Library, the Mullen Library of the Catholic University of America, the Howard Divinity School Library, the Pittsburgh Theological Seminary Library, and the American University Library. Sister Mary Winifred of the Community of the Ascension, an able researcher, logged countless hours in providing material for this book. Paul McMahon, Kevin DiCamillo, John Eagleson, and John Tintera of Crossroad Publishing Company were perceptive editorial professionals with whom to work.

I dedicate this book to the Very Reverend Nathan D. Baxter, dean of Washington National Cathedral, an old friend who emerged, as I did, from the Pennsylvania of the 1960s, a God-seeker whose search has led him across cultures and continents to find a vibrant national and global ministry, and with whom I share a deep interest in religion in Africa. The proverb on p. v is used as an epigraph in I. M. Lewis, *Saints and Somalis: Popular Islam in a Clan-Based Society* (Lawrenceville, N.J.: Red Sea Press, 1998).

KING AFONSO I
(MVEMBA NZINGA)

baptized 1491; d. 1543

Portugal was an expansionist European state in the Middle Ages, battling Islam and seeking sources of gold, spices, and slaves and a mythical priest-king, "Prester John," whose mysterious Christian kingdom was hidden somewhere in Africa's vastness. Prester John never existed, but a no less remarkable African king, Mvemba Nzinga (throne name, Afonso I) built an impressive state, a Kongo kingdom, which thrived during the first half of the sixteenth century.

Afonso was a visionary who sought to improve his people's religious, material, and educational conditions. Blessed by a time of relative peace and adequate territory, he concentrated on these goals instead of warfare, once he had secured his throne by executing a rival brother who also claimed it.

Through a local court scribe literate in Portuguese, Afonso left a voluminous correspondence in which he asked his Portuguese counterpart to send missionaries, teachers, and medical experts, but with mixed results. Despite his demonstrable adherence to Christianity, few priests ever materialized, the Portuguese who came as unskilled laborers were the flotsam and jetsam of empire, and the slave trade burgeoned. Afonso's opposition to it was nominal at best, primarily because its tentacles caught "even noblemen and the sons of noblemen and our relatives."

Qualified priests were hard to come by. Those sent from Portugal often died in the insalubrious tropical setting, others quickly settled with concubines, and still others joined the growing European slave-trading community. Even the most devout had difficulty for, as in Europe, the people followed the monarch's religion but retained an overlay of traditional beliefs which responded to their basic questions of life and death. Roman Catholic priests were called *nganga*, the same word used for traditional ritual practitioners, although their functions differed.

The medieval church's pageantry and ritual caught hold quickly in the capital, where the king was present at important services dur-

15

ing the liturgical year and often preached at Mass. Alfonso built a Catholic court, the structure of which could have fit in several Mediterranean countries, complete with titles, confraternities, and chivalrous orders. The large but grass-roofed cathedral in São Salvador was the most impressive building along the African coast and had a bell. Kongo dia Ngunga, Kongo of the Bell, was one of the capital's names.

As early as the sixteenth century the Portuguese began formation of an indigenous clergy, sending many young Kongolese to Lisbon for instruction. Although the difficulties of learning and functioning in Latin, cultural shock, and the demands of a celibate life greatly diminished their numbers, one of the king's sons, Henry, studied in Portugal, became an auxiliary bishop in 1521 at about age twenty-five, and returned to his country; he died a few years later with few traces of his activity.

His people knew Afonso as "the apostle of the Kongo," and in 1516 a Portuguese priest, Rui d'Aguiar, described him in an exaggerated yet purposeful account:

> His Christian life is such that he appears to me not as a man but as an angel sent by the Lord to this kingdom to convert it, especially when he preaches.... Better than we, he knows the prophets and the Gospel of our Lord Jesus Christ and all the lives of the saints and all things regarding our Mother the Holy Church.... He studies the Holy Gospel and when the priest finishes the Mass he asks for benediction. When he has received it he begins to preach to the people with great skill and great charity.... He punishes with rigor those who worship idols and he has them burned along with the idols.[12]

At his death, possibly two million people, half the population of the Kongo, had been baptized. But the picture was never one of unalloyed success. Hastings writes, "There is frequently a riveting intensity in Afonso's appeals for help, protests about the growing slave-trade and bad behavior of the Portuguese, a fierce fusion of Christian faith, modernizing intentions, regal shrewdness, and a bitterness with the reality in which neither his secular nor religious hopes were being realized."[13]

Following Afonso's death the Portuguese and Kongolese fought, the capital city and cathedral were destroyed, and the new king was beheaded, as was his chaplain, the first black Capuchin priest, Francisco de São Salvador Roboredo.

O God, *who raised up faithful servants to praise your name and advance your kingdom, we give thanks for the example of King Afonso I, who with steadfast faith and perseverance overcame great difficulties and built your church in the Kongo, where for centuries people have sung your praises. Amen.*

DR. JAMES EMMANUEL KWEGYIR AGGREY

West African Educator, 1875–1927

The surest way to keep a people down is to educate the men and neglect the women. If you educate a man you simply educate an individual, but if you educate a woman you educate a family.

—Dr. James Emmanuel Kwegyir Aggrey

James Emmanuel Kwegyir Aggrey was a Christian visionary and educator born in October 1875 in the Gold Coast, now Ghana, a Fanti whose father was a gold "taker," an expert who checked and weighed shipments of gold dust for a prominent African trader. In 1883 the youth was baptized a Christian in the Methodist Church, took the name of James, and entered the Cape Coast Wesleyan Methodist School. Aggrey was a brilliant student and soon was asked to teach in a distant school. "One of the things that kept me up was the faith that my old teachers had in me. And I prayed God to help me never to disappoint them," he wrote of his experience.[14]

By the time he was nineteen he was licensed to preach and was a skilled interpreter, translating sermons and hymns into Fanti and editing the Bible translations of others. Shortly after Aggrey was named headmaster of a local Wesleyan school, he was given a scholarship to America. The young African was sent to Livingstone College in Salisbury, North Carolina, the chief college of the African Methodist Episcopal Zion Church, the sponsoring church. Aggrey was a born student, equally proficient in the classics and sciences. He mastered German, French, Latin, and Greek, in addition to English. (Later he acquired a working knowledge of Japanese and Spanish.)

While at Livingstone, Aggrey met the love of his life, Rose Douglas of Portsmouth, Virginia, who would be his companion and mother of their three children. At this time Aggrey pursued graduate studies in divinity and education and a correspondence course in osteopathy, and served as pastor of two small Carolina churches. An intensely focused preacher, he told his poor rural congregation, "Don't expect people to bring you money. Help yourselves; rear chickens. White people want eggs; and good eggs, they don't care whether they are a white man's or a black man's." "There's gravy in his sermons," the congregation responded, "plenty of good strong meat, but gravy too." Under Aggrey's leadership, the congregation members improved their self-esteem; many became better educated and obtained productive jobs.

Aggrey's next intellectual port of call was Columbia University in New York City, where he began work on a doctor's degree. At this time the Phelps Stokes educational trust was preparing a pioneering survey on improving education in Africa and asked Aggrey to join the study mission visiting ten West African countries. While in the Gold Coast after a twenty-two-year absence, he visited his mother and many relatives, was greeted as "our great brother from America," and was installed as Linguist, the same office his father had held in traditional society.

Constantly exhorting Africans to higher achievement, he said, "Remember, my brothers, to love and to work." And he often quoted a biblical text from Exodus (4:2), where God asked Moses what was in his hand and Moses replied, "A staff." Start with such tools, he said, work the land, and build for the future. "The land that grows things for the white man will grow things for the black man." Speaking frequently of the need for races to work together, he remarked, "You can play a tune of sorts on the white keys, and you can play a tune of sorts on the black keys, but for harmony, you must use both the black and the white."

Aggrey was invited back to the Gold Coast in 1924 as assistant vice principal of the colony's new flagship educational institution, the Achimoto school and college, which was the personal project of the colonial governor, Sir Gordon Guggisberg. Aggrey set about the task with customary vigor, even donating his own library of twenty-five hundred books to the school, hammering nails, and meeting with parents, students, and faculty. At the school's opening on January 28, 1927, the governor paid tribute to him, and the modest Aggrey, when asked to say a few words to the students, exhorted them, "Let's Go, Eagles! Let's Go, Eagles!" which became the school's rallying cry.

Aggrey returned to Columbia to resume his doctoral thesis in June 1927, but speaking demands interfered with his writing time. He was both a voice for racial cooperation and for improved education in Africa, and he told audiences, "Only the best is good enough for Africa," adding, "You can never beat prejudice by frontal attack. Always flank it. You can catch more with molasses than you can with vinegar."

Death cut him down on July 30, 1927, in Harlem Hospital. Dr. Ansel Phelps Stokes, canon of Washington Cathedral and president of the Phelps-Stokes Fund, spoke at Mother Zion Church. He said Aggrey did for Africa what Booker T. Washington did for America. On August 7, a large crowd gathered at Achimoto School for a memorial service, after which the students chanted in unison Aggrey's call for education and self-fulfillment, "Let's Go, Eagles! Let's Go, Eagles!"

We praise you, Creator God, for the life of James Emmanuel Aggrey, whose lively witness taught people to help themselves, to love and to work, so they might soar like eagles and play together, white keys and black keys, for the furtherance of your kingdom. Amen.

ARCHBISHOP
PETER J. AKINOLA

Nigeria, b. 1944

❀❀❀❀❀❀❀❀❀

Halfway down Douala Street in Abuja, Nigeria, the populous West African nation's new federal capital, is a walled compound of tin-roofed cement buildings, Bishopscourt, headquarters of The Most Reverend Peter J. Akinola, D.D., archbishop, metropolitan, and primate of the Church of Nigeria (Anglican Communion) and bishop of Abuja, the national capital. In 1979 the rulers of Africa's largest state, seeking to overcome differences between North and South, Moslem and Christian, desert and rain forest, moved the capital from crowded coastal Lagos to the largely unsettled interior. Flat and dry, Abuja was "big bush," a barren, parched setting, before government ministries began heading north. Now it contains the massive headquarters of the federal government and housing for civil servants.

Of medium height, Bishop Peter is a prelate of fierce energy, punctuating his carefully organized and vigorously delivered sermons with lively gestures, dramatic pauses, and carefully drawn word pictures that provoke audible responses from congregations. The church faces daunting problems. Nigeria's population is estimated at 120 million people; both Muslims and Christians claim a slight majority, and among the Christians there are 15 million Anglicans. World Bank estimates place per capita GNP at $260, and average life expectancy at fifty-two years.

"Our church is the fastest growing Anglican church in the world," the archbishop began, "faster growing than Canada, Great Britain, and the United States combined." Using a text recommended by one of his six children, at his installation the prelate spoke on "Behold, I am doing a new thing." "Nigerians must find a way out of this big jungle of sin, greed, and selfishness of Nigerian life," he said, lamenting "the level of corruption in this country." He presented the church with a five-point vision statement encompassing spirituality, evangelism, institution building, external mission, and finances. "Your destiny is in your hands," he told Nigerians, adding, "God is colorless. To answer many of our problems we must have sheer hard work."

Peter J. Akinola was born in Abeokutain, in Nigeria's thickly veg-
etated South, in 1944. His father died when he was four years old,
"and I have no memory of him. Later people told me he was a good
and decent man." Money was lacking for school, so an uncle in the
far North helped Peter find a job. A conventional Christian, Peter
sang in the church choir, taught Bible classes, and graduated to lay
reading lessons at the evening service.

By 1968 he had moved from a job as a postal worker to becoming
a skilled carpenter and cabinetmaker, with his own shop and show-
room and several employees. He was doing well, but strange dreams
intruded. "I found myself telling my age-mates and friends not to
drink, go to the cinema, have many girl friends. I heard them saying,
'Look, Bishop, if you don't like our lives, get out of here.' "

"Then one fateful day in October I came to my workshop. A
church representative was there with a letter asking the parish to send
two young men to Zaria for seminary training. My uncle, who had
brought me there many years ago, said, 'Peter, the church council met
and looked around the whole church and you are the only one they
recommended. You should go for the interview.' I could not refuse my
uncle." Peter was accepted by the Theological College of Northern
Nigeria, and after study there was ordained and, in 1978, assigned
to Suleja, an isolated truckers' stop, a crossroads on the North-South
road. The parched region had just been designated Nigeria's capital,
and Peter headed out on his Honda motorbike to visit newly arriving government workers in their homes. "Parlor churches" formed,
Christians met regularly in living rooms or under large trees, and
truckers made their *buketria*, or cafeteria, available to Protestants and
Roman Catholics for Sunday worship. In 1979 Peter left Suleja for
three years at Virginia Theological Seminary, where he had dreams of
returning as a seminary professor. But instead in 1981 the bishop assigned him back to Suleja for three more years. "I cried and I cried and
said, 'No way!' In Nigeria, the bishops assign clergy and the bishop
said, 'We need a pioneer, someone who is not only a pastor but a
builder.' " It was a time of explosive growth for the church. Government workers, many of them Anglicans from elsewhere in Nigeria,
poured into Abuja. Catechists and lay readers headed out as missionary teams into villages on Friday nights and returned on Sunday
evenings, preaching wherever they could find listeners.

In November 1989 Peter became bishop of Nigeria's twenty-sixth
diocese. (There were seventy-six by 2000). And he was enthroned as
head of the church in the nation's new capital. The diocese's crest

contains a Bible, cross, and yams, a Nigerian food crop. The three sprouting yams represent the Trinity and new life in Christ.

Bit by bit the church added additional institutions, medical dispensaries, schools, rural development projects, and a large primary school. Bishopscourt includes an office block and meeting rooms, clergy housing, and a five-bedroom bungalow for the archbishop (who has six children), plus a ninety-room guesthouse to provide relatively cheap accommodation to Christian visitors to the nation's capital, with proceeds being used for mission work.

O Christ, the carpenter's son, build your church with the strong hands of faithful workers everywhere. Let your people pray and then see the fruit of their labor, an earthly vision of that city without walls where you abide and where dwell the faithful departed of all races and ages. Amen.

ROLAND ALLEN

Missionary, Mission Theorist, 1868–1947

Christ has given the apostles a world-wide commission, embracing all the nations; but intellectually they did not understand what He meant. They found that out as they followed the impulse of the Spirit.

—Roland Allen, *Pentecost and the World*, 1917

Roland Allen, a young English missionary, first in North China and later in East Africa, sought to change drastically the entire colonial and paternalistic system of mission governance. He became a leading missionary theorist and a controversial, prophetic challenger of the existing order.

The son of an Anglican clergyman, Allen was a graduate of St. John's College, Oxford, and then trained at the Leeds Clergy Training School before being sent by the Society for the Propagation of the Gospel in Foreign Parts (SPG) to China. Allen was ahead of his time in his theological views, and his personality managed to alienate most colleagues with whom he came in contact. After eight years in China, he resigned and returned to a parish in England, said it was a non-Christian place, and left it as well. Allen spent the rest of his life writing about mission issues and serving as a nonstipendiary minister, the model for ministry he favored from his reading of the New Testament. Drawing on 1 Peter 4:10, he argued that priesthood belonged inherently to all Christians.

He believed that indigenous peoples should be given control of their own churches — including control of finances — and responsibility for supporting their own churches. In a 1902 report he wrote:

> The continued presence of a foreigner seems to me to produce an evil effect. The native genius is cramped by his presence and cannot work with him. The Christians tend to sit still and let him do everything for them, denying all responsibility. . . . I should feel disposed to group all foreigners together in one place to avoid having them reside in more places than can be helped. A visit of two or three months stirs up the Church. Long continued residence stifles it.[15]

He also proposed that local churches raise up their own spiritual leaders and present them to the bishop for ordination. Their devotion and commitment to the Christian Gospel and the support of their friends and neighbors should be the primary qualification for ordination. Allen wanted most clergy to earn their incomes from secular work, the tentmaker model St. Paul followed in the New Testament. His best-known book is *Missionary Methods: St. Paul's or Ours?* (1913), and in it and other works he was a tireless promoter for the autonomous self-funded, self-directed, locally led church.

Allen's feisty temperament made waves among the Nairobi settler community. While he was in Kenya during World War II he told the settler community not to wrap the Bible in the Union Jack, lest both be thrown out together, and when a local Colonel Blimp issued a blanket denunciation of everything German, Allen dueled back in the local paper, "I might ask him whether he 'hates' all drugs invented by German chemists, whether he 'hates' all German music; blind hatred is not Christian."

During a 1935 sermon in All Saints' Cathedral he urged the settler community to be their own ministers:

> Sooner or later many of you, and your children, will go up country. There, Sunday after Sunday, you will have no Church to go to. You know that. Well then, what are you going to do? ... Will you say, ... "The Church is here where I am"? Would that person be "fighting a battle on Christ's behalf against the sloth which says, "If there is no chaplain to do things for us, we can do nothing, but hold a dance or a tennis tournament." You have the secret. You know what is the Christian fight, and that you are fighting it, and that Michael and all his angels are on your side.[16]

Eventually the local English bishop forbade Allen to preach, although he could celebrate the Eucharist. Among Africans he was a revered figure, called *Bwana Mzee* (the old gentlemen) for his mane of white hair.

Allen completely turned traditional missionary attitudes on their ear. In his emphasis on an immediate, intense, local experiencing of prayer and community, he lessened the need for hierarchical control of the institutional church. In his total trust of local congregations to raise up ministers, he presaged the sort of Canon III (locally ordained) ministries now recognized in Alaska and certain parts of the United States where seminary-trained clergy are not available. In his trusting of the Holy Spirit and welcoming of local leadership, Allen expressed ideas that a later generation of liberation theologians and post–Vatican II mission strategists would find important to the future of world mission.

> *To preach the Gospel requires that the preacher should believe that he is sent to those whom he is addressing at the moment, because God has among them those whom He is at the moment calling; it requires that the speaker should expect a response.*
> — *Missionary Methods: St. Paul's or Ours?* (1913)

ST. ANTHONY OF EGYPT

Hermit, Abbot, c. 250–356

Anthony, the spiritual father of some of the greatest figures of early Christian North Africa, was the barely literate son of a prosperous Egyptian village merchant. The religious tutor of such leading personalities as Athanasius, Jerome, Basil, and Augustine of Hippo, as an orphan of twenty, he was struck by the biblical admonition, "If thou wilt be perfect, go and sell all that thou hast." This is what Anthony did, living from simple gardening and the charity of others for the rest of his life.

Anthony began his new life by moving to an ancient Egyptian tomb not far from his village, where he lived for several years, prayed intensely, and fasted. In addition to welcoming visions of angels, he wrestled with powerful demons that, following an attack, left him for dead. Athanasius, responsible for the Creed that bears his name and Anthony's first biographer, wrote:

> All at once the place was filled with the phantoms of lions, bears, leopards, bulls, serpents, asps, scorpions, and wolves. And each moved according to the shape it had assumed. . . . And the noises emitted simultaneously by all the apparitions were frightful and the fury shown was fierce. . . . Anthony, pummeled and goaded by them, made bold to say, 'Do not delay! Up and at me! If you cannot attack, why excite yourself to no purpose?' So, after trying many ruses, they gnashed their teeth, because they were only fooling themselves and not him.[17]

In about 294 A.D. Anthony, after having made sure things were running well in the monastery he had established, headed east toward the Red Sea to a desolate place near a spring of fresh water, where he established a new hermitage. Passing caravans and shepherds left him gifts of dates, bread, and, delicacy of delicacies, packets of onions. There may have been as many as ten thousand monks and twice that number of nuns living in the desert in Anthony's time. The desert, it must be emphasized, was not the empty place of a Clint Eastwood film. Its trade routes were numerous, and its oases were well known.

Soon fame of Anthony's teachings spread; the distant Emperor Constantine asked for his prayers, and there are early records of people renting camels to make the long trip to his hermitage. Wild animals were his constant companions. A charming story recounts Anthony's relationship with the animals in an era when bearbaiting and torturing of animals was a widespread form of entertainment:

> At first wild animals in the desert coming for water often would damage the beds in his garden. But he caught one of the animals, held it gently, and said to them all: "Why do you harm me when I harm none of you? Go away, and in the Lord's name do not come near these things again." And ever afterwards, as though awed by his orders, they did not come near the place.[18]

Such tales of monks' encounters with animals were numerous: an aging monk fed a starving lion with dates, another shared his evening meal regularly with a she-wolf, still another taught an ibex, a desert antelope, which plants to eat and which to avoid.

Before he died, at the venerable age of 105, Anthony gave away his few earthly possessions: his hair shirt, which he wore as a means of constant mortification of the flesh, an old cloak, and the two sheepskins on which he slept or which he used for covering at night. He wrote, "So farewell, ye that are my heartstrings, for Anthony is going and will not be with you in this world any more" and asked his two closest followers to "shelter in the ground, hide in the earth the body of your father. And please do your old friend's bidding in this also: that none but you only shall know the place of his grave."

Anthony of the desert, the desolate places sprang to life, and beauty appeared in the barren landscape; wild creatures sought your presence, and you welcomed them. So might we follow you and Christ to the desert places and find them a source of life. Amen.

NANA ASMA'U

West African Islamic Religious Poet,
1793–1864

⊗⊗⊗⊗⊗⊗⊗⊗⊗⊗

The remarkable West African poet Nana Asma'u was a daughter of the Islamic jihad leader Shehu Usman dan Fodiyo. She grew up to be a deeply religious person, seeking to follow the *Sunna*, the "right way" demonstrated in the life of the Prophet Muhammad, and was active as a scholar, teacher, and social reformer. Asma'u was a member of a mystical Sufi community that was part of the Qadiriyya order, which had its origins with an Islamic saint, Abdulqadir Jelani (d. 1166) of Baghdad. Her education was in the classical Islamic tradition, with emphasis on memorizing the Koran and on leading a life of prayer. Dan Fodiyo, who led the jihad in Northern Nigeria, was also an author and prayerful person who carried his large library of Arabic manuscripts with him by camel or horseback. Drawing on his library, gradually his daughter became accustomed to the norms of religious discourse and learned to write in Arabic, Fulfulde, Hausa, and Tamachek. Asma'u was married to a high court officer of the Sokoto Caliphate, raised six sons, and wrote works of prose and poetry. In the disruptive wake of the Sokoto jihad, Asma'u was active in welfare efforts and in organizing women teachers to propagate Islamic values, especially through the sanctification of life by constant daily prayer.

Asma'u's literary legacy includes a remarkable collection of religious poems, many of them used to educate initiates to Sufi practice. "So Verily" (1822) is an Islamic Te Deum to a munificent God.

> *Lord God Almighty, all Powerful, he who asserts there is more*
> *than one god will perish.*
> *One God, Almighty, nothing is perfect except it comes from*
> *Him.*
> *Come to God, receive His generosity: all good things are derived*
> *from Him.*
> *Anyone who says he requires nothing of God is either ignorant*
> *or an unbeliever.*

*Everyone who seeks God's help will receive it, for God allows
      people to make requests.*

*I pray God will show me the Way of religion and that I will
      keep to it until I die.*

*God is Pure, and forgets nothing: those whom He forgives find
      peace.*

*May He bless us and show us the Path, and may He help us to
      remain one people.*

*We pray for victory and that the rebellion of Ibra may be
      overcome.*

We pray, too, for forgiveness in this world and the next.

*Call upon God always, so that things which are too difficult
      may be made easy.*

*Pray to God, do your meditations, praying for forgiveness and
      giving thanks.*

*Look at His generosity! It is unbounded, His munificence is
      infinite.*

We give thanks to God and pray for our Lord of the Universe.[19]

ST. ATHANASIUS

Bishop of Alexandria, Teacher of the Faith,
293–373

If we think of Egypt as the gateway for the church to make its way into Africa, then the port city of Alexandria becomes a pivotal place, and Athanasius, a fourth-century figure, a central player in the drama of expanding Christianity. Athanasius, bishop and saint, probably was ordained at an early age, which would have been common at that time, for he appears to have been engaged in substantive controversies as a fairly young cleric. The age was one of violent disputes over issues that a modern audience can hardly find exciting. Still, it was a time when the church was hammering out the original statements of doctrine, stakes were high, winners won big, and losers were banished or excommunicated.

In this early theological superbowl Athanasius squared off with another Alexandrian priest named Arius, who preached that the Son of God was not eternal and a figure comparable in substance to God the Father, but in fact was an invention of God the Father and that all the Son's supposed power was not distinct from the power and personality of the Father. Athanasius set out to have Arius's doctrine declared heresy and its author banished. In his essay *On the Incarnation* he detailed his basic position, commonly accepted now among Christians. Athanasius said that Father and Son were coeternal and coequals and used the technical term *homousios* to describe their relationship.

This position was accepted at an important early gathering of most Christian leaders called by the emperor Constantine at Nicaea in 325 A.D. "They are two," Athanasius wrote, "for the Father is Father, and the Son is not the same, but again, the Son is Son, and not the Father himself. But their Nature is one, for the Begotten is not dissimilar to the Begetter, but his image, and everything that is the Father's is also the Son's." The position is elaborated more clearly in the Creed of St. Athanasius:

And the Catholic Faith is this: That we worship one God in Trinity, and Trinity in Unity, neither confounding the Persons, nor dividing the Substance.

For there is one Person of the Father, another of the Son, and
another of the Holy Ghost.

But the Godhead of the Father, of the Son, and of the Holy
Ghost, is all one, the Glory equal, the Majesty co-eternal.

Such as the Father is, such is the Son, and such is the Holy
Ghost.[20]

Doctrinal controversies rarely end cleanly, and this one is no exception. Arius and some of his coterie were banished, but they lingered
to reappear several years later as the emperor had second thoughts
about accepting the new position Athanasius and his party had hammered through. In fact, with the return of Arius and a new emperor,
it was Athanasius's turn to head into exile, and he fled to Trier in 336
and to Rome in 339, not to return to Alexandria until 346. He was
driven into exile five times; in one instance he wrote, "I was seated
upon my chair, the deacon was about ready to read the psalm, the
people to answer 'For his mercy endureth forever.' The solemn act was
interrupted; a panic arose" as soldiers and police closed in on him.
In another instance, he fled to Upper Egypt, where he had numerous
supporters among the desert community of ascetics like Anthony and
Pachomius.

Controversy raged throughout his episcopate, church councils met
to carve out doctrinal positions, and Athanasius headed into exile
in 355. However, the Arian camp splintered, and when the Emperor
Constantius, its chief supporter, died in 361, Athanasius returned
again to power. Although he died a decade later in 373, by then he
had the support of several theological heavies, such as St. Basil and
St. Gregory of Nazianzus, and his position was in the ascendancy. Arianism was never quite defeated; it enjoyed a following in the outposts
of empire, principally among the Teutonic tribes that occupied much
of Western Europe and persecuted North African Christians. But with
the conversion of the Franks in 496, Arianism became a spent force.

Athanasius was a consummate activist rather than a systematic
theologian. His writings were aimed at winning debates against opponents; his manner was unyielding, his temper quick. But Athanasius
was on to something central to the newly emerging Christian faith;
the basic doctrines of Arianism could easy have disintegrated into a
vacuous polytheism, leaving Christianity one among many faith systems in the Mediterranean basin. Athanasius set out to prevent this
from happening, and his zeal was finally rewarded as his position
prevailed.

Ever-living God, whose servant Athanasius courageously testified that Jesus Christ is truly with us in the Word made flesh: grant us to see the glory of your Word and to grow in his likeness, that we may be fulfilled in the knowledge of you, the only God, through Jesus Christ our Lord. Amen.

—*Celebrating Common Prayer,* 445[21]

ST. AUGUSTINE
Doctor of the Church, North African Bishop,
354–430

🕸🕸🕸🕸🕸🕸🕸🕸

Thou madest us for thyself and our heart is restless until it rests in thee.
Grant me, Lord, to know and understand which is first — to call on thee
or to praise thee. And again, to know thee or to call on thee. For who can
call on thee, not knowing thee? For he that knoweth thee may not call on
thee as other than thou art. Or is it better that we call on thee that we may
know thee?   — A Prayer of St. Augustine[22]

Augustine was born in Tagaste, near Constantine, in what is now Algeria and spent thirty-five years as bishop of Hippo, a North African
port. He is best remembered for his restless, probing mind and his
writings, which include a defense of the emerging Catholic faith, a
profound exploration of the religious aspects of the human personality, and an all-encompassing Christian doctrine of creation. Some
ninety-three books, three hundred letters, and four hundred sermons
that remain represent only a fraction of his total production. Pac-
ing about, Augustine kept teams of stenographers and copyists busy.
A key to approaching Augustine is to remember that he was a pas-
sionate, fiercely energetic thinker; efforts to slice off an aspect of his
writings and claim them as a final systematic statement of his belief
are almost always inadequate.

Augustine's father was a pagan minor Roman local official, and
his Berber mother, Monica, an active Christian. At about age sixteen,
Augustine entered into a fifteen-year happy liaison with a woman who
bore him a son, Deodatus, who later died as a teenager (see p. 37).
At the same time, Augustine developed a lasting friendship with a
wealthy local landowner who both bankrolled his future education
and acted as a surrogate father. In 371 the bright lights of Carthage
attracted the young scholar, and Augustine pursued his education
there for three years. He later returned as a teacher, until in 383 A.D.
he set off for Rome for a five-year sojourn in Italy.

It was during this time that Augustine was converted from being
a nominal to an active Christian, from leading the relatively carefree
life of a young Roman professor of rhetoric to following the monastic
life. He recalled coming upon the biblical text "Be clothed in Jesus

Christ" and saying, "The very instant I finished that sentence, light was flooding my heart with assurance, and every shadow of doubt evanesced."

Sex was a continuing concern to Augustine. Obviously he had a satisfactory relationship with his female partner of fifteen years, for he continued to brood about the subject. True, he never adopted the emperor Marcus Aurelius's view that sexual contact was but "release of slime by rubbing a woman's innards" but in one dialogue between himself and Reason he acknowledges being tormented the previous night by "imagined caresses soliciting you with old bitter-sweetness."

During Lent in 387 Bishop Ambrose, another giant of the church, baptized Augustine in Milan. The preparation was a long one. The candidates went unbathed through Lent and wore penitential hair shirts. Eventually they bathed on Thursday in Holy Week, the event being variously compared to Noah's Flood or the passage of the Red Sea. After praying through the night of Easter Eve, at dawn they faced the sun and were led to a pool for baptism.

After his final return to Africa (388–430) Augustine produced some of his most productive work, writings that would give him a place as Africa's most original theological mind. Here he set out on the dual tasks of both expounding his own Christian beliefs and, like other early church figures, sharply refuting opposing schools of thought. Three themes dominate his later writings, the doctrine of the Trinity, where his position placed him in opposition to the then-flourishing heretical religions, God the creator, and the depths of the human mind in relation to sin and salvation.

During this time Augustine was elected bishop of the North African seaport town of Hippo, spurred on by a local Greek bishop who needed help. Election to the episcopate was not the elaborate process it is today. The nearly seven hundred North African prelates were often little more than parish administrators, some of whom were selected by acclamation from congregations lacking leadership. Wearing the simple monastic garb he was accustomed to, Augustine was consecrated a bishop in 395 at age forty-one. He had been a priest four years, a baptized Christian for eight.

Augustine set about his busy work as church leader, reformer, chider of heretics, and builder of a diocese and monastery, but news from Rome was ominous. In 410 Alaric the Visigoth sacked the Eternal City, sending shock waves to the ends of empire. One of Augustine's most-remembered books, written in the shadow of Rome's fall, was *The City of God*, a volume of twenty-two books composed over fifteen years. In it he stressed the need for justice amid political chaos. "What is a political regime, when devoid of justice, but organized crime?" he asked. In the work he contrasts Christ's body, interpreted as the Christian community with sinners in its midst, and Satan's body, sinners with a few Christians among them. Garry Wills remarked, "This is an eschatological vision of what is going on in human history — the growing toward a final harvest that separates saints and sinners."[23] In the work, Augustine also answered critics who blamed the fall of the Roman empire on the rise of the Christian religion. Augustine roundly dismissed such reasoning, arguing instead that mortal kingdoms come and go and that fidelity to God's laws and the practice of personal piety and a prayerful life are required for individual and collective survival in any civic setting.

> *Late have I loved thee: O Beauty so ancient and so new; late have I loved thee: for behold thou wert within me, and I outside; and I sought thee outside and in my unloveliness fell upon those lovely things that thou hast made. Thou wert with me, and I was not with thee. I was kept from thee by those things, yet had they not been in thee, they would not have been at all. Thou didst call and cry to me to break open my deafness: and thou didst send forth thy beams and shine upon me and chase away my blindness: thou didst breathe fragrance upon me, and I drew in my breath and do now pant for thee: I tasted thee, and now hunger and thirst for thee: thou didst touch me, and I have burned for thy peace.*   — St. Augustine[24]

ST. AUGUSTINE'S
UNNAMED PARTNER
AND THEIR SON, GODSEND

d. c. 400

Augustine spent fifteen years with one woman "and with her alone, since I kept faith with her bed." Most likely Augustine was only sixteen or seventeen when he took up with a local North African girl, a Catholic from his hometown of Tagaste. Augustine did not want to have a child, but did, and scattered throughout his later writings are affectionate comments obviously about his son. He delighted in the youth and contrasted his loving education with his own harsh exposure to the world of learning. For instance he attributes these words to a happy child: "I learned [to speak] as a baby, not inhibited by fear of punishment, surrounded as I was by coddling nurses, laughing games, and happy play. I learned without others' punitive insistence that I learn, from my own heart's need to deliver what I was laboring forth to the outer world.... I picked up words from anyone who spoke to me, not just from tutors, and I somehow did labor forth my feelings in others' ears. Unfettered inquisitiveness, it is clear, teaches better than do intimidating assignments."[25] In such a commentary, Augustine clearly had in mind his harsh father and harsher tutors who beat him for his inability to learn Greek. He was clearly determined to see a different, more loving pattern of learning in his own son and in his own students.

Some time after Augustine and his family arrived in Italy, he sent his partner back to Africa, where, devout Christian that she was, she lived a life of consecrated continence. This was triggered by an arranged marriage for Augustine engineered by his mother, Monica, who had negotiated an advantageous union with a Christian heiress, a girl under twelve years of age. (Augustine took a temporary mistress between the time he sent his original partner home and the marriage.) Such arranged marriages were common; the issue was not love but property and in this case Augustine was "trading up." It was not without remorse that he abandoned his partner of fifteen years: "Since she was an obstacle to my marriage, the woman I lived with for so long was torn out of my side. My heart, to which she had been grafted, was lacerated, wounded, shedding blood."

Marriage to his original partner would have been difficult. Roman law forbade marriage with persons of a lower class, and Augustine, although he kept delaying it, was feeling himself gradually called to a life of celibacy, the proper route for an aspiring philosopher who could devote all his energies to the pleasures of the mind and to God. His position henceforth would be that the purpose of sex was procreation, not mutual pleasure.

We know little about the woman. Did she go willingly back to her people? Did Monica tell her it was best for her and for Augustine? We will never know. Some would argue that it was irresponsible for the future saint to abandon a faithful partner with a teenaged son. But suppose he had stayed with her. Would he have emerged as the most brilliant thinker of the early church? Probably not. Would he have been an excellent North African master of classical rhetoric and a Christian philosopher of the first order? Most likely. In any case, this unknown woman gave him a brilliant son, who died at age sixteen, and she was very probably a loving, constant companion to one of the church's most original minds.

We give you thanks, O God, for the faithfulness of an unknown woman, for her care of Augustine and their son, for their family life together, and for the memory of their separate lives, which find their completion in you, the author and finisher of our faith. Amen.

ST. JOSEPHINE BAKHITA

Religious, Former Slave, Sudan and Italy,
1869–1947

I received the Sacrament of Baptism with such joy that only angels could describe. . . .

If I were to meet the slave-traders who kidnapped me and even those who tortured me, I would kneel and kiss their hands, for if that did not happen, I would not be a Christian and Religious today.

—St. Josephine Bakhita

From slave to saint is how the life trajectory of Mother Josephine Bakhita reads. Born in 1869 to a loving family in a Sudanese village, as a small child she was kidnapped, sold as a slave, and mutilated and tortured by her captors. In a first-person narrative she wrote, "One day I unwittingly made a mistake that incensed the master's son. He became furious, snatched me violently from my hiding place, and began to strike me ferociously with the lash and his feet. Finally he left me for half-dead, completely unconscious. Some slaves carried me away and lay me on a straw mat, where I remained for over a month." Next she was sold to a Turkish general, whose mistress beat her frequently and had her tattooed in over sixty places. The incisions were cut with a razor and salt was rubbed into the cuts, producing terrible, sustained pain. "I thought I would die, especially when salt was poured in the wounds. . . . It was by a miracle of God I didn't die. He had destined me for better things."

Finally, at age fourteen, she was sold to an Italian diplomat, who took her to Italy as a nursemaid. While there in 1888 she was instructed to stay with the child she was watching and, since the young girl was learning about the Christian religion from the Sisters of Charity, the Canossian Sisters in Venice, Bakhita received instruction as well. "The saintly sisters helped me know God, whom I had experienced in my heart since childhood," she wrote. "I had asked who could be the master of the sun, moon, stars — now at last I knew him."

A crisis came when the Italian diplomat's wife returned with her child to Africa. Bakhita was expected to accompany them dutifully, but she refused, preferring to stay with the sisters, seek baptism, and follow the religious life. High religious and civil authorities were contacted to support her refusal to return to Africa. Since slavery was illegal in Italy, Bakhita was able to remain in the convent, where she was baptized, confirmed, and received her first communion on January 9, 1890. After her baptism she kissed the font and said, "Here I became a daughter of God." Her utterances, following her baptism and entry in the religious life, were often ecstatic:

> "O Lord, if I could fly to my people and tell them of your Goodness at the top of my voice: Oh, how many souls would be won!"

> "When a person loves another dearly, he desires strongly to be close to the other: therefore, why be afraid to die? Death brings us to God!"

Bakhita joined the religious order on December 8, 1896, at age forty-one, where she served as convent cook, seamstress, sacristan, and doorkeeper. "You teach catechism. I will stay in the chapel and pray for you that you may teach well," she told the sisters. She remained active in the order until she died on February 8, 1947. "Do you wish to go to heaven?" a sister asked her shortly before Bakhita's death. "I neither wish to go nor stay," was her reply, "God knows where to find me when he wants me!" The Roman Catholic Church proclaimed her a saint on October 1, 2000.[26]

> *I have given everything to my Master: He will take care of me.... The best thing for us is not what we consider best, but what the Lord wants of us!*   —St. Josephine Bakhita

STEPHEN BIKO

South African Political Activist, Martyr,
1946–1977

We as blacks cannot forget the fact that Christianity in Africa is tied up with the entire colonial process. This meant that Christians came here with a form of culture which they called Christian but which in effect was Western, and which expressed itself as an imperial culture as far as Africa was concerned.   —Stephen Biko

Bantu Stephen Biko was only thirty years old when the South African police beat him to death. Of medium height and possessed with restless energy, a fiery orator and charismatic leader, Biko sped like a meteor to the top of the South African civil rights movement. The person who, had he lived, might have become South Africa's first black president became a prime target for the omnipresent security forces. They tracked his every move, often interrogated him, and frequently placed him under arrest or banned him from speaking in public, writing for publication, or receiving more than one nonfamily visitor at a time.

The man who would be considered the father of Black Consciousness, a movement he called "black self-reliance," was born on December 4, 1946, in King William's Town, South Africa, into an Anglican family. While a teenager, he wrote to a family friend, a white Anglican priest, Aelred Stubbs, while wrestling with the question of finding or abandoning a faith. After graduating from the Roman Catholic Marianhill secondary school in Natal in 1965, he enrolled in medical school in Durban, but soon his energies were devoted to politics. From the start, Biko was clear in his call for black political and cultural autonomy in South Africa. "The whites were doing all the talking and the blacks listening," he said. Disenchanted with a moderate multiracial student group, in 1968 he became the first president of the all-black South African Students' Organization (SASO). Biko preached a twofold message: apartheid subjected South African blacks not only to grievous political, economic, and social injustice, but also caused blacks to think, feel, and act as inferiors. He was among the first South African black leaders to say publicly that white liberals could not be their voices, that blacks must raise their own collective consciousness and esteem and take their own place in claiming their freedoms.

When asked, "How does Christianity fit in with black consciousness?" Biko replied:

I grew up in the Anglican Church, so this matter is an important one for me. But it is a troublesome question, for in South Africa, Christianity for most people is purely a formal matter. We as blacks cannot forget the fact that Christianity in Africa is tied up with the entire colonial process. This meant that Christians came here with a form of culture which they called Christian but which in effect was Western, and which expressed itself as an imperial culture as far as Africa was concerned.[27]

Banned in 1973, Biko was arrested four times during the next two years and was often held for months at a time without trial. He was seized at a roadblock on August 18, 1977, and jailed in Port Elizabeth. Held naked and manacled, he was subjected to ruthless interrogations and beatings, suffered severe brain damage, and died after being transported in an unconscious state nearly 740 miles in the back of a truck to Pretoria. A medical report prepared in 1998 disclosed, "On September 12, Stephen Biko died on the floor of a cell in Pretoria central prison, naked and alone. The post mortem examination showed brain damage, ... extensive head trauma ... and various external injuries. The medical treatment was subsequently described by a judge of the Supreme Court as having been 'callous, lacking any element of compassion, care or humanity.' "

Police denied any mistreatment of their prisoner. Their lame alibi was that he was seized with rage and hurled himself against a wall. A subsequent inquest absolved the police of any wrongdoing, but in 1977 five former police officers confessed to Biko's murder. (They had received grants of amnesty from the South African Truth and Reconciliation Commission.)

Reflecting on Biko's importance to a generation of young South African blacks and on the international acclaim in which he was held, the well-known journalist Donald Woods concluded with a New Testament quotation appropriate for all of South Africa: "Weep not for me, but for yourselves and for your children."

At Biko's funeral, attended by fifteen thousand persons, Desmond Tutu, recalling the language of Martin Luther King Jr., said, "We are experiencing the birth pangs of a new South Africa, where all of us, black and white, shall walk tall. For all of us, black and white together, shall overcome, nay, indeed have already overcome."

O God our Father, whose Son forgave his enemies while he was suffering shame and death: Strengthen those who suffer for the sake of conscience; when they are accused, save them from speaking in hate; when they are rejected, save them from bitterness; when they are imprisoned, save them from despair; and to us your servants, give grace to respect their witness and to discern the truth, that our society may be cleansed and strengthened. This we ask for the sake of Jesus Christ, our merciful and righteous Judge. Amen.

— Prayer Book and Hymnal, 823

LOTT CARY

First American Black Missionary to Liberia,
Governor of Liberia, 1780–1828

∷∷∷∷∷∷∷∷∷∷

Born on a Virginian slave plantation, Lott Cary became a Christian convert at age twenty-seven. By 1813 he had saved the $850 needed to purchase his freedom and that of his two children. (He was a widower.) Cary had an unusual dream in that or any age: he wanted to carry the Christian Gospel to Africa, for which he gained the support of the Virginia-based African Baptist Missionary Society.

The American Colonization Society, a private group, founded Liberia, to which Lott Cary was attracted in the 1820s as a place to repatriate freed black slaves, but only three thousand such persons responded to the offer. In 1857, almost three decades after Cary's death, Liberia would be recognized as an independent republic. In a wider context, Cary represented a religion of biblical and civic enthusiasm, given not only to preaching the Gospel but also to directly influencing civic life. For freed slaves, such participation in political society is understandable; Cary's religion belonged to a brand of nineteenth-century evangelism from which the later social gospel emerged.

The first such American-African colonization effort took place in 1820 in Sierra Leone, but the settlers were devastated by malaria. Then on January 23, 1821, the black Virginian and a group of colonists set sail for Africa. The U.S. government, hoping to send freed slaves to a new republic in Africa, sponsored their voyage, a follow-up to the unsuccessful Sierra Leone venture. Cary explained his reasons for the voyage:

> I am an African, and in this country, however meritorious my conduct and respectable my character, I cannot receive the credit due to either. I wish to go to a country where I shall be estimated by my merits, not by my complexion; and I feel bound to labor for my suffering race.

Arriving in Africa, he explained his missionary strategy:

If you intend to do anything for Africa, you must not wait for the Colonization Society, nor for government; for neither of these are in search of missionary ground, but of colonizing grounds; if it should not sow missionary seeds, you cannot expect a missionary crop. And, moreover, all of us who are connected with the agents, who are under public instructions, must be conformed to their laws whether they militate against missionary operations or not.[28]

An activist, Cary helped found the new Liberia "Place of Freedom" settlement and the Providence Baptist Church, the first missionary Baptist church in Africa. He also built several schools and was named the settlement's health officer, an important post in such a pestilential climate. He worked hard with the sick and destitute and then became a popular leader at a time when the settlement's fortunes were low. Dissension was rife, supplies were exhausted, and the health of the dwindling band of colonists was deteriorating.

In August 1828 Cary was elevated to governor after the previous governor had died at age thirty-five, after naming Cary his successor. Cary's untimely death came that year in a freak explosion of gunpowder as he was preparing to defend the colony against attack. Eight persons perished in the explosion, and Liberia's arms supply was destroyed. The church he founded in Monrovia continues to exist 175 years later.

> *Everlasting God, whose servant Lott Cary carried the good news of your son to Liberia: grant that we who commemorate his service may know the hope of the Gospel in our hearts and manifest its light in all our ways, through Jesus Christ our Lord. Amen.* — Celebrating Common Prayer, 488

EUGÉNE CASALIS

French Protestant Missionary to Basutoland,
1812–1891

The French Reformed Church was an active presence in South Africa, primarily in Basutoland, and as was common among French Protestant missionaries, a few leading families tended to support the missions generation after generation.

One such person was Eugéne Casalis, who spent twenty-three years among the Basuto before returning to Paris to become head of missionary training for his church. Like many French raised in a Calvinistic tradition, Casalis learned as much of the fear of God as he did of the love of God in his early years.[29]

Casalis decided to become a missionary at age nine. He had been reading some of the missionary literature for children widely circulated in France by religious groups. The youth found what he called a "living sympathy" for Africans, triggered in part by an illustration in a story, "Gumal and Lina," in which a young African, surrounded by the forests, lifts his arms skyward and says, "I am a Christian." Accounts of the Spanish conquest of Mexico and Peru also aroused in him empathy for indigenous peoples.

Casalis arrived in South Africa on February 24, 1833, after an arduous three-and-a-half month voyage to the Cape. There he was met by the redoubtable John Philip (see p. 166), who welcomed a generation of new missionaries to South Africa even when they were not members of his own denomination. It was Philip who suggested that Casalis resume the work of earlier French missionaries among the Basuto, who had been scattered in a recent violent war.

Eventually the missionaries arrived at Thaba Nchu, the Black Mountain, where they led a service for some of the subchiefs of Moshesh, leader of the Basuto. The setting was one of spectacular beauty — brooding mountains, a vast plain filled with wildlife, and verdant pastures. Casalis, preaching in the idiom of that era, told the Basuto that the missionaries were servants of a high God, who had revealed himself to them through Jesus Christ and who offered blessings and salvation to those who accepted the divine message. One

46

sentence from his sermon: "If you will receive our message, you will be like the ostrich which rejects its old feathers in order to get more beautiful ones."

Next they met the paramount chief, Moshesh, at his palace high atop Thaba Bosiu Mountain. Entrance to the plateau on which the massive compound was situated was by a winding narrow path along a riverbed, easily defensible by warriors at the top. Moshesh was a commanding presence, a leader now in his middle years, possessed with gravitas and a trim, athletic body.

Casalis expressed the missionaries' sorrow at the loss of life the Basuto had sustained in recent wars, as suggested by the whitened bones visible on the plain. War was the product of human pride and evil, the missionary continued, but because they were representatives of God, their desire was to bring peace. A new era of peace and progress was theirs, Casalis said, if the Basuto would accept the missionary presence and the God represented by it. The missionaries asked for land and permission to operate among the Basuto. Moshesh readily supported them, and soon land was cleared, buildings were constructed, and European agricultural practices were introduced alongside indigenous ones.

"None of us experienced even the shadow of a regret for having left all that was most dear to us for the Lord," Casalis wrote. He and the French Protestant missionaries established a solid presence among the Basuto, making it easier for Roman Catholic and Church of the Province of South Africa missionaries to conduct their activity a decade later. Among the Basuto he was known as Mahloana-Matsoana, "The man with the small black eyes," and "the friend of Moshesh."

> *You only are my portion, O Lord;*
> *I have promised to keep your words.*
> *I entreat you with all my heart,*
> *Be merciful to me according to your promise.*
> —Psalm 119:57–58

ST. CATHERINE OF ALEXANDRIA

Martyr, early fourth century

⊗⊗⊗⊗⊗⊗⊗⊗⊗⊗

St. Catherine, legend has it, was well educated and of noble birth. While still a teenager, she admonished the Roman emperor Maximianus, violent persecutor of the Christians, for his cruelty. She also debated with his court's pagan philosophers and converted them to Christianity. The new Christians were immediately martyred, as was the emperor's wife on accepting baptism. Catherine was then broken on the wheel, which has become the symbol identified with her, and was beheaded, after which angels solemnly carried her body to Mt. Sinai, according to early accounts.

The Byzantine emperor Justinian founded a Greek Orthodox monastery on Mt. Sinai in 527, reportedly at the prodding of his wife. It resembled a Byzantine military structure, with thick granite walls. At that time, many religious establishments were constructed like fortresses; otherwise they would have no chance against raiders. In 570 A.D. a monk described the setting as "the abode of a multitude of monks and hermits who came to meet us bearing crosses and singing psalms and falling upon the ground to reverence us. And we did likewise, shedding tears." In 628 the Prophet Muhammad granted a Charter of Privileges to the monks of St. Catherine's Monastery, assuring them of protection, freedom of worship, and movement. The Charter said, "No one is to destroy a house of their religion, to damage it, or to carry anything from it to the Muslims' houses.... If a female Christian is married to a Muslim, it is not to take place without her approval. She is not to be prevented from visiting her church to pray."

The monastery has always had a symbiotic relationship with the local Muslim community. A small mosque, still used today, stands on its premises, and its guards historically have been local Bedouin Arabs, supported by the monastic community.

During the Middle Ages, Catherine became a cult figure, and pilgrimages were made from all over Europe to her resting place. But gradually interest waned, and the resident number of religious dwindled. Only a few aged monks remain as guardians of this once-popular international shrine, which distributed daily food for four hundred persons and bread for another thousand. A priceless collection of icons, some of them dating to the eighth century, are housed on the premises, as are thousands of manuscripts containing texts of the early church.

> *Almighty God, by whose grace and power the holy martyr Catherine triumphed over suffering and was faithful unto death, strengthen us with your grace, that we may endure reproach and persecution and faithfully bear witness to the same through Jesus Christ our Lord. Amen.*
> — *Celebrating Common Prayer,* 484

MOTHER CECILE

South African Religious Educator,
1862–1906

⸭⸭⸭⸭⸭⸭⸭⸭⸭⸭

Nothing helps one so much as to fix one's mind on Christ and let Him
teach one how, from the Manger to the Cross, Incarnate Love gave to the
uttermost. If we look long enough at that great fact, the nails may still be
iron, but there comes the grace and strength not to wish to come down
from our own cross.   — Mother Cecile

Sister Cecile, at age twenty-one, became the first member of the
Anglican Community of the Resurrection, which was established in
Grahamstown, South Africa. The nuns created a training college for
teachers and assisted in parochial, educational, and social ministries.
They also ran an orphanage, schools for colored children, St. Francis Xavier Mission for the Chinese community, an industrial training
school for African girls, a hostel, and similar institutions in what is
now Zimbabwe.

The impetus for such missionary activity came from a woman born
to a privileged English home, Annie Cecelia Isherwood, daughter of
Captain and Mrs. Isherwood of Hillingdon Lodge, Uxbridge, a family that traced its lineage to a signer of the Magna Charta. Cecelia's
loving home was torn asunder by the death of her mother when Cecelia was only eight, and that of her father five years later. She was
then raised by her brother and devoted family friends, General Sir
James and Lady Browne. She attended the fashionable London parish of St. Peter's, Eaton Square, where conversations with a sensitive
and supportive rector led to her confirmation, a life of parish work,
and her being set apart as a deaconess. Invited by Bishop Webb of
Grahamstown, South Africa, to join him in that diocese, she became
part of the effort to expand the Anglican Church there.

After arriving in South Africa, she witnessed the striking need for
prison reform. Adults and children were herded together, and stray
children were locked in cells with hardened offenders. The young social reformer's intense lobbying led to a parliamentary commission
being named to investigate the problem. Meanwhile, she founded
an orphanage in Grahamstown and a home for unwed mothers in
Port Elizabeth. At the request of Bishop Webb, she agreed to be-

come the first member of the Community of the Resurrection of Our Lord, the second Anglican sisterhood to take root in South Africa. Cecile became a life-professed nun at age twenty-five in 1887. While the community found an attractive property, Eden Grove, near the Grahamstown Botanical Gardens, the nuns lived barely at a subsistence level to pay the mortgage. In the early years, they possessed only one cloak and pair of shoes for wear in bad weather, and only one lamp for communal use at night. An indigenous priest gave a small donation to the nuns, "the ladies with their heads tied up."

By all accounts, her chief work was the Grahamstown Training College, which prepared European women to work with Africans. Not only did she raise private funds for it, but arranged for state support as well. Both English and Dutch girls were admitted. (Admission of African young was not a possibility in the late nineteenth century.) She died in 1906 of a painful and incurable illness. Her testimony was:

We must never forget that Our Blessed Lord Himself first looked out in human form upon this world of ours in the face of a little child; and we want to nurture and train his children for Him, that their life and their work here on earth may be a steadfast looking up to the Face of Our Lord Jesus Christ.

— Mother Cecile[30]

JOHN CHILEMBWE

Central African Pastor-Revolutionary,
d. 1915

🙨🙨🙨🙨🙨🙨🙨🙨🙨

Let the rich men, bankers, titled men, storekeepers, farmers and landlords go to war and get shot. Instead the poor Africans who have nothing to own in this present world...are to die in a cause which is not theirs.
— John Chilembwe on the eve of World War I

The modern Malawi banknotes show a thin, intense face, with focused eyes and determined, parched lips. The person is John Chilembwe, well known as an early nationalist-revolutionary who died in an abortive 1915 uprising. Chilembwe spent his life as a Central African pastor, constantly rebuffed by the white political-religious establishment until he saw armed revolution as the only option open to him.

Chilembwe entered the mission world in 1892 as a cook in the Zambezi Industrial Mission. Joseph Booth, a British missionary, adopted him and took the youth to America, where he studied at Virginia Theological Seminary in Lynchburg, Virginia. Chilembwe returned to Nyasaland (now Malawi) in 1900, sponsored by the Negro Baptist Convention. The Providence Industrial Mission, which Chilembwe directed for fourteen years, was highly successful, consciously modeled on the Booker T. Washington school of self-help. Several hundred children attended mission schools, and the African Industrial Society, which Chilembwe founded, taught local people vocational skills. "He devoted himself to schools and agricultural improvement, to hygiene, health, and temperance. He was the archetypal Improver. An asthmatic with failing sight, he was a most unlikely revolutionary," Elizabeth Isichei concludes.[31]

Next door to these expanding enterprises were the Bruce estates, a sprawling plantation owned by Scots. The missionary David Livingstone's son-in-law ran this development set in choice highland agricultural lands. A classic settler-native conflict evolved. The plantation needed cheap labor and hired from Chilembwe's community, offering low salaries and demanding working conditions. European planters had expropriated land for their great estates, and Africans could be summarily ordered to move or be required to pay land rents. Building permanent homes was never a possibility, nor was the prospect of planting crops or trees.

In short, the settler government viewed the expanding Christian communities as landless squatters. Grass-hut churches near the modest dwellings were apparently burned by estate management, and tensions mounted. Famine struck between 1912 and 1914, and hut taxes on Africans rose. Then came World War I, which meant the disruption of African societies through forced recruitment of soldiers and porters and through European warfare fought locally by African troops wearing European uniforms. Chilembwe described the situation in a letter to the editor of the *Nyasaland Times*, which brought the issue's swift confiscation:

> A number of Police are marching in various villages persuading well-built natives to join the war. The masses of our people are ready to put on uniforms ignorant of what they have to face or why they have to face it.... Will there be any good prospects for the natives after the end of the war? Shall we be recognized as anybody in the best interests of civilization and Christianity after the great struggle is ended? ... In time of peace the Government failed to help the underdog. In time of peace, everything for Europeans only. And instead of honor we suffer humiliation.... But in time of war it has been found that we are needed to share hardships and shed our blood in equality.[32]

What happened next was a desperate, violent uprising of the disenfranchised, the sort of short-lived revolts that sprung up in Vietnam against French rule or in India against the British. On January 23, 1915, Chilembwe led a party of armed Africans onto the agricultural estate, where, acting on impulse, they decapitated one of the bosses, William Jervis Livingstone, and bore his head to the church in a nearby town. The revolt sputtered but lasted until February 4. As government forces approached, the revolt collapsed. Its leaders were captured and hanged. Chilembwe was killed on February 3, 1915, by a small police patrol that stumbled on him as he fled toward Mozambique.

Like such jacqueries anywhere, Chilembwe's revolt raises questions. Why did a pastor turn suddenly into a violent insurrectionist? Was it his personal condition of being in debt and his embittered attitude toward colonialism? Did his desperate group expect divine assistance? "Let us strike a blow and die," was the movement's motto, deliberately chosen after the example of the American insurrectionist

John Brown. Adrian Hastings has remarked, "Chilembwe has proved vastly more powerful in death than in life: the strangest of mini-risings largely unsupported in a land not excessively ill governed has become in the retrospect of mythological history a famous expression of proto-nationalism and Christian resistance."[33]

> *O Lord in whose hands all your children find the divine justice that eludes human understanding, we commend to your mercy the peoples of East Africa of all races, languages, and social conditions. Remove such hatred as infects their hearts, and give them wisdom and patience that can come only from you, the eternal God in whom our voiceless strivings find fulfillment. Amen.*

CLEMENT OF ALEXANDRIA
Father of the Church, c. 150–c. 215

Although born in Athens sometime during the third century, Clement moved across the Mediterranean to Alexandria, the intellectual, political, and economic center of Egypt, where he became one of the leading theological figures of his age. Of pagan birth, once Clement became a Christian he founded a school to instruct new believers. In about 202 Clement fled Alexandria for Palestine during a time of persecutions and did not return. His talented student, Origen, took over the school.[34]

Coming from Athens, Clement knew the Greek language and philosophy well. He was both a mystic and a sharp polemicist, defending the newly spreading Christian religion. Clement drew on the Old Testament prophets and on the Incarnation, the word becoming flesh in Jesus the Christ, in several of his writings.

In *Paedagogus*, an instructional work for the newly baptized, he described the details of Christian morality in the daily life of a believer, including rules of etiquette and personal behavior. Other works treat the relationship of Christianity to Greek culture; here Clement laid the foundations for a school of Christian humanism, arguing the compatibility of much Greek secular knowledge and philosophy as "the servant of theology." Philosophy, Clement believed, contained a partial truth and was a gift of God, which led to further truth. The mystical way of ascending toward Christ is another avenue to finding divine truth. The church, baptism, and the Eucharist, so central to later generations of Christian thinkers, receive little attention from the author, whose energies, like many of his generation, were aimed at contesting Greeks and pagans.

Clement was also an early writer about the two cities, the City of God and the political state, an idea Augustine would develop two centuries later. For Clement, the Christian's first duty was to live as a citizen of heaven, and then as a citizen of the earth. Should a conflict between the two arise, Christians should follow the "higher law" of God, he argued.

Almighty God, who enlightened your church by the teaching of your servant Clement: enrich it evermore with your heavenly grace, and raise up faithful witnesses, who by their life and teaching may proclaim the truth of your salvation, through Jesus Christ our Lord. Amen.

— *Celebrating Common Prayer*, 485

FRANÇOIS COLLIARD

French Missionary to South Africa,
1834–1904

❀❀❀❀❀❀❀❀

Life was never easy for the French Protestant missionary François Colliard, who spent most of his professional life among the Basuto people of South Africa. Born of Huguenot stock in France, Colliard was an introverted, introspective bookish youth who grew up in the starkly Calvinistic setting of the French Reformed Church.[35] His first three years in Basutoland were spent alone, awaiting the arrival of his bride-to-be, Christina Mackintosh, the strong-willed daughter of an Edinburgh minister. The nearest mission station was nearly fifty miles away, and there were no Christians among the Basuto. Eventually a three-room hut was built, and an ox was killed and roasted as a celebration, to which Colliard's African neighbors were invited. Although Colliard had difficulties with the local chief, his stay was assisted by the friendship of a valued African colleague, Nathaniel Makatoko, nephew of the great king Moshesh, a Christian and a supporter of the missionary through the years.

As a preacher, the French missionary used local proverbs and fables to illuminate Gospel points. In one diary entry he wrote of employing illustrations of the Grasshopper, the Ant, and the Bee, which were crowd-pleasers. As his knowledge of the language improved, he wrote Christian songs for use during planting and harvesting cycles and at other times in the people's lives. The local people, used to singing, asked him to "weep" on the accordion he brought from France.

With Christina's arrival on January 3, 1861, life took a decided upturn for Colliard. Although the Colliards spent the first five years of their married life together at the mission station, they often traveled to outlying regions by wagon, which Christina made attractive with rugs and curtains. Of their wooden wagon, Colliard exclaimed, "It is the eighth wonder of the world!" She traveled frequently with her husband and was an active participant in his activities. Once she gathered the mission women with her and sat sewing under a tree waiting for a chief who had threatened to throw them down a crag to change his mind. In another instance, her husband sent her to negotiate safe passage for the mission party across hostile land, since she was a skilled negotiator with local peoples.

In April 1866 Boer soldiers from the expanding Free State were at war with the Basuto, and the French missionaries, whom the Boer did not trust, were expelled. Finally, in 1869 they were allowed to return, and they stayed another five years, after which the Paris Mission Society asked them to commence work in Barotseland in the northern Transvaal. Here Colliard and his party were rejected by four major chiefs and narrowly escaped a massacre. Local people systematically rebuffed them, until they happened upon a Sotho-speaking ethnic group on the Zambezi River.

Colliard was fifty when he returned to Barotseland in 1884. Bloody local wars prevented his wife from joining him for three years. In 1866 Lewanika, a shifty local king, invited him to work among the Barotse. Lewanika never converted to Christianity but constantly tried to manipulate the missionary to his advantage. On several occasions Colliard stood up against the tyrannical ruler. For example, once one of the king's ministers was falsely accused, forced to strip, and then made to crouch down in the burning sand while enemies shouted accusations against him, demanding that he be bound and slain. "You shall not kill that man," Colliard yelled above the din. "You can kill me first," and he called the accused victim "a servant of God and a minister of mercy."

Colliard was gravely ill by 1904, and the faithful Barotse surrounded his house, singing hymns until his death. His last will and testament, addressed to the Protestant churches of France, adjured them never to "renounce the rich harvest reserved to the sowing they have accomplished in suffering and tears." The balance sheet on Colliard's work is mixed. He did not convert vast numbers of Africans to the Christian faith, but the sensitive student of local customs did build a cadre of faithful Christians who planted the seed for future evangelism. Through his translations he earned the respect of many local people preparing for the next generation of missionary activity.

Almighty God, you call your witnesses from every nation to reveal your glory in their lives. We thank you for the example of François and Christina Colliard and their companion Nathaniel Makatoko, Christians in South Africa, whose steadfast patience and perseverance helped advance your kingdom. This we pray in the name of Jesus, the Good Shepherd. Amen.

DANIEL COMBONI

Missionary Bishop to Egypt and the Sudan,
Founder of the Comboni Missionary
Congregations, 1831–1881

Some people would consider Daniel Comboni a failure when he died in Khartoum in 1881. The missionary priest had been working actively in or for Africa for over thirty years and had produced a continent-wide strategic document, *Plan for the Regeneration of Africa*, but had little to show for it. Over a hundred of the priests he recruited had died, most of his Sudan missions had failed, were struggling, or would soon be wiped out by the Muslim Mahdi. But a century later, the Combonians and Comboni Sisters were a strong missionary order in Africa and Latin America. Comboni ranks, with Venn, Libermann, and Lavigerie, as one of the handful of nineteenth-century figures claiming an encompassing missionary vision. His was a long-term strategy: "The missionaries will have to understand that they are stones hid under the earth, which will perhaps never come to light, but which will become part of the foundations of a vast, new building."[36]

Born in a small town in Italy in 1831, Comboni always wanted to be a priest, developed a strong interest in Africa, and participated in an expedition to the south of the Sudan in 1857. Tropical illnesses decimated the small group and, as he lay dying, the father superior said, "If it should happen that only one of you be left, let him not give up or lose confidence.... Swear to me that you will not turn back." "Africa or death," Comboni answered. (He was the first mission's only survivor and returned to Italy to recover his health.)

What was the best way to conduct missionary work in Africa? Comboni wrestled with the question, and in 1864 while in Rome he wrote *Plan for the Regeneration of Africa*. Facing the issues of climate and disease head on, as well as the problem of African students' cultural adaptability to Europe, Comboni recommended that all European missionary orders should combine resources (this was in the heyday of the "scramble for Africa" and went against prevailing trends). Together they should build institutes in favorable climactic zones throughout the continent. Here Europeans could come to teach and Africans to learn, not only as religious, but as lay teachers and craftspersons as well. When institute courses were completed, Africans and Europeans would then head to the interior together, but the Europeans would leave after a few years, to be replaced by other Europeans or not, depending on the need. "The regeneration of Africa by means of Africa itself seems to me the only possible way to Christianize the continent," Comboni wrote.

As might be expected, the French refused to participate in such a plan, although Rome found it attractive and encouraged the Italian missionary, who then created the Cairo Institute, with schools for girls and boys and a hospital, as the first such launching pad. (It would be his only one). The Verona Sisters and Verona Fathers came a few years later, and by late 1871 Comboni returned to the Sudan to set up operations himself. He was named vicar apostolic of Central Africa in 1877.

The task Comboni faced in Africa in the 1870s was complicated by the slave trade. Slavery was big business in Central Africa, with large, well-armed caravans of recruiters who bribed Egyptian officials to let them move freely from the interior to port cities, where they sold their human cargo. Comboni fought hard against slavery, was given his own small army to combat the traffickers, closed the El Obeid slave market, and hunted down some of the slave raiders. But he was only one person against an established industry.

With Comboni was the first African priest to work in Central Africa, Fr. Pius Hadrianus, a Benedictine. Soon another African priest, Fr. Antonio Dubale, was running a model village for freed slaves in El Obeid. A trained Nubian catechist, product of the Cairo Institute, was dispatched to work among this important southern Sudan ethnic group. The Nubians had a rich culture, were anti-Islamic, and were a logical target for mission work.

Comboni was a major figure in African religious life, training African missionaries, combating the slave trade, establishing a small number of solidly conceived mission stations in Sudan, and, most importantly, establishing the Verona Fathers and Sisters, which went through various reorganizations to emerge as the Comboni missionary congregations. Comboni was beatified in Rome on March 17, 1996.

Look on those who revere you, O God, on those who trust in your merciful one. Heal our sad divisions and our enmities,

O Lord, help us to reject the ways of violence. Then shall dawn break over the desert; then shall your children from north and south in Sudan sing your praises, Holy one whom we know by many names. Amen.

ERNEST CREUX
AND PAUL BERTHOUD

Swiss Missionaries to South Africa,
1845–1929 and 1847–1930

※※※※※※※※※※

> I see in front of me all that can be described as the most hideous, physically, but Jesus loves them, we love them in His love, and, in return, their poor suffering hearts are filled with love and gratitude.
> — Ernest Creux, of a South African leper community

Switzerland is a small country of purposeful people and, though its missionary presence was never a large one, its members engaged in carefully planned mission activity. Such was the case of Ernest Creux and Paul Berthoud, two late nineteenth- and early twentieth-century missionaries who worked among the Thonga-speaking people of the northern Transvaal and the Ronga-speaking people of Mozambique.[37] In all, nearly three hundred houses of worship were built in the two locations during the missionaries' long stay in Africa, and they were known as well for their work among lepers, prisoners, and the mentally ill.

Both came from the Free Church of the Canton of Vaud, the region near Geneva. Creux was impulsive and poetic, an intuitive pastor; Berthoud was the careful planner and organizer, the conceptualizer of the duo. Since their own denomination did not at that time have a missionary program, the pair was sent to the University of Edinburgh to learn English and something about medicine. In 1875 Creux, Berthoud, and their families set out for an inland posting among the Gwamba people. Boer hostility to the ethnic group was strong. One elder said, "They are thieves, liars, tricksters, and apart from this, they speak a very difficult tongue." "These are just the kind of people we are looking for," one of the missionaries replied. "Didn't Jesus come to seek and to save the lost?" By July 9, 1875, the missionary caravan of thirty-nine persons, with two babies in their midst, and over a hundred beasts arrived in the mountainous Spelonken district, which reminded them of Switzerland. Despite the difficulties of having no home and few supplies, they set about building a mission station. Their plans were brutally interrupted in their second year, when Creux and Berthoud were seized and placed in protective custody by the suspicious Boers, who were at war with a local tribe.

The women were left to run the new mission for several months. In 1879 and 1880 a malaria epidemic struck, killing Mrs. Berthoud and, one by one, her five children. Meanwhile, three of Creux's children died from diphtheria. Despite tragic setbacks, the sponsoring missionary organizations redoubled their efforts on behalf of the South African mission. A local evangelist was ordained for work among the Gwamba people in Portuguese territory and Paul's brother, Henri, came to South Africa as well. Meanwhile, Berthoud continued his recuperation in Switzerland, printing a book of translations of biblical passages and hymns in the local language. Creux, still in Africa, was asked to mediate a dispute between the Transvaal government and the Bavenda people, who refused to pay taxes to the invader.

A feature of the Swiss missions was the active recruitment and training of African clergy, but in Creux's region, setbacks were experienced. The influx of gold miners brought severe social disruptions, with rootless male workers paid high wages and seeking strong drink. The fragile stability of the tranquil Christian communities was threatened; the mission salaries could not compete with the miners' wages, and other distractions were multiple.

By century's end the mission stations were established on solid ground. Creux remained now in Pretoria as director of activities. He also ministered to more than four hundred Africans condemned to the scaffold by the South African government and to a leper community as well. Of the lepers he said, "I see in front of me all that can be described as the most hideous, physically, but Jesus loves them, we love them in His love, and, in return, their poor suffering hearts are filled with love and gratitude." Berthoud remained in Mozambique. His triumph was construction of a church that held twelve hundred persons, but he faced the bitter loss of his second wife as well, a victim of dysentery.

> *Lord, you have been our refuge*
> *from one generation to another.*
> *Before the mountains were brought forth*
> *or the land and the earth were born,*
> *from age to age you are God.*
> —Psalm 90:1–2

SAMUEL AJAYI CROWTHER

African Bishop of the Niger Territories,
c. 1806–1891

৪৪৪৪৪৪৪৪৪৪

The whole proceeding seemed to myself like a dream. . . . At the conclusion
of the blessing, the whole church rang with *ke oh sheh* — so be it, so let
it be.
— Bishop Crowther commenting on one of the first services
conducted in the Yoruba language, 1844, in Freetown, Sierra Leone

He had a gift for languages and helped translate the Bible and *Book of
Common Prayer* into Yoruba, a major language of Nigeria, and into
other dialects as well. As an explorer he received a gold medal for
his West African discoveries. As a missionary he founded schools and
training colleges and steadily built local congregations, encouraging
them to improve their lot with commerce in cotton and agriculture. In Canterbury Cathedral on St. Peter's Day 1864 Samuel Ajayi
Crowther was consecrated first bishop of the Niger Territories, a position he held for the next twenty-seven years until death claimed him
in 1891.[38]

The teen-aged Crowther was captured during a Nigerian civil war
and sold to Portuguese slave traders. But the vessel transferring him
to America met a British antislavery patrol, and he was taken to Freetown, Sierra Leone, where he was educated at a Church Missionary
Society (CMS) school and baptized in 1825. After a brief visit to
England he returned home and studied to be a schoolteacher at the
recently opened training college, Fourah Bay Institute. Crowther's in-
telligence and conscientiousness made him stand out, and when an
expedition to the Niger region was proposed in 1841, he was invited
to join it as a catechist. The journey was no Discovery Channel holi-
day trip. Well-armed slave traders controlled much of the region, and
malaria (mal-air or "bad air") was a constant threat.

Impressed with Crowther's ability, in 1842 the CMS sent him to
their Islington, England, training college. Ordained a priest in 1843,
he returned first to Sierra Leone and then to Yoruba land. At that time
British mission policy encouraged indigenous churches to take responsibility for their own activities under local leadership. An African

diocese was decided upon as part of mission strategy, and Crowther, thoroughly Victorian in outlook, was named its bishop.

The 1880s were the high noon of British imperialism, and policy shifted sharply under the leadership of colonial administrator Sir George Goldie, who wanted to keep trade entirely in British hands and religious missions led only by British missionaries. The growing African commercial infrastructure was thus left high and dry. Crowther became a bishop with no clearly defined diocese, with British subalterns who would not accept his authority and who subverted his activities, often in a mean-spirited, unchristian manner.

The formative years of Crowther's episcopacy were marked by constant sniping and undercutting from European associates. Although he opposed slavery, he did not speak out against polygamy, perhaps concluding that of all the issues facing a missionary bishop, this was not one with which he would have much success. His enemies charged that he misused mission funds, was a weak leader, and failed to discipline the morally corrupt members of his African clergy. Crowther's response to the last accusation was that he did act through admonition and such devices as temporary suspension from ministry or relocation of offending clergy; thus he hoped to maintain a base while he hoped to recruit a more able future round of ministers.

Crowther's European opponents argued that he could never be a bishop to whites because he was "too much a native"; neither would Africans accept him because he was a former captive, not a member of a noble family. Headquartered in Lagos, Crowther was never bishop in the colonial capital, but had vague responsibilities in an undefined part of the interior. Crowther has been called "a little man with nerves of steel, whom incessant work did not seem to wear." Reflective and introspective in temperament, his shy, soft-spoken pastoral manner was loving and compassionate. He was also courageous; once as a bishop he was captured by a local chief who demanded a ransom of two hundred slaves for his release. Crowther flatly refused. The bishop's opposition to the slave trade was unequivocal. He called it "a great abomination in the sight of God."

Crowther had been caught in a whiplash between two distinctly different policies. Originally, the CMS had wanted to create African missions led by trained Africans, but all that changed by the 1880s and the "scramble for Africa." Britain was there to rule now. Despite the difficulties, Crowther's achievement was considerable, missions were expanded, the Church of England's sacred books were translated into local languages, and local clergy and lay leadership were installed throughout the region. Crowther bore his difficulties patiently and never wavered as a Christian, thus creating a base from which a later generation of indigenous Anglican clergy would emerge to control their own ecclesial destinies, albeit not until the 1950s.

Other African Christians, watching the way he was treated, left the Church of England and formed the United Native African Church. CMS blindness contributed to the emergence of a distinct form of African Christianity often called Independency. Local churches sprung up all over the continent, mirroring the theology, liturgy, and organization of the churches from which they emerged, but, denied any substantive role in the original churches, they became independent bodies under local leadership. Their numbers proliferated in the twentieth century; they became a distinctive feature of Africa's religious landscape.

We praise you O God, for the life and witness of Samuel Ajayi Crowther, bishop of your church. Through his steadfast perseverance and fortitude in the face of adversity, he planted the seeds that grew in another generation, plentiful as the stars, abundant as the harvest, raising up a church in Nigeria and West Africa to proclaim the living Christ among us. Amen.

ALEXANDER CRUMMELL

"Missionary at Large of the Colored People,"
Liberia, Sierra Leone, 1819–1898

❀❀❀❀❀❀❀❀❀

> I saw Alexander Crummell first at a Wilberforce commencement season.
> . . . Tall, frail, and black, he stood, with simple dignity and an unmistakable
> air of good breeding. I began to feel the fineness of his character, his calm
> courtesy, the sweetness of his strength, and his fair blending of the hope
> and truth of life. — W. E. B. Du Bois

Alexander Crummell, who spent twenty years as a missionary in
Liberia and Sierra Leone, was born in New York City on March 3,
1819. After study at the Mulberry Street School and high school in
New York, he transferred to Canaan, New Hampshire, to a school
founded by the abolitionists, which was destroyed by an angry local
mob. After further study in Whitesboro, New York, and Boston, he
was ordained a minister at age twenty-five. Excluded from the ranks
of white clergy in his Episcopal diocese, he moved to England, where
he completed an A.B. degree at Queens College, Cambridge, in 1853.

Next he spent twenty years as a missionary in West Africa, serving
as professor of Mental and Moral Science at the College of Liberia.
Crummell supported the vision of a black Christian republic of freed
slaves, but became disillusioned with political life in Liberia, and his
health failed.

In 1880 Crummell founded St. Luke's Episcopal Church in Washington, D.C., and the American Negro Academy. He was a prolific essayist for nearly two decades. His books include *Future of
Africa* (1862), *Greatness of Christ* (1882), and *Africa and America*
(1892). A tireless activist, Crummell maintained a strong interest in
African missions. He believed that the best way for Africans to improve their situation was through acquiring "civilization," that is, a
classic Western education. If Africa "is ever regenerated the influences and agencies to this end must come from *external* sources.
Civilization . . . never springs up, spontaneously, in any new land. It
must be transplanted."[39]

Crummell believed that African-Americans were ideal candidates
to be missionaries to Africa. Crummell observed, "There is a tropical
fitness, which inheres in our constitution, whereby we are enabled . . .

to sit down under an African sun; and soon, and with comparative ease, feel ourselves at home." African-Americans also knew the "sorrow, pain, and deepest anguish" of slavery and thus demonstrated a special empathy with Africa. "The hand of God is on the black man, in all the lands of his distant sojourn, for the good of Africa. This continent is to be reclaimed for Christ. The faith of Jesus is to supersede all the abounding desolations of heathenism."[40]

The last two decades of the nineteenth century were times of mission expansion. Over a hundred black American missionaries went to Africa. Their viewpoints differed little from those of their white contemporaries. "Africa for Christ" was their rallying cry, but their message contained a basic contradiction; an attraction to the nobleness of native culture on the one hand and an aversion to heathenism on the other.

Crummell reflected the view of Africa as a "dark continent" prevalent among Americans of his time. Yet, like many African-American missionaries, he had high hopes for Africa. Christianity and civilization, he believed, together opened the road to a future of hope and progress.

> *Christ for the world we sing!*
> *The world to Christ we bring*
> *with loving zeal;*
> *the poor, and them that mourn,*
> *the faint and overborne,*
> *sin sick and sorrow-worn,*
> *whom Christ doth heal.*[41]

ST. CYPRIAN

Bishop of Carthage, Martyr, c. 200–258

The Word of God was led, wordless, to the Cross.
— St. Cyprian

A well-educated pagan lawyer, Cyprian became a priest after his conversion in his middle years and, two years later, a bishop. (The church was growing, leadership was in short supply, and bishops were numerous.) The early years of his episcopate coincided with the Roman persecutions of 250–251, and Cyprian went into hiding for over a year. Shortly after the persecutions, a devastating plague wracked the Carthage diocese, and he urged church members to be exceptionally generous in ministering to their afflicted sisters and brothers.

The Roman persecutions were revived in 257, and Cyprian was exiled to a small coastal town near Carthage and then confined to his villa in the main city. He remained at peace during his trial and in the moments before he was beheaded. Observers recalled that he had once written, "The Word of God was led, wordless, to the Cross."

Cyprian left an unusually large collection of letters; they provide glimpses of the vigorously expanding North African church, as well as Cyprian's reflections on the role of a bishop as a caring pastor and leader, although subject to the backbiting of a small minority of the clergy. Cyprian's pastoral attentiveness and his simple, clear, practical faith helped prepare his people for martyrdom, anticipated by early Christians.

Cyprian was part of a synod of North African bishops that met periodically to clarify doctrine and deal with questions of church administration. The African church was a lively, growing body, possessed of some of the finest minds in Christendom, and exercised intellectual parity with the wider church in Europe and Asia Minor until the Arab invasions of the seventh century virtually wiped it out.

In church councils Cyprian was unequivocal in his opposition to deviant points of view on doctrine and on bishops, priests, and congregations who adopted unorthodox positions about the faith. He wrote, "There is only one church founded by Christ and entrusted to the apostles as leaders. She remains one even after having spread

69

throughout the world, ... just as the sun's rays are many, yet the light is one, and a tree's branches are many, yet the strength deriving from its sturdy root is one. So, too, many streams flow from a single stream."

Despite his fierce advocacy of the unity of the church, Cyprian did not blindly support the primacy of the bishop of Rome as head of the church. In the early church, the role of bishop of Rome was in development and not so clear-cut as its supporters maintain today. African bishops stressed the collegial nature of the episcopate. While they traced their roles and powers to Peter "on whom the church was built," Cyprian believed that Peter was only an example of how all shepherds of the church should act, and that the chair of Peter, occupied by the bishop of Rome, was worthy of respect but could claim no special powers. As the churches in North Africa eventually declined under Arab pressures, power shifted to Rome, the role of the bishop of Rome increased, and the argument became historical.

Lawyer, priest, and martyr — Lord we uphold the example of Cyprian of Carthage before your throne of grace. May he who wrote "the Word of God was led, wordless, to the Cross" be our intercessor, and that of a troubled world, before your divine presence. This we ask in the name of Christ our mediator and advocate. Amen.

ST. CYRIL OF ALEXANDRIA

Bishop and Doctor of the Church,
c. 375–444

Born in Alexandria, Egypt, Cyril received an excellent religious and humanistic education in one of the world's most cosmopolitan cities of its day, but his intellectual arrogance and stubbornness caused him difficulties. Cyril pillaged and closed the churches of a heretical group with which he quarreled, expelled the Jews from Alexandria, and sparred with the Roman prefect Orestes. Cyril fought with almost everyone and spent much of his later life quarreling with various heretics. To the modern reader, such fierce disputes appear senseless, and rational people willing to seek common cause over a cup of tea could have settled many, but that was not the atmosphere of fourth-century Alexandria. Emerging Christianity was one of several competing religious and philosophical systems, and within Christianity there were divergent doctrinal tendencies, each with strong advocates. What would later become orthodoxy was then being hammered out on the anvil of sharp discourse among church leaders.[42]

One of Cyril's first disputes was with the Nestorians, another Christian group with distinctive theological views about the nature of Christ. Nestorians argued Christ was two separate persons, one human, the other divine. Orthodox Christians believed Jesus Christ was both fully human and fully divine. The early church often used the Greek word *Theotokos*, God-bearer, for Mary, the mother of God. The Nestorians rejected this term, arguing that God could not have been born from a human being, and preferred the term *Christokos*, Christ-bearer, which Nestor thought was a clearer expression of the dual nature of Christ. Both they and Cyril were reacting against others who used the word *anthropotokos* (man-bearer), which they asserted denied the combined (for the Orthodox) or dual (for the Nestorians) divinity and humanity of Christ. If Jesus was only human, Cyril and his followers argued, and God was elsewhere, the Incarnation, the word become flesh, would be meaningless. Cyril plunged into the debate with sharp invective, addressing one document "To Nestorius, the new Judas."

Cyril's prickly nature was demonstrated when a council denounced his handling of the Nestorian question and deposed him as bishop, placing him under guard for three months. The pope intervened, declaring his support for Cyril, who emerged as a local hero in Alexandria. Nestor, his rival and powerful patriarch of Constantinople, retired to a monastery, and Cyril, fueled by his earlier experiences, went on to write extensively about the nature of Christ. He was a prolific writer, and from his pen poured forth a stream of biblical commentaries, letters, sermons, and theological discourses, for which he was eventually named a doctor of the church, meaning an important contributor to its body of doctrine.

Lord of all life and power, who through the mighty resurrection of your son overcame the old order of sin and death to make all things new, grant that we, being dead to sin and alive to you in Jesus Christ, may reign with him in glory. Amen.
                                         — Celebrating Common Prayer, 18

THE DESERT PEOPLE

c. 250–500

⸙⸙⸙⸙⸙⸙⸙⸙⸙

O athletes of God, let not your souls be faint.
— Paul of Petra

The desert has a special place in Christian spirituality. There was desert land not far from the holy city of Jerusalem and only a short distance from the Galilean countryside as well. A place to which Jesus and his followers frequently withdrew, it was also the site where John the Baptist, last in the line of great prophets, appeared to herald the Messiah's presence, citing another desert prophet, Isaiah, who had proclaimed: "The voice of one crying out in the wilderness: 'Prepare the way of the Lord, make his paths straight.'"

Jesus may have spent years of preparation for his ministry in a desert monastery, and just before his tumultuous final three years of public ministry, he was tempted by Satan in the wilderness, where the Devil offered him tangible power and influence if he would abandon his messianic role. Jesus, alone in the desert, rejected the offer. "Then the devil left him, and suddenly angels came and waited on him" (Matt. 5:6)

Angels were other occupants of desert spaces, clouds of them, flights of angels winging through the cloudless air, combating devils, singing God's praises, and ministering to a growing number of Christians who came to the desert as solitary hermits, in communities, or as temporary pilgrims.

The time of the desert fathers (called here the "desert people," for the numbers included many women) was c. 250 to 500 A.D., a time when several thousand monks lived individually as hermits or in communities (cenobites), primarily in three regions of Egypt; Thebaid, the Nitrian Desert, and Middle Egypt between the Nile and the Red Sea, where St. Anthony of Egypt (see p. 27) also lived. The barren wilderness was alive with prayerful communities, and toward the end of this period, their numbers grew into the thousands, many of them humble Coptic peasants attracted by the forceful message of the saints who were dwelling in huts and caves or simple monasteries.[43]

Barbarian raids on the small, isolated monastic communities

73

were common. The monk Ammon described one such raid near Alexandria, where thirty-eight monks were killed in 380 A.D.:

> For who, even if his heart were of stone, would not weep for the holy martyrs who had grown old in the garb of Christians, flung upon the ground in merciless suffering; each one of them struck down, one with his head cut off and another [cleft in twain and another] with his head split in two. What can I say about the number of merciless blows which struck the saints who were killed limb by limb and were flung upon the ground?[44]

African Christianity has a unique affinity with desert spirituality; for one thing, there are deserts everywhere, especially in Egypt and the Nile region, but also in North Africa, the Sahara, and further south the Kalahari, with innumerable wildernesses in between. Andrew Walls, a Scottish missionary who spent many years in Africa, once said, "You do not have to interpret Old Testament Christianity to Africans; they live in an Old Testament world," a world full of desert spaces, a place where the spirituality of the desert finds responsiveness.

In the early centuries, thousands of Christians in Egypt, facing Roman persecution, fled to the desert, living in caves or large holes hewn in rocks, a common form of lodging, or in small buildings made of stone with roofing of dried reeds. An early account spoke of a land "so swamped with monks that their chants and hymns by day and by night made the whole country one church of God."

Usually these dwellings were near sources of water; the monks needed water to drink and to irrigate their crops of barley, onions, and other vegetables. Hermits led a life of ascetical simplicity, often depriving themselves of food and even mutilating their bodies in self-denial. They called themselves "athletes of Christ," by which they meant those who trained constantly for the competition and engaged their enemy the Devil in races, wrestling matches, and mortal combat. St. Jerome, a leading figure of the desert ascetics, wrote:

> *O Desert, bright with the flowers of Christ! O Solitude, whence come the stones of which the Apocalypse, the city of the Great King, is built! O Wilderness, gladdened with God's especial presence! What keeps you in the world, my brother, you who are above the world? How long shall gloomy roofs oppress you? Oh, that I could behold the desert, lovelier to me than any city.*[45]

OLAUDAH EQUIANO
Freed Slave and Author, 1745–1797

One of the most remarkable early slave narratives comes from a young Igbo villager who was sold by his own people into captivity at the age of eleven. Olaudah Equiano made the middle passage, was a plantation slave in the West Indies and Virginia, and spent time in the British navy and on a slave-trading ship run by a Quaker merchant, before buying his freedom in 1766. He then was active in the antislavery movement, became a baptized Christian, hoped to study for the ministry, married an English woman, presented an antislavery petition to the queen, and lectured extensively throughout the British Isles.[46]

His book is called *The Interesting Narrative of the Life of Olaudah Equiano, or Gustavus Vassa, the African, Written by Himself,* first published in 1789.[47] The volume gained a strong following in England among the abolitionist community. John Wesley, founder of Methodism, read it; a white abolitionist called it "more use to our cause than half the people in the country." The work went through eight English editions during the author's lifetime and became an international bestseller.

Equiano had been shipwrecked in the Caribbean, stuck in Arctic ice, saw Mt. Vesuvius erupt, and met some of the religious and emancipation leaders of his time. Modest, witty, and unassuming, he considered himself "neither a saint, a hero, nor a tyrant." Equiano learned to read and write aboard a British ship. A British officer had purchased him in 1757, and while bound for England he struck up a friendship with a white Virginian, Richard Baker, who taught him to read and write.

The story of his personal growth parallels the accounts of Equiano's own widespread travels. He had hoped to be freed by his British master, but was sold instead into further slavery, this time to a Quaker merchant who conducted a trade in sugar and slaves between the West Indies and the American South. The new master, Robert King, promoted Equiano to increasingly responsible positions in his human trade, allowing him to purchase his freedom on July 10, 1766.

A strong religious strain is woven through Equiano's narrative, beginning with his observations about the spiritual universe of his native Igbo culture:

> As to religion, the natives believe that there is one Creator of all things, and that he lives in the sun, and is girted round with a belt that he may never eat or drink; but, according to some, he smokes a pipe, which is our own favorite luxury. They believe he governs events, especially our deaths or captivity; but, as for the doctrine of eternity, I do not remember to have ever heard of it; some however believe in the transmigration of souls to a certain degree. Those spirits which are not transmigrated, such as our dear friends or relations, they believe always attend them, and guard them from bad spirits and their foes.[48]

During his first visit to England in 1757–1758 two English women, the Guerin sisters, introduced Equiano to Christianity. The narrative qualities of the Old Testament attracted him, as did the similarities between Hebrew and African societies. A vision of the dying Christ saving him was pivotal for Equiano, then sailing off Cadiz on October 6, 1774. Equally important was his self-assigned guilt at his failure to save a slave friend, John Annis, from death in the West Indies. (Annis, with Equiano's help, had petitioned the British courts for freedom, arguing that once he set foot on English soil he was free, since slavery did not exist in England.) Meanwhile, the slave's owner, not waiting for the court's decision, spirited Annis off to the West Indies, where he had him tortured to death.

In 1779 the freed African sought ordination by the bishop of London to be a missionary to West Africa but was rejected by the prelate. Equiano knew the principal English abolitionists, and his *Narrative* became an important weapon in their hands. Here was a lucid first-person account describing the evils of slavery. By 1788, the movement gained momentum, and tens of thousands of signatures were pouring in to Parliament. On March 21, 1788, Equiano delivered a petition of his own to Queen Charlotte, wife of George III. It was during this time that proponents of slavery tried to discredit Equiano's *Narrative*, arguing that the author was not from Africa but from the West Indies, but their efforts were to no avail. The work endured as a major slave narrative, along with comparable works like the *Narrative of the Life of Frederick Douglass, an American Slave, Written by Himself.*

O God, you made us in your own image and redeemed us through Jesus your Son: Look with compassion on the whole human family; take away the arrogance and hatred which infect our hearts; break down the walls that separate us; unite us in bonds of love; and work through our struggle and confusion to accomplish your purposes on earth; that, in your good time, all nations and races may serve you in harmony around your heavenly throne; through Jesus Christ our Lord. Amen.

—Prayer Book and Hymnal, 815

FARID ESACK
South African Muslim, b. 1959

Dr. Farid Esack is a well-known South African Muslim religious leader and a former member of the Call of Islam, an interreligious movement for racial and gender equality. He is a controversial writer, especially among fundamentalists of any faith tradition. His books, *Qur'an, Liberation, and Pluralism* (1997) and *On Being a Muslim: Finding a Religious Path in the World Today* (1999) are deeply reflective, witty, and draw on several religious traditions for their insights. In 1997 President Nelson Mandela appointed Dr. Esack to the Commission on Gender Equality, a deliberative body created by South Africa's post-apartheid constitution. Esack has lived in Germany and England, lectured in the United States, taught Islamic studies in the Roman Catholic St. Patrick's Technical High School, Karachi, Pakistan, and been a columnist in publications as diverse as *Al Qalam* (South Africa), *As-Salamu Alikum* (New York), and *Islamica* (London). The following excerpts are from his book *On Being a Muslim: Finding a Religious Path in the World Today*:

> One of the most meaningful ways in which some of us in the Call of Islam have experienced communication with Allah has been in a small group of close friends. Fairly common in Christian circles — in fact I first picked up the idea from a group of Christians in Pakistan — this way of praying to Allah was also practiced by the earliest Muslims. . . . Words, of course, only work if accompanied by works. While Allah is the Cause of Causes and the Originator of all the natural laws and, therefore, at liberty to suspend all or any of His laws and respond to us without our intervention, this is not His divine pattern. We turn to Him before we experience His nearness. To invoke a text that seems to have worked well for me during my own Meccan crucible — "To those who strive towards us, to them we shall show the way" (K. 29:69).
>
> Neither is it a question of trusting in Allah *but* tying up your camel; it's one of trusting in Allah *and* tying up your camel. He desires that we strive and call upon Him; not call upon Him

but strive. These two actions are not mutually exclusive, as if our striving is our side of the deal and our calling Him a reminder that He must complete His side of the deal: the very ability to strive comes from Him. To call upon Him without having exhausted what He has already given us is a rejection of His grace.

What if all of these words and works fail to open windows, let alone doors? One can be desperate for Allah to respond to one's calls and seemingly fulfil all that is possible for a young person in this day and age....I have often felt that I was met with a deafening silence. Alas, rather belatedly I have discovered I do not control the agenda.

Timing, my sister, timing. We do what we must do; the timing is Allah's.[49]

God! There is no God but He; the Living, the Eternal; Nor slumber seizeth Him, nor sleep; His, whatsoever is in the Heavens and whatsoever is in the Earth! Who is he that can intercede with Him but by His own permission? He knoweth what hath been *before them and what* shall be *after them; yet nought of His knowledge shall they grasp, save what He willeth. His throne reacheth over the Heavens and the Earth, and the upholding of both burdeneth Him not; and He is the High, the Great!*

–Surah 2:256[50]

STS. FELICITAS AND PERPETUA AND COMPANIONS

Martyrs at Carthage, d. 203

❀❀❀❀❀❀❀❀❀❀

Felicitas and Perpetua, two young North African Christian women, and three companions were thrown to wild animals and killed for their faith at Carthage on March 7, 203. A gripping account of their last days remains, written by Perpetua, a twenty-two-year-old woman of noble birth and the mother of a small child.

A local Christian in Carthage collected the narratives and added a commentary, making this vivid account one of the earliest and most dramatic documents of martyrdom. *The Passion of St. Perpetua, St. Felicitas, and Their Companions* was widely read in the early church as an instructional document on how Christians should face persecution.

Felicitas and Perpetua and their companions lived during a time of persecution of Christians under the Roman emperor Septimus Severus (193–211). Perpetua's father was an elderly pagan, her mother a Christian. Felicitas, her household slave, was pregnant at the time of their arrest. The women were baptized and then led off to prison.

The young woman recalled the harshness of their life behind bars, and Perpetua was anxious for her small child as well. Eventually Perpetua's mother was allowed to visit her with Perpetua's young son, whom she was allowed to nurse and keep with her in prison. Meanwhile, Perpetua's father tried to persuade her to abandon her Christian faith. At their trial the Christians refused to offer sacrifices to the Roman gods for the emperor's safety. After being scourged, they were thrown to the wild beasts, the men to a boar, bear, and leopard, the women to a wild heifer. Once animals wounded them, the Christians were killed by swords. Perpetua wrote the following live-witness account:

•

A few days later we were lodged in the prison, and I was much frightened, because I had never known such darkness. What a day of horror! Terrible heat, owing to the crowds! Rough treatment by the soldiers! To crown it all I was tormented with anxiety for my baby. But Tertius and Pomponius, those blessed deacons who ministered to us, paid for us to be moved for a few hours to a better part of the prison and we obtained some relief. All went out of the prison and we were left to ourselves. My baby was brought and I nursed him, for already he was faint for want of food. I spoke anxiously to my mother on his behalf and encouraged my brother and commended my son to their care. For I was concerned when I saw their concern for me. For many days I suffered such anxieties, but I obtained leave for my child to remain in prison with me, and when relieved of my trouble and distress for him, I quickly recovered my health. My prison suddenly became a palace to me and I would rather have been there than anywhere else.

Then my brother said to me: "Dear sister, you are greatly privileged; surely you might ask for a vision to discover whether you are to be condemned or freed." Faithfully I promised that I would, for I knew that I could speak with the Lord, whose great blessings I had come to experience. And so I said: "I shall tell you tomorrow." Then I made my request and this was the vision I had:

I saw a ladder of tremendous height made of bronze, reaching all the way to the heavens, but it was so narrow that only one person could climb up at a time. To the sides of the ladder were attached all sorts of metal weapons: there were swords, spears, hooks, daggers, and spikes; so that if anyone tried to climb up carelessly or without paying attention, he would be mangled and his flesh would adhere to the weapons.

At the foot of the ladder lay a dragon of enormous size, and it would attack those who tried to climb up and try to terrify them from doing so. And Saturus was the first to go up, he who was later to give himself up of his own accord. He had been the builder of our strength, although he was not present when we were arrested. And he arrived at the top of the staircase and he looked back and said to me: "Perpetua, I am waiting for you. But take care; do not let the dragon bite you." "He will not harm me," I said, "in the name of Christ Jesus." Slowly, as though he were afraid of me, the dragon stuck his head out from underneath the ladder. Then, using it as my first step, I trod on his head and went up.

Then I saw an immense garden, and in it a gray-haired man sat in shepherd's garb; tall he was, and milking sheep. And standing around him were many thousands of people clad in white garments. He raised his head, looked at me, and said: "I am glad you have come, my child." He called me over to him and gave me, as it were, a mouthful of the milk he was drawing; and I took it into my cupped hands and consumed it. And all those who stood around said: "Amen!" At the sound of this word I came to, with the taste of something sweet still in my mouth. I at once told this to my brother, and we realized that we would have to suffer, and that from now on we would no longer have any hope in this life.[51]

> *Holy God, as you gave great courage to Perpetua and Felicitas and their companions, so grant that we may be worthy to climb the ladder of sacrifice and be received into the garden of peace, through Jesus Christ our Lord. Amen.*
>
> — *Celebrating Common Prayer,* 437

GONVILLE FFRENCH-BEYTAGH

Dean of Johannesburg Cathedral,
Human Rights Prisoner, 1912–1991

Gonville Aubie ffrench-Beytagh was born on January 26, 1913, in Shanghai, son of an expatriate Irish alcoholic cotton company executive and a South African mother. After the family had broken up, the youth returned to South Africa to live with his mother. While there he underwent a religious conversion on Christmas Eve in Johannesburg Cathedral, where the dean had locked the door to keep drunken revelers from the Midnight Mass:

> It was a hot night [December is midsummer in South Africa] and as the doors had been closed, the air was completely still. I knelt at the communion rail, and as I knelt there I felt a very strong cool breeze — and that was all. I do not think that at the time I had any idea what the word "breath" or the word "wind" means to the Christian, or even that the Greek word for the Holy Spirit means breath. I did not even think of Jesus breathing the spirit on his disciples. All I know is that this breath, or wind, which I felt, had a meaning and a content for me which I have never been able to communicate to anyone else, and still cannot describe.[52]

Deciding to enter the ministry, in January 1936 at age twenty-four he enrolled in St. Paul's Theological College, Grahamstown, Eastern Cape Province, and was ordained in 1939. After serving in a mining town, ffrench-Beytagh became increasingly disillusioned with apartheid schemes for "separate development" and "partnership," for both systematically excluded blacks and coloreds from full participation in the life of South Africa. An interlude as dean of the cathedral in Salisbury, Rhodesia, from 1954 to 1964 removed him from the growing maelstrom of South African politics, and when he returned in 1965 it was to a world where almost all whites who had spoken out for freedom had been imprisoned or exiled. In 1971 ffrench-Beytagh publicly called the "South African way of life" the "South African way of death," and in January 1971 the dean was arrested. He spent his fifty-ninth birthday in jail, was brutally interrogated, and on November 1 convicted and sentenced under a state terrorism act for allegedly possessing African National Congress leaflets with titles like *We Bring You a Message, These Men Are Our Brothers, Our Sons, The ANC Says No to Vorster and His Gang,* and *Freedom.* (He was later expelled to England, where he died twenty years later.)

A United Nations report stated, "The charges against the Dean were that he opposed apartheid — a policy which all member states of the United Nations have described as a criminal affront against the conscience and dignity of mankind — and that he had provided humanitarian assistance to people imprisoned for their opposition to apartheid and their families."

In his prison diary the Dean wrote:

Early that morning (and every morning afterwards) I stood in front of a piece of wall between the two barred and grilled high windows, which was the nearest thing to a cross that I could find in the cell. I faced it as I would an altar and said what I could remember of the Mass. Later when I had my office book [a *Book of Common Prayer,* with the daily Bible lessons for matins and evensong], I could read part of an Epistle or Gospel as well, but from the first morning I said the Creed, and prayed generally where the Prayer for the Church comes, and made a short confession; then I said the *Sanctus* by heart and made a spiritual communion. This is something I have never really experienced before, though I have read about it and advised people to do it. But I can say with complete certainty that the communion that I received then was as real as any communion that I have ever received sacramentally.[53]

On the night he was handed over to suffering and death, our Lord Jesus Christ took bread; and when he had given thanks to you, he broke it, and gave it to his disciples, and said, "Take, eat: This is my Body, which is given for you. Do this for the remembrance of me." After supper he took the cup of wine: and when he had given thanks, he gave it to them, and said, "Drink this, all of you: This is my Blood of the new Covenant, which is shed for you and for many for the forgiveness of sins. Whenever you drink it, do this for the remembrance of me."
— *Book of Common Prayer and Hymnal,* 362–363

CHARLES DE FOUCAULD

Hermit and Martyr in the Sahara,
1858–1916

Your vocation is to shout the Gospel from the rooftops, not in words, but
with your life.   – Charles de Foucauld

His life was the stuff of a French opera. An orphan, and later a graduate of the military academy Saint-Cyr, he was passionately in love with a beautiful mistress. Then his regiment left for Algeria, where the desert and its people fascinated him. The fashionable Parisian agnostic next converted to Christianity, abandoned a successful military career, became a Trappist monk, and journeyed to the Holy Land. He later returned to Africa as a solitary hermit monk, where he lived among the poorest of the poor. His final years were spent in North Africa, most of them in the middle of the Sahara, where anti-French rebels assassinated him on December 1, 1916.

Such was the legacy of Charles Eugène, viscount of Foucauld, born in 1858 and left an orphan six years later. The Foucaulds were a titled family whose sons had fought honorably in French wars and whose family motto was "Never Retreat." Charles was admitted to Saint-Cyr, where he spent more time in escapades than in preparing for a military career among the elite of French soldiery. After graduation Charles broke with Mimi, his mistress, and became a soldier, but nagging religious questions now filled his consciousness. "My God, if you exist, make your existence known to me," he prayed, and sought the guidance of a well-known spiritual director who told him to make his confession and receive communion, and he would become a believer. Actually, it worked. Charles later wrote of the experience, "As soon as I believed there was a God, I understood that I could not do anything other than live for him. My religious vocation dates from the same moment as my faith."

Armed with a comfortable inheritance, he headed for the Holy Land, where he visited sacred sites. He joined a Trappist monastery in Armenia, and stayed there for nearly seven years. Charles increasingly concentrated on imitating what he called "the hidden life of Jesus," who lived among the poor. Employed as a custodian in the convent of the Poor Clares in Nazareth, he wrote, "I have now the unutter-able, the inexpressibly profound happiness of raking manure." After seeking ordination in France in 1901, he returned to North Africa to live the remaining fifteen years of his life. Charles hoped to found a community of Little Brothers (and later Little Sisters) whose lives would be spent among the poor. None joined him in his lifetime, but by the 1970s more than 250 Brothers and 1,000 Sisters lived in small "fraternities" in different nations; a union of priests in secular voca-tions was launched in 1952, followed by two groups for lay women and men.[54]

Although he had mustered out of the army, Charles retained links with its members. In 1905 an old military comrade invited him on an expedition deep into the Sahara, where Charles built a hermitage in the remote oasis village of Tamanrasset. He lived simply among local people, dressed in a white robe. While he wrote a Tuareg dic-tionary and maintained respect for Islam, his was not of a scholarly bent. Nor did he seek to convert local peoples, but to live a life of Christian compassion among them. Villagers called him a *marabout,* or holy man.

Subsisting on a diet of local dates and meal, he lived in a small house of stones and reeds. Here he kept the reserved sacrament ex-posed before a lamp. Pictures of him taken in these years reveal a balding, gaunt figure, missing several teeth, skin parched, eyes burn-ing with intensity. Seeking to emulate the hidden life of Jesus and to welcome all humanity, he wrote:

> I want to accustom all the inhabitants, Christians, Muslims, Jews, and nonbelievers, to look on me as their brother, the uni-versal brother. Already they're calling this house "the fraternity" (*khaoua* in Arabic) — about which I'm delighted — and realizing that the poor have a brother here — not only the poor, though: all men.[55]

His death was complicated by his close association with the French military. Arms were stored in his hermitage, which by 1916 had meter-thick high walls. French military patrols stopped there, and to them and the Arabic-speaking populations Charles was a local French agent. The Senoussi tribesmen who killed him were using World War I as an opportunity to purge their homelands of foreign infidels. On the evening of December 1, 1916, a local person, bribed by the invaders, knocked on his door, pretending to deliver some mail. Armed rebels forced their way in, held the priest captive, ransacked the place, and shot him in the head.

It was the destiny of Charles de Foucauld to die in obscurity, and it was not for many years that he became a spiritual presence, one attracting both readers and actual followers. The austerity of his life and teachings would attract only a selective following, and the hidden life of Jesus, which he found at the core of the Gospel, was not a mainstream theme for most clergy. Near the end of his life, he summarized his faith:

> *Jesus came to Nazareth, the place of the hidden life, of ordinary life, of family life, of prayer, work, obscurity, silent virtues, practiced with no witnesses other than God, his friends and neighbors. Nazareth, the place where most people lead their lives. We must infinitely respect the least of our brothers.... Let us mingle with them. Let us be one of them to the extent that God wishes...and treat them fraternally in order to have the honor and joy of being accepted as one of them.*[56]

MOHANDAS K. GANDHI

Nonviolent Religious Leader, Martyr,
1869–1948

The only tyrant I accept in this world is the still small voice within. What
you do is of little significance. But it is very important that you do it.
— Mohandas K. Gandhi

Mohandas K. Gandhi, perhaps the last century's leading figure for
world peace, was an Indian whose religious and political ideas were
formulated in South Africa during the twenty-one years he spent
there. During that time the young lawyer-turned-spiritual leader ar-
ticulated his concept of Satyagraha, "truth force," a philosophy of
nonviolent noncooperation with a concomitant willingness to endure
suffering if required. Of this movement, Gandhi wrote, "None of
us knew what name to give to our movement. I then used the term
passive resistance in describing it. I did not quite understand the im-
plications of passive resistance as I called it. I only knew that some
new principle had come into being."[57]

Born in India in 1869, Gandhi arrived in Africa in April 1893 as
a twenty-four-year-old lawyer representing a Durban Indian business
executive in a commercial lawsuit. Photos of the time show him as a
dapper, well-groomed young man with alert eyes and a pleasing countenance, but his legal success went hand-in-hand with his encounters
with harsh British racial laws. Indians could not own land, and where
they could live and trade was severely restricted. Protests were triggered by British refusals to allow Indian refugees from the Anglo-Boer
War in the Transvaal (1899–1902) to return to their homes.

In September 1906 three thousand members of the Johannesburg Indian community gathered to denounce a law requiring them
to be fingerprinted and carry registration certificates. Later protests
extended to a local law forbidding Indians from reentering the Transvaal. A subsequent court decision declined to recognize Hindu and
Muslim marriages as valid, reducing married women to concubines
in the eyes of the law, making their children illegitimate, and refusing
them inheritance rights. Such struggles occupied Gandhi from 1906 to
1915. By then he was a leading political activist, having founded the

Natal Indian Congress. Originally reluctant to enter politics, Gandhi said, "If I seem to take part in politics, it is only because politics encircles us today like the coil of a snake from which one cannot get out, no matter how much one tries. I wish therefore to wrestle with the snake."

Reflecting on the situation he faced in South Africa, Gandhi said, "I was, with my countrymen, in a hopeless minority, not only a hopeless minority but a despised minority. If the Europeans of South Africa will forgive me for saying so, we were all Coolies [a derogatory term for Indian laborers]. I was an insignificant Coolie lawyer. At that time we had no Coolie doctors. We had no Coolie lawyers. [I was] the first in the field. Nevertheless [I was] a Coolie." Gandhi had faced the indignation of being ordered into the van compartment of a local train even though he had purchased a ticket for a first-class seat. And because trams were generally reserved for Europeans, the young lawyer walked long distances to and from work each day.

A Hindu, Gandhi quoted frequently from the Bible. Gandhi could not accept claims that Jesus Christ was the sole source of salvation, remarking that the behavior of many Christians, including those he encountered in South Africa and India, left him wondering about how their conduct represented claims to universal truth. Likewise, Gandhi was attracted to the suffering of Christ as a valid means of redemption for humanity, but could not accept its messianic aspects.

Detractors called him a "secret Christian," and the religious leader remarked, "If I have read the Bible correctly, I know many men who have never heard the name of Jesus Christ or have even rejected the official interpretation of Christianity who will, probably, if Jesus came in our midst today in the flesh, be owned by him more than many of us."

Gandhi's intensely political nonviolent methods also attracted the black liberation movement in South Africa, and founders of the African National Congress in 1912 adopted some of his doctrines in their own protracted struggle against racist laws and practices. Much later, in 1952 the ANC and the South African Indian Congress joined together in their passive resistance to apartheid. Martin Luther King Jr. patterned much of his civil rights movement after Gandhi, as did other resistance leaders elsewhere in the world.

To believe in something, and not to live it, is dishonest.
— Gandhi

POPE GELASIUS I

Pontificate 492–496

Africa's third pope was Gelasius I, whose pontificate extended from 492 to 496, and who did as much to promote dissension between church and state and East and West as he did to clarify doctrine and order. It was Gelasius's lot to become pope at a time of intense political and theological struggle within the church. High on the list was the continuing Donatist controversy in North Africa, in which a regional church sought independence for its theology and church structure, which Rome opposed. A similar struggle took place in the East, where a group of Christians disputed the doctrine of the Trinity and argued that Christ had only one nature. Additionally, there was a movement by the Byzantine emperor toward caesaropapism, the concept that religious and political rulers were combined in one authoritative person. Thus doctrinal questions were braided into issues of power and authority, as they usually are in the life of any church.

Gelasius advanced the idea that papal power, given its divine origins, was superior to temporal power, an attitude that persisted in the papacy for centuries. In response to a challenge from the Roman emperor, he wrote, "There are two powers by which this world is chiefly ruled: the sacred authority of the priesthood and the authority of kings." (It was during Gelasius's reign that the title "Vicar of Christ" was first assumed by the pope).

Gelasius made no compromise with opponents, ordering the library of a heretical group be burned before the doors of St. Mary Major Church in Rome. He was equally unyielding in his dispute with leaders of the Eastern Church, striking the name of one of their schismatic leaders from church records. This contributed to deteriorating relations between the two main branches of Christendom and to their enduring separation.

They were faithful until death and God has given them the crown of life.

> —Antiphon to the Benedictus, Feast of a Saint

ROBERT GRAY

Bishop of the Church of the Province
of South Africa, 1809–1872

※※※※※※※※

When Robert Gray arrived in South Africa in 1847, it was as Anglican bishop in a diocese of over two hundred thousand square miles and with only a handful of clergy. Within a quarter century the number of dioceses had increased to six, and educational institutions were built, including Diocesan College (Rondebosch), St. George's Cathedral Grammar School (Cape Town), and the "Sunflower" (Zonnebloem) College for African and Colored Students.

On January 30, 1847, Gray, at that time secretary of the Society for the Propagation of the Gospel, was invited to accept the bishopric of either Cape Town or Adelaide, Australia, by the Colonial Bishoprics' Fund. Gray picked South Africa and was consecrated in Westminster Abbey. He spent nearly a year raising funds and missionary personnel for South Africa, arriving there on Sunday, February 20, 1848.

Shortly after arrival, he purchased a wooded estate not far from Cape Town, which became Bishopscourt, the home of subsequent clerical leaders of the diocese. As was true of so many missionaries, his wife was an immense asset. In addition to running the large estate, she raised their children, entertained a stream of guests, answered much of her husband's correspondence, designed several mission churches, and kept their personal and church accounts. Gray was often absent. One episcopal visitation took four months and another nine months, while covering four thousand miles, earning Gray the sobriquet "the post-cart bishop."

Mrs. Gray sometimes accompanied her husband. A description of her in one such visitation is contained in *Robert Gray, First Bishop of Cape Town:*

> Dressed in a dark green plaid dress, with a large gray felt hat, trimmed with an ostrich feather, she accompanied the Bishop on his long exacting journeys through the immense diocese. . . . With her she took her little sketch book, pencils and paints, and her delicate little pictures of the country may still be seen. As they

went up, she painted the little, high-shouldered Gothic churches, which she had designed and which stand to her memory today.[58]

Gray returned to England in 1852 and preached over three hundred sermons in support of fund-raising for his expanding diocese. He also arranged for the vast territory to be divided into smaller dioceses, which presented both opportunities and challenges. On the positive side, new dioceses and mission stations proliferated, and in 1870 South Africa's first provincial synod was held. On the negative side, Gray was faced with the kind of power struggles endemic to church hierarchies. Bishop Gray became involved, through no desire of his own, in a famous heresy trial. In 1863 he excommunicated the bishop of Natal, J. W. Colenso, who had been presented on charges of heresy. The bottom-line issue was that Colenso, in several published works of biblical commentary, had disavowed much of the content of traditional sacramental theology and also denied that there was eternal punishment. Moreover, reflecting the biblical criticism of the mid-nineteenth century, he disputed the authorship of some books of the Bible and, for good measure, did not actively insist on the divorce of the wives of polygamous males when the men converted to Christianity. Colenso, clearly, was one huge target for his opponents.

The doctrinal squabble was never the real issue. It masked a struggle for power. Colenso argued that Gray had no authority to deprive him of office. Meanwhile, he scrambled to take title to church lands and monies, something allowed by local courts. Not to be outdone, Gray appointed another bishop as bishop of Maritzburg and Natal, a "new" diocese that by design was coterminous with the diocese Colenso claimed. The case took several years to thread its way through the courts, but the Privy Council found that Gray lacked authority to take the actions he did.

Gray's health was failing, and he died in 1872. He is most remembered as a solid builder of the church but, as sometimes happens to bishops, bedeviled by power controversies brought on by opponents.

> *Alleluia! Christ feeds his flock in every age.*
> *O come, let us worship.*
> —Preparation Prayer, Feast of Bishops

HAGAR, SLAVE WOMAN OF EGYPT, AND HER SON, ISHMAEL

❀❀❀❀❀❀❀❀❀

> And as she sat opposite him [her son] she lifted up her voice and wept. And God heard the voice of the boy; and the angel of God called to Hagar from heaven, and said to her, 'What troubles you, Hagar? Do not be afraid; for God has heard the voice of the boy where he is. Come, lift up the boy and hold him fast with your hand, for I will make a great nation of him.
> —Genesis 21:16–18

The story of Hagar is deeply troubling, with no easy resolution. An Egyptian slave woman, Hagar has been driven away into the desert with Ishmael, her baby, the child her Hebrew mistress, Sarah, forced her to have in her stead, and then rejected. All this came about because Sarah, to her great surprise, bore a son in her old age, something no one ever expected. Now Sarah's elderly husband, Abraham, founder of the Hebrew people, had his own heir. The dynasty would continue.

Carrying a son for a mistress was not an unusual practice in ancient Egypt. Infertility was widespread, and such a solution was perfectly legal. For her part, Hagar was pleased to have become pregnant by Abraham and then, in a moment of dime-novel drama, "looked with contempt on her mistress" (16:4), which made Sarah furious. "Then Sarah dealt harshly with her, and she ran away from her" (16:6).

Enter Yahweh, who dispatches an angel to order Hagar back to Sarah's household. "Return to your mistress and submit to her" (16:9) in turn for which "I will so greatly multiply your offspring that they cannot be counted for multitude." The son was called Ishmael ["God hears"]. "A wild ass of a man, with his hand against everyone, and everyone's hand against him; and he shall live at odds with all his kin" (16:11–12) is how Ishmael was described.

After Sarah's delivery of her own son, Isaac, the rejected Hagar and her small son, Ishmael, were banished to the wilderness. The expulsion was triggered when "Sarah saw the son of Hagar the Egyptian, whom she had borne to Abraham, playing with her son Isaac. So she said to Abraham, 'Cast out this slave woman with her son; for the

93

son of the slave woman shall not inherit along with my son Isaac' "
(21:8–10).

Sarah and her son were driven into the wilderness of Beersheba.
Soon their small supply of water gave out and the mother, in extremis,
left her baby under a bush to die. She sat down in weakened condition
about a bowshot away and made a final plea with Yahweh, "Do not
let me look upon the death of the child" (21:16). Yahweh replied he
would make the boy the leader of a great nation (Muslims regard
Ishmael as a protoancestor). Hagar was one of only three women in
the book of Genesis to hold a dialogue with God, who either provided
her with a source of water or gave her eyes to see water that was
already there, depending on the interpretation.

Yahweh, Abraham, Sarah and Isaac, Hagar and Ishmael all figure
in the Genesis accounts of early Israel. In a larger context, Hagar
represents the dispossessed, a woman marginalized by history, lacking
position, land, or prospects. In this regard, she is like many African
women, cast into a demanding world to work, bear children, and
survive as best she can. Yet her story has its positive aspects as well.
Hagar saw God, and God provided for her and her son. She was given
water in the desert, and Ishmael was promised a responsible role as
head of a nation.

Her destiny in the land east of Eden was, like Cain's, to live by the
sweat of her brow, although, unlike Cain, she committed no grievous
sin. Consigned to bondage, her endurance prefigured the later deliverance of Moses and the Hebrew people from slavery in Egypt. Hagar
was a determined woman, a survivor, for whom life held both major
losses and real victories.

> *My soul proclaims the greatness of the Lord,*
> *my spirit rejoices in God my Savior,*
> *for you, Lord, have looked with favor*
> *on your lowly servant.*
> *From this day all generations will call me blessed.*
>   —Magnificat (Luke 1:47–48)

JAMES HANNINGTON
Bishop and Martyr, 1847–1885

The nineteenth century was the century of missionary expansion. Fired by evangelical zeal to share the good news of God in Christ, missionaries pushed through African jungles and deserts, learned local languages, and braved pestilential climates to create schools, hospitals, and churches. Some were killed, others contracted debilitating diseases, but by the century's end a global missionary presence was in place. The picture of missionary expansion was by no means a triumphal journey. Disease and martyrdom claimed great numbers. For example, James Hannington became bishop of Eastern Equatorial Africa in 1884 at age thirty-seven and began a tragic voyage toward Uganda. Shortly before arriving at the court of the suspicious *kabaka* (king), Mwanga, he and his party were seized by the ruler's soldiers and jailed. Hannington wrote on July 22:

> The outlook is gloomy. . . . Starvation, desertion, treachery, and a few other nightmares and furies hover over one's head in ghostly forms, and yet in spite of it all, I feel in capital spirits. Let me beg every mite of spare prayer. You must uphold my hands, lest they fall. If this is the last chapter of earthly history, then the next will be the first page of the heavenly — no blots and smudges, no incoherence, but sweet converse in the presence of the Lamb.

He was held prisoner by a regional ruler near the Uganda border and wrote:

> 28th. 7th day. A terrible night; first with noisy, drunken guards, and secondly with vermin, which have found out my tent and swarm. I don't think I got one hour's sleep, and woke with fever fast developing. O Lord, do have mercy on me, and release me! I am quite broken down and brought low. Comforted by reading 27th Psalm. Fever developed very rapidly . . . soon was delirious.
>
> Evening. Fever passed away. Word came that Mwanga had sent three soldiers, but what news they bring they will not yet let me know. Much comforted by the 28th Psalm.

29th (8th day). I can hear no news, but was held up by the 30th Psalm, which came with great power. A hyena howled near me last night, smelling a sick man. I hope it is not to have me yet.[59]

Soon the bishop and his fifty porters were led out and killed. Widespread persecution of Christians followed, many being killed or sold to Arab slavers. The Anglican Church, of which Hannington was a bishop, uses this prayer to commemorate his death:

Precious in your sight, O Lord, is the death of your saints, whose faithful witness, by your providence, has its great reward: We give you thanks for your martyrs James Hannington and his companions, who purchased with their blood a road to Uganda for the proclamation of the Gospel; and we pray that with them we also may obtain the crown of righteousness which is laid up for all who love the appearing of our Savior Jesus Christ; who lives and reigns with you and the Holy Spirit, one God, for ever and ever. Amen.[60]

IMAM ABDULLAH HARON

Islamic Leader,
Murdered by South African Police,
1924–1969

More than 250,000 persons attended the funeral of Imam Abdullah Haron, who became a South African martyr alongside Steven Biko, when he died under arrest on September 27, 1969. South African police cynically announced his death was caused by "falling down stairs." Arrested on the eve of the celebration of the Prophet's birthday and held without charges for over four months, Haron had developed a national following as a progressive Islamic cleric, friend of young people, skilled mosque leader, and figure in the interfaith and anti-apartheid communities.

Since Islam does not have ordained clergy, he earned his living as a regional sales representative for a chocolate company. He started a program of telling children stories in the mosque, after which each was given a chocolate. An active Sunday morning swimmer, he also played cricket and rugby and was an affable, likable figure.

From his base at Cape Town's Stegman Road mosque, he steadily protested the South African government's policy of apartheid, one of the few mainstream Muslim voices to consistently oppose institutionalized racism. A member of the nonpolitical Muslim Judicial Council, he had friends in such activist groups as Black Sash, the Pan Africanist Congress, and the Claremont Muslim Youth Association. Haron was also active in preaching Islam in black townships and was a link between Muslim and non-Muslim communities. He supported a greater role for women in mosque life and invited them, plus African socialists and African nationalists, to speak at his mosque.

Following his death, a memorial service was held at St. George's Anglican Cathedral, Cape Town, and another was held in the crypt of St. Paul's Cathedral, London. In death, his life and personality have made him a figure for the ages, where people struggle against oppression, and of South Africa's victory over apartheid. At a commemorative service, Imam Shaheed Gamieldien quoted from the Koran:

O you who believe! Seek help
with patient perseverance
and prayer: for God is with those
who patiently persevere.
And say not of those
who are slain in the way
of God: "They are dead."
Nay, they are living,
though you perceive (it) not.
                    —Surah 2:153–154[61]

THE PROPHET HARRIS
(WILLIAM WADE HARRIS)

Evangelist, Liberia and Ivory Coast,
c. 1865–1929

❀❀❀❀❀❀❀❀❀❀

> God has sent me to proclaim that the time has come when he wants to deliver you from the power of the devil who ruins you, makes you foolish and kills you. The time is fulfilled, the devil is conquered here also, therefore burn all your fetishes, all your greegrees and your amulets, and I will baptize you in the name of this God who is your Father, of his son Jesus Christ who has died for your sins, and of the Holy Spirit who will change your hearts.[62]

With this message William Wade Harris, an itinerant evangelist and prophet, wandered between his native Liberia and the nearby Ivory Coast and Ghana in the second decade of the twentieth century, preaching a message of repentance and attracting hundreds of thousands of followers. And, although he never saw himself as founding an independent church, by century's end large numbers of West Africans joined "Harris churches" and kept his message and memory alive.[63]

Born of Grebo parents in Liberia in about 1865, Harris began life as a bricklayer and deckhand on British ships working the West African waters. Later, he was an interpreter for the Liberian government and then a mission schoolteacher. Originally a Methodist, he became a catechist for the Episcopal Church at one point before striking out on his own. Harris was arrested for attempting to overthrow the Liberian government and for supporting traditional Grebo interests. Charging that government customs agents cheated them out of their scanty earnings, the Grebo also felt pressured by the growing number of Liberian-Americans who controlled the country and preferred British rule instead. Harris hoisted the Union Jack and was jailed for doing so.

While in prison in 1910 Harris received a vision, presumably from the Angel Gabriel, that set him on his course as a solitary prophet in 1910. "You are not in prison," the Angel said. "God is coming to anoint you. You will be a prophet. . . . You are like Daniel." Harris was a striking figure with a powerful orator's voice. "It seems as if God made the soul of Harris a soul of fire. You cannot be in his presence for long without realizing you are in contact with a great personality," a contemporary said of him. Sometimes coifed in a Sudanic turban and dressed in a long white robe with crossed white bands across the breast, he carried a cross-like staff and Bible in one hand, and a gourd rattle in the other. With a hollowed-out gourd he baptized possibly a hundred thousand persons in one year.

Harris's manner of attracting converts was simple. He and some disciples would enter a village, singing songs and making sounds with their gourd rattles. After a crowd assembled, Harris preached, and if people accepted his message about renouncing the religion of fetishes and greegrees and accepted the Christian God, he baptized them and placed his Bible on their heads. If a traditional spirit possessed someone during the rite, Harris asked him or her to touch the cross he wore while he prayed and sprinkled the person with water.

The Prophet led a simple personal life and made no attempt to attract a following for himself. When word spread that the cross he carried was as powerful as a fetish, he broke it and fashioned a new one of local wood, telling people the wood had no power of its own. It was God who gave the people new life through baptism, he preached; the water or the gourd which carried it had no power of their own. Harris was no accommodationist, and his message was one of unequivocal rejection of traditional religion for the Christian God. He was a healer as well and Harris reputedly had the power to call down fire from heaven. There were stories of traditional religious shrines bursting into flame when he entered a village. Once, when a village would not hear his message, it was attacked by baboons.

While in the Ivory Coast, he attracted a growing following and preached unequivocally against World War I. This brought him into direct conflict with French colonial authorities, who had large recruitment quotas for African troops, *tirailleurs*, to be delivered to the conflagration in Europe. His insistence on keeping the Sabbath holy also clashed with French demands for laborers to build roads and public works. Eventually he was deported back to Liberia in 1915 and denied reentry to the Ivory Coast.

European missionaries were of a mixed mind about Harris. Some resented such an uneducated charismatic figure attracting large crowds and baptizing converts with no prior preparation. Others rejoiced that Harris's work helped fill their own pews, for his message was that converts should seek neighborhood churches. By the late twentieth century the Ivory Coast, with a population of five million

people, was estimated to contain a million Muslims, 500,000 Roman
Catholics, 200,000 Protestants, and a million Harrists.

> *You did not choose me but I chose you and I appointed you to
> go out and bear fruit, the fruit that shall last.*
>
> —Antiphon to the Benedictus,
> Feast of Apostles and Evangelists

TREVOR HUDDLESTON

"Bishop Trevor of Sophiatown,"
1913–1998

If you think of Desmond Tutu, think of Trevor Huddleston. Together they are two leading spiritual presences opposing apartheid in South Africa and pointing a new way for reconciliation and the country's moral future. And they knew one another well. Huddleston, as a Community of the Resurrection monk, visited the sickly Tutu, confined to a hospital bed for two years as a youth with tuberculosis. Later Tutu named his first child "Trevor" and remembered the lanky monk: "He was so un-English in many ways, being very fond of hugging people, embracing them, and in the way in which he laughed. He did not laugh like many white people, only with their teeth; he laughed with his whole body, his whole being, and that endeared him very much to black people. And if he wore a white cassock it did not remain clean for long, as he trudged the dusty streets of Sophiatown with the little urchins with grubby fingers always wanting to touch him and call him 'Fader' with obvious affection in their little voices."[64]

Attracted to the Anglican monastic Community of the Resurrection as a young man, Huddleston was ordained and became part of the order in 1939. At that time the community had extensive missionary programs, parishes, schools, and training colleges in Southern Africa, and in 1943 the thirty-year-old Huddleston was assigned to Sophiatown, a black residential part of Johannesburg; the assignment changed his life. More than 3.5 million persons had been thrown from their residences during the government's effort to remove "black spots" in white regions and to forcibly vacate Africans from choice land. Huddleston was one of the active voices who organized constant protests against the government's action.

Huddleston came to know most of the leaders of the African National Congress (ANC) and was a constant, active figure with them and others in protesting South Africa's restrictive racial practices. At the same time, he responded to the vibrancy of local culture. He asked musicians from the Johannesburg Symphony Orchestra to play in the school playground, and Yehudi Menuhin gave a concert at the church. The priest organized a school jazz band, which allowed a generation of South African musicians to find a following. Hugh Masekela, who would become a great jazz trumpeter, received his first instrument from Huddleston, who obtained it as a gift from Louis Armstrong. Later, realizing that European artists were playing primarily to segregated audiences, the priest organized a boycott of European and American performers coming to South Africa. It helped South African jazz and folk music develop its own unique voice, since its musicians had almost no direct contact with outsiders.

After thirteen years in South Africa, in 1956 Huddleston was recalled by his community to England to be novice master for the order. Meanwhile, he continued to speak out against apartheid and attend meetings in London. He and Julius Nyerere, later to be the first president of independent Tanzania, spoke at the founding meeting of the Anti-Apartheid Movement in London, and later he became the organization's president. Much to his surprise, he was elected bishop of the rural diocese of Masai in Tanganyika, where he learned the Swahili language at age forty-nine. He stayed eight years until in 1968 he was named a suffragan bishop of Stepney, in a poor part of East London. After ten years he was elected bishop of Mauritius and soon thereafter archbishop of the Anglican Province of the Indian Ocean, where he stayed until 1983. (Friends thought "most of my parishioners were fish," he joked.)

Although seventy years old, Huddleston, despite a history of diabetes, showed no signs of tiring. He led a massive protest against the visit of P. W. Botha to Britain in June 1984. The Artists Against Apartheid event he organized in 1986 attracted top rock stars and an audience of over a quarter-million. The "Nelson Mandela Freedom at 70" concert he planned in 1988 was broadcast to an audience of over one billion persons.

After his return to England Huddleston was given an apartment in St. James' Church, Piccadilly, where he could conduct his anti-apartheid activities and take services from time to time. It was my habit to attend morning Eucharists there when in London. I had just returned from South Africa and arrived for the eight o'clock Wednesday morning service. The great Christopher Wren era sacristy door opened, and there emerged the unmistakable profile of the lanky, ascetic figure, sparse and prophet-like in his liturgical gestures. Only two or three persons were at the service, and afterward we chatted. I told him of my meetings earlier in the week in South Africa with Desmond

Tutu and of the situation there. "Please write the Africa prayer for me," I asked in leaving. With firm hand and carefully spaced letters he wrote the prayer that he composed many years ago and that is still used widely in churches:

> *God bless Africa,*
> *Guard her children,*
> *Guide her leaders and*
> *Give her peace for Jesus Christ's sake. Amen.*
> — Trevor Huddleston, CR
> 25-8-1987

ST. ANNE-MARIE JAVOUHEY

Founder, Sisters of St. Joseph of Cluny,
Missionary to Africa, 1779–1851

※※※※※※※※※

I want to be there especially where there is danger and suffering.
— St. Anne-Marie Javouhey

Possessed of strong determination, a superb organizer, and an inspirational pastor, Mother (later Saint) Anne-Marie Javouhey earned a lasting place in church history for her opposition to slavery, for founding the missionary order of the Sisters of St. Joseph of Cluny and for being responsible for the early ordination of African Roman Catholic priests. Being a strong-willed, successful woman, she raised the ire of bishops who found her a threat.

Anne-Marie Javouhey was born in a devout farm family shortly before the French Revolution and grew up in the tumultuous and often anti-Christian setting of Napoleonic France. In 1812 she and eight companions acquired a house in Cluny, and their fledging order took the name of the Sisters of St. Joseph of Cluny. In addition to founding several houses in France, the sisters were responsible for the revival of missionary life in parts of the French overseas empire, especially in Africa. One of the most important mission stations was Senegal, and in 1822 Mother Anne-Marie arrived to spend two years there, but she fell gravely ill. The nuns founded hospitals and a Christian village, a settlement for ex-slaves, which failed when decimated by an epidemic.

The French nun realized the future of the church in Africa must be in African hands. She arranged for young Africans to study in France, and in 1840 three Senegalese priests were ordained. She also organized a seminary where Africans could receive most of their religious education in Africa. As was the case with Fr. Libermann, with whom she corresponded and later exchanged ideas on missionary strategy, church activity was part of a wider effort to "civilize Africa, to make an agricultural people, laborers, and of course honest and good Christians."

She had plans for an interracial religious community, but this was more than the local French bishop in Senegal could handle, and the

105

order folded following a tuberculosis epidemic. Meanwhile, the energetic Javouhey sought funding and support for a struggling new
French missionary order, the Holy Spirit Fathers, that became a major
presence in francophone West Africa.

Her next field of action was the insalubrious colony of French
Guyana, where the French government asked her to colonize the
country's interior. In 1828 she arrived with thirty-six sisters and a
group of freed African emigrants and soon had a self-supporting
settlement launched with agricultural, commercial, educational, and
religious institutions in place. Several hundred freed Africans joined
the colony. Local French priests denied her access to the sacraments
during her stay, causing her to leave Guyana in 1843. In France,
the bishop of Autun was part of a rumor campaign against her and
claimed he was superior general of her community.

Being a woman leader in a male hierarchical church is never easy,
and it was very hard to be a pioneer woman leader in the mid-
nineteenth century. But she endured, though in declining health, and
at the time of her death in 1851, more than three hundred of her
missionary sisters were at work, mainly in Africa. She had founded
over thirty houses throughout France during her forty-four years in
charge of the congregation. She was canonized by the Roman Catholic Church in 1961, and the place where she first settled in Africa on
the island of Gorée was kept as a memorial to her work, not far from
the infamous slave pens that were so much a part of African history.

*Almighty God, by whose grace St. Anne-Marie Javouhey, kin-
dled by the fire of your love, became a burning and a shining
light in your church: inflame us with the same spirit of discipline
and love, that we may ever walk before you as children of light,
through Jesus Christ our Lord. Amen.*
                                                    — *Celebrating Common Prayer,* 487

JOHN KAISER

Priest, Murdered in Kenya, 1932–2000

By all accounts, the August 2000 shooting death of Fr. John Kaiser was a political assassination. The body of the seventy-two-year-old Minnesota native who had spent nearly thirty-six years as a Roman Catholic missionary priest in Kenya was found with a shot in the back of the head near his pickup truck.[65] It had been left abandoned on a rural road northwest of Nairobi, Kenya's capital. Kaiser was a human rights activist who frequently denounced corruption and immorality in public, naming names and citing facts. He had recently accused a powerful Kenyan minister of state of sexually violating a minor. The girl had reportedly sought the priest's counsel, and Fr. Kaiser told her to contact a lawyer. A case was opened against the cabinet minister, who was charged with statutory rape.

The Kenyan government claimed the priest committed suicide, saying a shotgun was found near his body and a round of ammunition in his pocket. But it would be extraordinarily difficult for a person to shoot himself in the back of the head with a shotgun, and the pathologist's reports fixed the blast that killed him as coming from a distance.

Political assassination is a feature of modern Kenyan life. "Who in Kenya is desperate enough to kill Fr. Kaiser, and why now?" the head of the Kenyan Human Rights Commission asked, adding, "They could only be powerful people who saw him as a moral thorn in the flesh." In one instance, Kaiser accused two government ministers of fomenting ethnic violence in 1992 and 1993 when an estimated two thousand Kikuyu people died in the internal conflicts.

Kaiser's outspoken advocacy for human rights and in particular the rights of his parishioners earned him many powerful enemies. He had received death threats and had recently assisted two women from his parish to contact the Kenyan Federation of Women Lawyers after they said another cabinet minister had raped them. "Fr. Kaiser always loved the truth," a Kenyan bishop said. "Because he witnessed to the truth, and some powerful people feared the truth, he was killed."

A parishioner from Kaiser's church in Lolgorian said, "I feel very badly offended because he has always assisted my children. He was always very helpful to the congregation. Because of that, we loved him very much."

At the martyred priest's funeral in Nairobi's basilica, Apostolic Nuncio Giovanni Tonnucci told the congregation, "The church, through pitiless violence, has once more been deprived of one of her ministers. Let no one have any doubts about it: we are celebrating a religious occasion; we are reflecting on a religious assassination, not a political one. Fr. Kaiser has been murdered because he was, and in the eternity of God still is, a Catholic priest who preached the Gospel. Those who killed him, those who planned his killing, wanted to silence the voice of the Gospel."

The priest's life and martyrdom highlight an eternal dilemma for the Christian. Should the Christian life be one of silent prayer, avoiding conflict and public positions on injustices that a single individual is powerless to do much about? Or is the way of Jesus to confront principalities and powers, as Jesus did the traditional authorities, who then caused him to be crucified?

O God, your faithful servant John has gone to his rest. May the example of his stubborn courage in the face of oppressive power be an example to those who uphold human rights and human dignity in Kenya and elsewhere. Turn the leaders of all nations to a vision of your kingdom, where all your children may dwell in safety, laughter, and peace. Amen.

KHAMA BOIKANO

South African Chief and Christian Leader,
c. 1840s–1920s

❀❀❀❀❀❀❀❀❀

I am trying to lead my people according to the Word of God, which we have received from you white people, and you show us an example of wickedness.
—Khama Boikano

Khama Boikano, or "Khama the Good," was a paramount chief of the Bamangwato, a Bantu-speaking South African tribe. His kingdom was five times the size of England and Wales combined, and he ruled it for over fifty years. Khama's baptism in 1858 put him in conflict with his father, who saw the Christian religion as acceptable to whites, but not fitting the personality of Africans.[66] Additionally, Khama rejected the power of traditional diviners and healers, which brought him in conflict with tribal leaders. However, his skills as a warrior and hunter stood him in good stead, and he led his people to several important military victories.

Like many Christian converts, Khama balanced his activities as a tribal chief and the demands of his new faith. He rejected the demand for male circumcision, which caused controversy with tribal elders. Likewise, he opposed arranged marriages that benefited lineages rather than representing a lasting commitment between a woman and man. "I refuse on account of the Word of God to take a second wife," he told another chief, whose response was to burn the huts of two of Khama's sons.

Khama supported the work of missionaries. When a school was vacant for three years because the mission teacher was on home leave, Khama ran the school in the missionary's absence. He replaced traditional animist rituals with Christian prayers, for example, the annual planting ceremony. He allowed the people to hold their traditional service, but then he asked the missionaries to bless the plants as well.

The Bamangwato leader also criticized traditional chiefs who encouraged the sale of cheap brandy, often fortified with tobacco juice, and profited from its sale. When he found some drunken white traders, he arraigned them before the native court and told them, "You think you can despise my laws because I am a black man. Take

109

everything you have, strip the iron off the roofs, gather all your possessions, and go! I am trying to lead my people according to the Word of God, which we have received from you white people, and you show us an example of wickedness."

The chief began each day with prayers with his immediate entourage, after which he sat under a palaver tree to serve as judge, give orders, and make decisions, as runners arrived with news. Sometimes European traders came to his court, asking for permission to set up a store in his territory. At other times traditional shamans and diviners discussed with him the conducting of their ceremonies, which Khama allowed, as long as they did not conflict with the new Christian God's teachings. Once during a prolonged drought, people clamored to their leader to reintroduce traditional rainmaker practices. Khama's answer was that he failed to see how a traditional god who ate grain porridge could help people in such a dire circumstance.

His later decades were filled with activity. The South African chief traveled to England to oppose the division of his kingdom between the Cape Colony and a chartered company. The missionaries supported him in his position, which prevailed. In 1914 Khama was responsible for building a large new stone church and a nearby school. And the chief, to keep warring mission factions from competing in the territory he governed, approved only the presence of a single mission group, the London Missionary Society, in his lands. He also encouraged his own people to act as Christian missionaries among neighboring ethnic groups.

Khama Boikano was an important African leader advancing the Christian religion among his peoples. His conflicts were ones that thousands of other African leaders encountered: joining the church but alienating his father, negotiating intense competition among missionaries, deciding how much leeway to allow traditional diviners, rainmakers, and other ritual practitioners, and being caught in a power struggle between the European colonial government and a chartered company.

O God, we march to Zion, but over a stony path, son set against father, daughter against mother, Catholic against Protestant, European against African, traditional healers against converts. Help us to work through our conflicts, as did Khama Boikano, that we may be found worthy, with the redeemed of Africa and elsewhere, to stand before you in that new Jerusalem, of which you are a part, ever Jesus Christ our Lord. Amen.

SIMON KIMBANGU

Imprisoned Congolese Religious Leader,
Founder of Kimbanguist Church, c. 1889–1951

❀❀❀❀❀❀❀❀❀❀

I was in prison upcountry;
when I returned, they imprisoned me again.
To Kimbangu I complain.
The justified will carry his body
to be honored in the promised city.[67]

Simon Kimbangu, who spent less than five months in 1921 as a self-proclaimed prophet, died in 1951 after enduring thirty years in solitary confinement in a Belgian Congo jail. But a half-century later the separatist church he founded has several million followers, continues to grow, and has spread to other African countries. How does one explain the attraction of Kimbanguism? In part such movements gain a following in stressful settings, and both the Belgian Congo and Zaire were not lacking in economic, political, medical, and cultural stress. Another attraction is that the religion was well organized, preached a sound traditional biblical message, and did good works. In the long run, the success of Kimbanguism was in the centrality of the biblical message delivered in a specifically African context.

Kimbangu grew up in a British Baptist Missionary Society mission in the southwest of what was then the Belgian Congo and was baptized with his wife in 1915. Hoping to become a teacher and evangelist, he was denied this career path because he did not meet mission educational standards. The rejected Kimbangu began having visions calling him to be a prophet and healer. On April 6, 1921, he began a healing ministry that attracted thousands of followers among the Bakongo of the Lower Congo.

As many as ten thousand persons a day headed for Nkamba, Kimbangu's native village. His followers were pleased that Bibles and hymnals were soon sold out all over the country shortly after Kimbangu began to preach. "Since the first coming to Congo there was never seen such a buying of the book of God," they said. Some Protestant and Catholic missionaries, possessed of far less favorable conversion statistics, were jealous and sought his arrest. Originally rejected by the missionaries, Kimbangu's movement had both anti-white and anti-mission-church aspects. Its founder emerged as his own person and head of a church separate from missionary control. Fearing that this religious realignment might have political overtones, the always-suspicious Belgian authorities arrested Kimbangu. After a trial for insurrection and subversive activity, he received a harsh sentence, 120 lashes, and death.

Kimbangu's movement, called Ngunzism, spread like wildfire throughout the Congo and surrounding countries. Its diffusion was aided inadvertently by the Belgian colonial officials who sought to defuse it by deporting thousands of Kimbanguists to every part of the country. This spread Kimbanguism everywhere, giving it an instant foothold in places it might not have reached for years. In addition to the preaching and healing ministry, the church also organized agricultural cooperatives, youth programs, and schools. From the 1920s to the 1950s it existed mainly as an underground movement, suffering sustained persecutions. The number of Kimbanguist martyrs has been estimated at 150,000 persons — a figure impossible to confirm.

The irony is that Kimbangu was a conventional puritanical Christian who tried to maintain good relations with the mission. He preached obedience to civil authority and a strict moral code based on the Ten Commandments, eschewed polygamy, rejected the use of tobacco and alcohol, including local palm wine, forbade dancing, and repudiated the paganism of traditional religious practices. It would be difficult to imagine a more strait-laced conventional ethic. European missionaries protested his death sentence, which was commuted to life imprisonment. Despite repeated appeals for his release, he died in prison in Elizabethville in 1951.

In a poignant 1923 letter, Pauline in mood, some imprisoned Baptist deacons, part of the Kimbangu camp, wrote their nominal European supervisors, who had been critical of their practices:

> As for what you say that we are following a "new teaching," this is not so, our Teacher.... As for the sentences given us, some are for ten years, some twenty, others for life. When these sentences are finished, we cannot go back to our own country; we must die here. But as for us, these tribulations and these sentences "cannot separate us from the love of Christ and of God, nor can any other tribulation."... We assure you we have not broken a single State law, nor been disrespectful to our rulers. "We give to the Governor that which is due the

Governor.... " *We are well in body and in spirit. Two deacons died at Thysville in 1921....They died through being much beaten. Others also died, but there is no time to give their names....We get beaten with canes and have other troubles, but Jehovah is our shepherd.*[68]

APOLO KIVEBULAYA

East African Pastor and Missionary,
c. 1864–1933

⁂⁂⁂⁂⁂⁂⁂⁂⁂

Who befriended the Abambuti [forest people]?
Who loved them greatly?
It is Apolo Kivebulaya,
A great lover.

—Pygmy hymn

Apolo Kivebulaya spent decades building the church in East Africa, going by foot through dense forests, patiently becoming the friend of rural farmers and pygmies, learning their languages, eating their food, sleeping in their huts, and translating the Gospels into local languages.[69] After one such visit with Europeans in which 115 persons were confirmed, the pygmies told him, "How good God is to join us together with the Europeans. We have never before seen so many Europeans together [five!] and they greeted us with faces that did not despise us." A person of consistent energy during his thirty-eight years as a missionary, he was fond of quoting a local proverb: "He who waits till it goes by spears the tail," or "Procrastination is the thief of time."

It was in 1894, when he was about thirty years old, that Kivebulaya asked for baptismal instruction from the missionaries. His reading had led him to the catechism, and he fixed on the biblical phrase "Go ye into all the world and preach the Gospel." He selected the baptismal name Apollos, "the eloquent man, well-versed in the Scriptures" (Acts 18:25). Kivebulaya was not a traditional name, but meant "the thing from England," referring to Kivebulaya's scarlet military jacket, which may have been given to him by an English officer. Armed with Bible, sleeping mat, and such possessions as he could carry, the new Christian set out into the countryside as a teacher. "I started work preaching the things of God. God was very kind to me in all my work for Him.... I found fifty readers ... and they were building a small church thirty feet long ... so I found great joy from preaching and teaching the Gospel.... It was quite different from anything else." Later he would be ordained deacon and priest in the Church of England.

Soon Kivebulaya was asked to be a missionary in the nearby Congo. Here the missionary teacher, with his box of reading sheets and Gospels, set out on one of his lengthy bush visitations. Local opponents of the African Christians were numerous, fearing that the Christians would instruct the region's women to become independent and to question traditional authorities. Kivebulaya described one attack: "They came with spears and sticks and surrounded my house, and I was inside it. They stuck the spears through the walls, as a fisherman would spear fish in a basket trap. They were afraid to come into the house, in case I had a spear, but I had none. Then I started to pray. When they could not break through they left off."

As was the case for many Africans, aspects of Kivebulaya's belief came to him in visions. Several times he saw a man standing beside him, a brother who urged him to go preach in the forest "because I am with you." Once, during a dark moment when he was pursued by enemies, Kivebulaya wrote,

> Jesus Christ appeared to me in a dream in the night when I was doubting if I could endure being bound and prodded with spears, and my house being burned, being beaten every day and reviled and looked at with evil eyes. These were the things that were driving me from the Congo. When I was thinking about these things I saw Jesus Christ shining like the sun, and He said to me, "Be of good cheer, I am with you." I answered and said: "Who is speaking to me?" He replied the second time saying, "I am Jesus Christ. Preach to my people. Do not be afraid." These were the things of my dream and they are quite true. Since that year until now when I preached to the people they turned quickly from their customs and repented.

As he grew old, he asked to be buried with his head toward the forest, for it was the custom to bury people with their head pointed toward their home. "I am still going toward the forest to preach the Gospel; even now my spirit is toward my work." His earthly possessions were two cows, which he gave to a church, while asking that his table, chairs, and kettle be sold to pay teachers' salaries. He died on May 30, 1933.

A prayer in the Luganda language was found after Kivebulaya's death in a small pocket diary he always carried with him:

O God and Father,
and His Son Jesus Christ,
and the Holy Spirit,
may you give me a blessing while in this world,
while you lead me through the forests,
through the lakes and mountains,
so that I may do your work among your people,
Grant that I may be loved by you
and by your people. Amen.[70]

FESTO KIVENGERE

Ugandan Bishop and Evangelist, 1919–1988

Festo Kivengere, "the Billy Graham of Africa," was a Ugandan Christian leader who faced the wrath of the brutal dictator Idi Amin. Unlike Janni Luwum, who had been killed by Amin, Kivengere and his family fled the country. He returned after Amin's downfall to continue an active ministry until his death by leukemia in 1988.

Born in 1919 in a rural setting among the semi-nomadic rural pastoralists of southwest Uganda, Festo Kivengere belonged to a pagan ruling family. He spent his early life as a cattle herder, where he would read children's books about Jesus while herding calves. At about age ten he joined a mission school established in his village and was eventually sent away for higher education, after which he returned to his village as a teacher. Converted to Christianity during a revival meeting, Kivengere became a pastor and eventually Anglican bishop of Kigezi. After study in England and a trip to Australia he was asked to translate into Swahili the sermons of the American evangelist Billy Graham, who developed such confidence in Kivengere that he told him, "Don't bother to translate literally. You know what I mean — get that across." Kivengere and Graham became lifelong friends. The young African evangelist shared the platform with Graham on American revival tours and eventually formed his own African Evangelic Enterprise.

His own growth in the church coincided with the increasing excesses of the ruler who has been called "Africa's Hitler," and Kivengere was forced to flee his country. But he was not bitter because of the experience. He wrote a book called *I Love Idi Amin* in which he wrote, "On the cross, Jesus said, 'Father, forgive them, because they don't know what they are doing.' As evil as Idi Amin was, how can I do less toward him?"

Kivengere had met with Idi Amin to voice his opposition to the killing in 1973 of three men from his diocese by a government firing squad on a trumped-up charge:

> February 10 began as a sad day for us in Kabale. People were commanded to come to the stadium and witness the execution.

117

Death permeated the atmosphere. A silent crowd of about three thousand was there ready to watch. I had permission from the authorities to speak to the men before they died, and two of my fellow ministers were with me. They brought the men in a truck and unloaded them. They were handcuffed and their feet were chained. The firing squad stood at attention. As we walked into the center of the stadium, I was wondering what to say. How do you give the Gospel to doomed men who are probably seething with rage?

We approached them from behind, and as they turned to look at us, what a sight! Their faces were all alight with an unmistakable glow and radiance. Before we could say anything, one of them burst out: "Bishop, thank you for coming! I wanted to tell you. The day I was arrested, in my prison cell, I asked the Lord Jesus to come into my heart. He came in and forgave me all my sins! Heaven is now open, and there is nothing between me and my God! Please tell my wife and children that I am going to be with Jesus. Ask them to accept him into their lives as I did." The other two men told similar stories, excitedly raising their hands, which rattled their handcuffs.

I felt that what I needed to do was to talk to the soldiers, not to the condemned. So I translated what the men had said into a language the soldiers understood. The military men were standing there with guns cocked and bewilderment on their faces. They were so dumfounded that they forgot to put the hoods over the men's faces! The three faced the firing squad standing close together. They looked toward the people and began to wave, handcuffs and all. The people waved back. Then shots were fired, and the three were with Jesus.

Forgiveness, reconciliation, and proclamation were the three cornerstones of Kivengere's ministry, which continued until his death. Uganda, the country with perhaps the largest number of martyrs per square kilometer in Africa, also has one of the densest populations of active witnessing Christians.[71]

Almighty God, ruler of all nations, we give you thanks for the steadfast witness of your servant Festo Kivengere. Through his life we learn of your enduring presence among us; through his death we know that pain and fear are left behind at the gate of your eternal kingdom, where dwell the blessed dead in life everlasting, with Jesus Christ our Savior. Amen.

JOSEPH KIWANKU

*First African Roman Catholic Bishop
of Modern Times, d. 1966*

❁❁❁❁❁❁❁❁❁

By now, you Africans are missionaries to yourselves.
— Pope Paul VI during a 1969 visit to Uganda

In the transition from European to African governance in the Roman
Catholic Church in Africa, pride of place in East Africa went to
the Masaka Diocese of Uganda, where a visionary European bishop,
Henry Streicher, began promoting African leadership to the episcopacy in the 1920s. As early as 1925 in his five-year report to Rome he
advocated naming an African vicar apostolic for the region. Surpris-
ingly, Rome answered in the affirmative and designated the region's
prime real estate — the Masaka District — for African leadership.
This was in the middle of the long-established White Fathers mission
territory, and when they heard of the Vatican's action, local African
clergy responded with "Tulidde Budda — we have eaten Buddu" (the
region's name). "It is ours!" A tug-of-war had been going on between
those who favored Africanization of the episcopate and those who opposed it. It is a clash that has been duplicated in many denominations
in numerous other countries as well. Adrian Hastings has written,
"At every point in this process, Streicher...and Masaka itself were
far ahead of anything else in African Christianity, and success was
possible only because on the one side Streicher was so very unusual in
both his vision and his perseverance and on the other the local clergy
as a group thoroughly justified his confidence. They formed indeed
an exceptionally able, well-educated, and responsible body."[72]

An African doctor of canon law who had received a *summa cum
laude* mention for his oral examinations, Dr. Joseph Kiwanku, who
had also entered the White Fathers missionary order, was named
vicar apostolic in 1939. Pius XII consecrated him in Rome on the
Feast of Christ the King, along with another African bishop, Ignance
Ramarosandratana of Madagascar, and the first six Japanese bishops. An Indian cardinal assisted at the consecration. For the next
twelve years Kiwanku was the only African Catholic diocesan bishop
continent-wide, nor did any black Anglican hold a comparable posi-

tion. Kiwanku became a diocesan bishop in 1953 when Masaka was designated a full diocese. "He proved a model bishop," Hastings said of him, "who worked with laity, pressed forward with the education of his clergy, gave sage political advice, and tempered episcopal autocracy with basic democracy through the development of elected parish councils and school parent associations. Few missionary bishops achieved so much."[73]

In January 1961 Kiwanku was named archbishop of Kampala. On Mission Sunday 1964 the Ugandan prelate celebrated the canonization of the Roman Catholic martyrs of Uganda with the pope at the Vatican. It was also a celebration of his own twenty-fifth anniversary as a bishop. He was taken ill during a session of Vatican II and died on February 22, 1966.

During Pope Paul VI's 1969 African visit, he remarked while in Uganda, "By now, you Africans are missionaries to yourselves." Africans, established as priests in many parts of the continent, proved their worth not only in that role but increasingly as bishops, and soon other dioceses, Catholic and Anglican, throughout Africa came under local leadership.

Almighty God, the light of the faithful and Shepherd of souls, who sent your servant Joseph Kiwanku to be a bishop in the church, to feed your sheep by the word of Christ and to guide them by good example: give us grace to keep the faith of the church and to follow in the footsteps of Jesus Christ our Lord. Amen.   — *Celebrating Common Prayer, 486*

LACTANTIUS

Christian Apologist, North Africa,
c. 240–c. 320

Christianity has always had to compete for a place among other world religions and belief systems. In addition to formal, established religions, the world in ancient times was filled with developed and half-baked philosophical systems which attracted attention, such as cynicism, skepticism, materialism, and fatalism. It was into such a world in North Africa that Lucius Caelius (Lactantius) was born in about 240. Growing up in a pagan intellectual environment, at some point he became a Christian, which caused him to lose his position in the persecutions of 303. It must be remembered that changing faith then was not like changing brands of cars now. Such shifts often involved the loss of jobs and, at times, lives, especially for those who accepted the newly emerging Christian religion.[74]

Lactantius was a vigorous defender of the now-spreading Christian faith. In one work he linked the harmony of God's creation with the wonders of the human body at work, a not unexpected position, since many early Christian writers saw a direct link between the human body and the cosmos and argued that through God both could be in harmony. In other writings he attacked pagan ideas then circulating in North Africa; as a writer, he depended more on logic and confronting the weaknesses in the pagan positions than he did on an appeal to Scripture or church doctrine.

A feature of such early Christian apologists is their unequivocal stands: the just were saved; those who erred or grossly sinned faced eternal damnation. No tolerant ambiguity here. In a work called *De Mortibus Persecutorum* (*On the Death of the Persecutors*, c. 315) Lactantius argued that God "protects justice and leads all ungodly men and persecutors without fail to their deserved punishment." In yet another work, *De ira Dei* (*On the Wrath of God*, c. 318), Lactantius cited examples of both an angry and a compassionate God in the Old and New Testaments to refute the arguments of those who said that an omnipotent God was indifferent to what went on in the universe. The name of Lactantius belongs to the long list of early North

121

African Christians who were scrappy intellectual combatants for the faith, helping to give it credibility in the vigorous intellectual milieu of early Mediterranean culture.

> *O God, by your Holy Spirit you give to some the word of wisdom, to others the word of knowledge, and to others the word of faith: We praise your Name for the gifts of grace manifested to your servant Lactantius, and we pray that your Church may never be destitute of such gifts; through Jesus Christ, our Lord, who with you and the Holy Spirit lives and reigns, one God, for ever and ever. Amen.*
>
> — Collect of a Theologian and Teacher,
> *Prayer Book and Hymnal*, 248–249

CHARLES MARTIAL ALLEMAND LAVIGERIE

Primate of Africa, Founder of the White Fathers and Sisters, 1825–1892

> We follow the flag of France, without ever concerning ourselves whose hands hold it.
> —Cardinal Lavigerie

He was larger than life, a religious leader seemingly cast for a nineteenth-century French opera. Cardinal Lavigerie was born in Bayonne, France, one of four children of a French customs officer. Interested in religion since childhood, he played at being a priest. Ordained in 1849, he obtained doctorates in letters and theology from the Sorbonne, where he became professor of history in 1854.[75] A skilled organizer with a keen interest in overseas missions, in 1860 he traveled to Syria where the Druses had killed large numbers of Syrian Christians. Lavigerie collected funds for their relief. Soon he became a consultant to the Vatican on Oriental Affairs, adviser to the pope. In 1863, at age thirty-seven, he was named Bishop of Nancy.

The conquest and settlement of Algeria was France's highest overseas priority in the 1860s, and the French government pushed for appointment of the energetic prelate as archbishop of Algeria. It was he who had said, "We follow the flag of France, without ever concerning ourselves whose hands hold it." He would be a pastor to the growing number of French settlers and troops arriving there, they reasoned, but Lavigerie had his own ideas. He took the continent of Africa for his diocese and saw himself as the successor to Augustine as its bishop. "I shall not seek one day's rest," he remarked on landing in Africa. In quick succession he built parishes, schools, and orphanages, and founded the missionary order of the White Fathers and the White Sisters. Interested in agriculture, he brought the Muscat grape to North Africa.

Skilled as any marshal of France at public ceremony, in 1872 he consecrated the basilica of Our Lady of Africa on the heights of Algiers, and from it each Sunday ships in the Mediterranean were solemnly blessed. It was from this setting that he sent waves of priests into Africa, dressed in modified Moorish garb of his design. The first three priests he dispatched across the Sahara in 1874 were killed; so was another group of three in 1881. Lavigerie then hired armed guards, dressed them in the colorful uniforms of the papal zouaves, and urged them to use their arms only when required. The long ceremonies he designed, the costuming, banners, movement, and music could have come from the Paris Opera.

In 1875 he established headquarters in the historic chapel of St. Louis of Carthage, where St. Louis, the only French monarch to die abroad, was buried while returning from a crusade. Lavigerie returned often to France and was a tireless fund-raiser. He would preach a rousing missionary sermon and then pass among the congregation in his cardinal's robes slowly taking up a collection.

Lavigerie made no accommodation to local religions. He called Islam "truly the masterpiece of the evil one," but at the same time he realized his missionaries would have great difficulty converting its adherents. That would not come in any numbers for over a century, he reasoned. Meanwhile, his priests should act primarily as compassionate neighbors, founding schools and hospitals or helping those afflicted by drought, pestilence, or famine. "We leave God to carry on, in His own good time. Our part is to do His will. Our greatest happiness, after all our sacrifices, is to hear Moslems exclaim: 'Really, what good people these French are!' " By 1879 his missionaries had reached Lake Tanganyika and Lake Victoria, and had established themselves in Zanzibar.

In later years, he concentrated on opposing the slave trade, visiting several European capitals in the 1880s to support antislavery societies and lecture publicly against slavery. Arthritis plagued him in old age, and he suffered bouts of depression. He prepared his tomb in the basilica of St. Augustine shortly before his death in 1892. Lavigerie contributed directly to the growing French missionary movement; by 1900, more than two-thirds of the Roman Catholic priests abroad, 4,500 out of 6,500, came from France. "God has chosen France for himself," Lavigerie commented, "and reserved [for it] the evangelization of the African continent."

> *The word of God is alive and active,*
> *And speaks to us of salvation.*
>
> —Antiphon to the Magnificat
> for Evening Prayer, Feast of a Bishop

FRANÇOIS LIBERMANN
French Catholic Missionary, 1802–1852

Faites-vous nègres avec les nègres.
(Make yourself black with the blacks)
—François Libermann

Jägel Libermann, scion of a Polish Jewish family, was on his way to becoming a second-generation rabbi when he was converted to Christianity. The twenty-year-old Alsatian talmudic scholar was influenced by David Drach, a leading Parisian Jewish intellectual, who had converted to Catholicism. On November 12, 1825, Libermann too was converted and was baptized a few days later. He took the name François for Francis of Assisi. Although he studied for the priesthood, Libermann was plagued with epilepsy and was not ordained until 1841 at age thirty-nine. He had only thirteen years of active ministry remaining, but in that time he became one of France's most important nineteenth-century missionary voices.

Shortly after his ordination he opened a novitiate for the Society of the Holy Heart of Mary to send priests abroad. The new priest had long been interested in France's black colonial world, having carefully questioned former missionaries who had served in Réunion, Madagascar, and Haiti. Initially only three missionaries appeared. Haiti and Mauritius became off limits for political reasons, and the long-established Holy Ghost Fathers claimed francophone West Africa as their territory. Meanwhile, Rome, in response to the antislavery movement, created the Vicariate Apostolic of the Two Guineas extending five thousand miles along the West African coast. Fr. Libermann contributed seven priests and three lay workers, who set out for Cape Palmas in 1843. As was often the case, death and disease decimated the missionary ranks. It was not until September 28, 1844, that the first permanent station was founded as St. Mary of Gabon. The site was called Libreville, the French counterpart to Monrovia, Liberia, and became a base against the slave trade.

In 1848 Libermann broke the impasse with the Holy Ghost Fathers. His order and the Holy Ghost Fathers merged. Libermann became head of the new Congregation of the Holy Ghost. The agreement included supervision of a seminary to train colonial clergy and — the most controversial point — plans to train an indigenous African clergy. Between 1869 and 1910 twenty-two Africans were ordained to the Roman Catholic priesthood.

Writing to his priests in Dakar and Gabon on November 19, 1847, Libermann enumerated his ideas about the missionary role of Christians in language paralleling that of St. Paul. In particular, he stressed the need for *kenosis*, the self-emptying of a person to stand in poverty and solidarity with Africans. Libermann drew on a passage in Philippians (2:5–11) that Christ, in entering the world, did not establish himself as an equal to God, but came as a servant. As such Christ was willing to be humiliated and suffer death on the cross. Here is Libermann's fullest statement of *kenosis* in a missionary setting:

> Empty yourselves of Europe, of its manners and mentality; make yourselves black with the blacks, then you will understand them as they should be understood; make yourself black with the blacks to form them as they should be, not in the way of Europe, but leaving them what is their own; behave toward them as servants would behave to their masters, adapting to the customs, attitudes and habits of their masters.[76]

Wracked by migraine headaches and the return of epilepsy, Libermann died in early February 1852. Although only fifty years of age and active in the mission field for little more than a decade, his prodigious energy, deep spirituality, and wide-ranging interests made his achievements among the most lasting in French missionary history: he championed an indigenous church with a carefully trained indigenous clergy and hierarchy; he advocated separation of the church from the French state; he exemplified personal holiness, lived out in a religious community; and he was a leader in a wider civilizing effort, the *mission civilisatrice* of French colonial officials.[77]

> *Polish Jew, training to be a rabbi, you found your way to Christ and to Africa. Scholar and organizer, whose earthly life was plagued by poor health, in the self-emptying of Christ who gave up all upon the cross, you found the model and mission of the church, one for your century and ours. Amen.*

DAVID LIVINGSTONE

Missionary, Explorer, Abolitionist, 1813–1873

> Neither civilization nor Christianity can be promoted alone; in fact they are inseparable. — David Livingstone

The best known of all European missionaries in Africa, with the exception of Albert Schweitzer, was David Livingstone, who was also the first European explorer to cross Africa from west to east. He was an unrelenting opponent of slavery, calling it "an open sore" at a time when it was still a staple in European-African trade. Although he is usually studied only as an explorer, Livingstone remained constant in his missionary vocation during his eleven years in South Africa. "We are forwarding that great movement which God is carrying on for the renovation of the world," he announced in 1854. "We are part of the machinery he employs... fellow-workers, co-operators with God."

Livingstone's time in Africa coincided with an outpouring of world interest in the continent, and his *Missionary Travels* went through fourteen editions, with over seventy thousand copies sold. In addition to exploration and evangelism, he contributed significantly to the study of Bantu linguistics, tropical medicine, botany, geology, and zoology. He most likely suffered from a manic depressive disorder, an inherited malady that left him at times gloomy and depressed and at others filled with enterprise and elation.

Livingstone arrived at the Cape on March 15, 1840, and was drawn increasingly to the interior, which meant sending his wife and children home to Europe. "I would never build on another man's foundation," he said. "I shall preach the Gospel beyond every other man's line of things." As he moved inland, Livingstone had the dual objective of both avoiding the growing Afrikaner incursions to the north, and confronting the notorious slave trade. Promote honest commerce, he reasoned, and the slave trade will decrease; African chiefs who gain European goods from human commerce would be attracted to stable, more regular commercial exchange. "Neither civilization nor Christianity can be promoted alone," he wrote. "In fact they are inseparable." Nevertheless, he retained constant respect for African institutions. "Jesus came not to judge," he said, adding, "Christianity does not give any license for assaulting the civil institutions of man." On one of his three lengthy expeditions, he came upon the Lunda people near the Zambezi River, whom he depicted with thoughtfulness:

> They seem to possess a more vivid conviction of their relation to the Unseen world than any of the Southern tribes. In the deep dark forests near their villages we always met with idols and places of prayer. . . . Here in the still darkness of the forest night the worshipper — either male or female — comes alone and prays to the gods (Barimo) or spirits of departed relatives and when an answer to the petition seems granted, meal or other food is sprinkled on the spot as a thanks offering.[78]

Livingstone's final years were not easy ones. Nevertheless, his faith remained strong, as recorded in his *Last Journals*. While waiting for carriers on his last journey to the interior in 1871 he wrote, "I read the whole Bible through four times while I was at Manyuema." His pocket testament would indicate that, apart from the Gospels, his favorite reading was in the Psalms, including Psalm 40 ("I waited patiently upon the Lord"), Psalm 43 ("Give judgment for me, O God, and defend my cause against an ungodly people"), Psalm 90 ("Lord, you have been our refuge from one generation to another"), Psalm 95 ("Come, let us sing to the Lord"), Psalm 113 ("Hallelujah! Give praise, you servants of the Lord"), plus the more familiar Psalms 23 and 121.

On March 19, 1873, the last year of his life, Livingstone recorded a prayer:

> My birthday. My Jesus, my King, my Life, my All, I again dedicate my whole self to Thee. Accept me and grant, O gracious Father, that ere this year is gone I may finish my work. In Jesus' name I ask it. Amen.

Livingstone was found kneeling by his bedside, dead of a fever, on May 1, 1873. African colleagues bore his body nearly fifteen hundred miles through difficult terrain, a nine-month journey from the interior to the coast; from there it was transported to London to lie in Westminster Abbey.

DR. MATTHEW LUKWIYA

Ugandan Physician, Ebola Victim, 1957–2000

> It is our vocation to save life. It involves risk, but when we serve with love, that is when the risk does not matter so much. When we believe our mission is to save lives, we have got to do our work.
>
> —Dr. Matthew Lukwiya

Dr. Matthew Lukwiya could have held a comfortable medical position in England, the Middle East, South Africa, or wherever talented African doctors go, but he stayed in Uganda instead and died a horrible death from the Ebola disease.[79]

Dr. Lukwiya, forty-two, was the medical superintendent of a large Roman Catholic missionary hospital in Gula, a small town near the Sudanese border in northern Uganda. He had grown up poor in the region, his father a fishmonger, his mother a market trader, but a succession of scholarships sent him to school and medical school, where he continuously emerged first in his class. "Dr. Matthew," as he was known to patients and staff, began his professional life as a staff physician at St. Mary's Hospital in Gula, a state-of-the-art modern hospital run by an Italian Roman Catholic missionary order. St. Mary's treated eighteen thousand patients a year and five hundred out-patients a day, including army and rebel soldiers in the troubled border region.

The physician was in Kampala, 250 miles away, when news of a strange disease spreading through the north and affecting hospital personnel resulted in his being recalled quickly to St. Mary's. Dr. Lukwiya was enjoying an interlude of study and family life after seventeen years of fourteen-hour workdays. However, he left his wife, Margaret, and their five children behind in the country's major city and headed back to his hospital. Margaret was an evangelical Protestant, and Matthew attended services with her twice a week in Kampala and became an active Christian himself.

Ebola, first identified in 1995 in the Congo, is transmitted through contact with infected body fluids, such as vomit, blood, or sweat. It had no known cause and no known cure. As might be expected, hospital personnel panicked. The nearly four hundred employees of

St. Mary's hospital were in revolt, and Dr. Lukwiya spent a day with them, inspiring some, cajoling others. He also took important steps to curtail the spreading epidemic, alerting authorities in Kampala to it, isolating victims in a special ward, and tightening safety precautions for medical personnel, whose bodies must be completely covered in protective gear before encountering patients. Dr. Lukwiya was one of the people who tried to make patients comfortable, but in doing so committed a fatal error, leaving his face uncovered. The mistake was not uncommon. Protective masks soon fogged up, making it difficult for doctors, who also wore gloves, to puncture veins and conduct other medical procedures.

Soon Dr. Lukwiya was a patient himself. At first he thought it was malaria or another fever-causing disease, but gradually the truth was known — he had contracted Ebola, the 156th recorded victim of the outbreak. His wife came north but could not touch her dying husband. The best she could do was sit at a distance, clad in protective gear, and hold his foot with a surgical glove. He died on December 5, 2000.

Reflecting on his life, the physician's widow remarked, "Matthew was not for worldly desires. He was just devoted to his patients. It was never business. It was just his patients. That was it." One Good Friday, when rebels from a bandit group called the Lord's Resistance Army came to kidnap an Italian nun for ransom, the African doctor persuaded them to take him instead, which they did for a week.

There never had been a question about what Dr. Lukwiya would do with his life. The brilliant physician wanted to stay in his native region and be a healer of people. He told his fellow medical professionals who were thinking of quitting, "It is our vocation to save life. It involves risk, but when we serve with love, that is when the risk does not matter so much. When we believe our mission is to save lives, we have got to do our work." In a weakened state just before his death, he said, "Oh God, I think I will die in my service. If I die, let me be the last," after which he sang "Onward, Christian Soldiers."

O Christ, healer of nations and peoples, we thank you for the medical professionals of Africa, surgeons and nurses, pharmacists and health educators, herbalists and midwives, especially those who combat the spread of AIDS, Ebola, and other infectious diseases. Bless especially the memory of those, like Matthew Lukwiya, who laid down their lives for their people, as you did. Amen.

ALBERT JOHN
MVUMBI LUTHULI
Zulu Chief, Nobel Prize Laureate,
1898–1967

※※※※※※※※

> The road to freedom is via the cross.
> — Albert John Mvumbi Luthuli

Chief Albert John Mvumbi ("Continuous Rain" in Zulu) Luthuli, a leading figure in South Africa's struggle against apartheid and Africa's first Nobel Peace Prize recipient, was a product of Christian mission schools. His father, John Bunyan Luthuli, was a missionary interpreter in Rhodesia, and Albert, supported by a scholarship and his widowed mother's earnings as a charwoman, attended an American Mission Board's teacher training college near Durban, South Africa. He was one of the school's first African teachers, but in 1936 he switched careers when he was elected chief of a five-thousand-person community in Groutville in Natal's sugar lands. (An uncle had previously held the position.) Elected to leadership positions in the wider community, Luthuli eventually joined the Institute of Race Relations, the Christian Council Executive, and, in 1945, the African National Congress (ANC), becoming president of its Natal branch.[80]

Discussing the intersection of politics and religion, Luthuli said, "I am in Congress precisely *because* I am a Christian. My Christian belief about society must find expression here and now, and Congress is the spearhead of the real struggle.... My own urge, *because* I am a Christian, is to get into the thick of the struggle with other Christians, taking my Christianity with me and praying that it may be used to influence for good the character of the resistance."

Throughout his career the Zulu leader experienced the increasing harshness of South African racial policies. As a local chief, he lived with a constituency to whom poverty and political impotence were part of life. In 1946 he joined protests against police violence that crushed a strike of African miners, leaving eight persons dead and over a thousand injured. While on a 1948 tour of the United States, sponsored by the Congressional Board of Missions, he warned of racial problems in South Africa and their effects on the Christian community.

During Luthuli's tenure as Natal ANC president, he led the organization to join with the South African Indian Congress in protesting racially discriminatory laws, for which more than eight thousand persons went to jail. When the South African government gave him an ultimatum to leave his post with the ANC or resign his chief's position, he declined to do either. "The road to freedom is via the cross," he told his opponents, who deposed and eventually jailed him. Meanwhile, his reputation among ordinary South Africans grew. He exuded a quiet authority and sought to rally South Africans to a democratic future. People respectfully called him "chief," and in 1952 he was elected national president of the ANC. This made him a marked man and, despite his efforts at nonviolence and pleas for racial harmony, Luthuli was arrested in a 1956 roundup of 155 persons and charged with high treason, promoting violence, or being a Communist. He was released in 1957 after a lengthy trial in which the charges could not be proven. Repeatedly arrested and banned to living in his neighborhood, in 1960 Luthuli burned his pass, the document all Africans were required to carry by police, for which he was arrested and fined. Nelson Mandela was his defense attorney, and, far from serving its intended purpose of repressing the Africans, the incident turned the world spotlight on the regime's repressive racial policies. By then Luthuli had become a respected international figure; he was named the Nobel Peace Prize winner in 1961.

The mid-1960s marked the rejection of Luthuli's nonviolence and pleas for interracial dialogue by militant South African blacks. At the same time, the South African government kept him under house arrest. He died on July 21, 1967, struck by a train at a crossing near the small farm where he lived, a revered elder figure of the global struggle against political, racial, and religious repression.

Luthuli's autobiography, *Let My People Go*, has become an African classic. Written in the darkest period of apartheid, it ends with this message:

> *The struggle must go on — the struggle to make the opportunity for the building to begin. The struggle will go on. I speak humbly and without levity when I say that, God giving me strength and courage enough, I shall die, if need be for this cause. But I do not want to die until I have seen the building begun. Mayibuye I Afrika! Come Africa, come!*[81]

JANANI LUWUM
Archbishop of Uganda, Martyr,
1922–1977

❀❀❀❀❀❀❀❀

The reality of Jesus overwhelmed me, and it still does.
—Janani Luwum at the time of his conversion

Janani Luwum was an unlikely subject to be one of the twentieth century's most prominent martyrs. A Ugandan teacher of simple, lively
faith, he did not seek, but was called to, leadership positions in the
Anglican Church in Uganda, until, as archbishop, it was his destiny
to confront one of the century's worst dictators, Idi Amin, and die a
brutal death for his church and country.[82]

The future martyr became a Christian at 12:30 in the afternoon of
January 6, 1948, when, as a twenty-six-year-old rural school teacher,
he was converted by a passing revivalist preacher and became one
of the *balokole*, or "saved ones." "Today I have become a leader in
Christ's army," he said. "I am prepared to die in the army of Jesus."
Little did he know what the future held. After seeking ordination
in 1956, he spent a year at St. Augustine's College, Canterbury, and
then moved with his wife and two children to an isolated parish of
twenty-four churches stretched over forty miles of bush land with only
a rickety bicycle for transportation. By 1969 Luwum was consecrated
bishop of the newly formed diocese of Northern Uganda.

The new bishop, his bicycle replaced by a car, traveled tirelessly
around the diocese, preaching in an earthy idiom. In one place he
told the congregation they were treating the Lord like the guest who
was invited to a great feast but was offered only a chicken head for
supper and left saddened at his reception by his people. In another he
compared the congregation to a hyena at a crossroads, loping down
different roads in search of the most bountiful prey.

Meanwhile, Idi Amin, once a cook in the King's African Rifles, a
frequently drunk and power-obsessed soldier, was coming to power.
With the arrival of Uganda's independence in 1962, the affable but
nearly illiterate Amin was catapulted into leadership of the new African nation's army. In 1971, while the elected president, Milton Obote,
was out of the country, Amin, a nominal Muslim, seized power

through a coup d'état. Soldiers filled the streets and signs went up: "Amin — Our Christ."

On February 14, 1977, the archbishop was summoned to the palace, where the president accused him of complicity in a plot to overthrow him, a charge Luwum denied. At 9:30 on the morning of February 16 Amin summoned several Anglican bishops. The diplomatic corps, high government officials, and civic and religious leaders were also invited to a Kampala hotel, where Archbishop Luwum and six other bishops were paraded before the crowd. Three thousand armed soldiers assembled in the background, and a cache of arms and several antiquated Chinese automatic weapons were displayed. As the clergy were forced to stand in the blistering heat, charges were read against the archbishop by a prisoner who had obviously been beaten.

"What shall we do with the traitors?" asked the vice president, presiding over the stage-managed "trial." "Kill them, kill them," the soldiers replied, echoing lines from another rigged trial two thousand years earlier. After the crowd was dismissed and the bishops were herded to a room in the presidential palace, the archbishop was told that the president wanted to see him. The others were free to leave. "I can see the hand of the Lord in this," Luwum said, and walked calmly from the room. It was the last words anyone heard from him.

A few details of the archbishop's last hours were pieced together. After refusing to sign a confession, he was taken to the infamous State Research Center, where he was stripped to his underclothes and thrown into a cell with prisoners waiting to die. When the detainees asked for his blessing, guards returned his cassock and cross to him, and he prayed with the condemned. Peace and calm descended on those behind bars, a survivor later reported. Eyewitnesses added that shortly before his death at 6:00 p.m. the archbishop prayed aloud for his captors.

Although the government forbade any memorial service for the dead archbishop, thousands of persons gathered at Kampala Cathedral. An empty grave was dug next to that of Bishop Hannington, a missionary bishop who had been martyred in the nineteenth century by Uganda's ruler (see p. 95). Spontaneously they sang the hymn the archbishop and two others reportedly sang shortly before their death:

> Daily, daily sing the praises
> of the City God has made....

Idi Amin later departed Uganda in disgrace, Janani Luwum has joined the noble army of martyrs, in the company of such modern companions as Martin Luther King Jr., Oscar Romero, and Dietrich Bonhoeffer. The archbishop of Canterbury in the presence of the queen dedicated a stone sculpture of Luwum and the others at Westminster Abbey in July 1998. Archbishop Janani Luwum stands now for the ages as the model of a faithful pastor who died for Christ.

> *Crown him, ye martyrs of our God,*
> *who from his altar call:*
> *praise him whose way of pain ye trod,*
> *and crown him Lord of all!*
> —From hymn "All Hail the Power of Jesus' Name,"
> *Prayer Book and Hymnal,* no. 494

THE MARTYRS OF THE
CHRISTIAN FRATERNITY

Buta, Burundi, 1997

❀❀❀❀❀❀❀❀❀

God is good and we have met Him.
— The Martyrs of the Christian Fraternity

The isolated, mountainous country of Burundi, often called "the Switzerland of Africa," has been the scene of some of Africa's bitterest ethnic violence, a spillover from the genocide in neighboring Rwanda. At about 5:30 in the morning of April 30, 1997, armed invaders allegedly from the Hutu rebel group CNDD (the National Council for the Defense of Democracy) attacked the Roman Catholic Seminary at Buta, killing forty young seminarians between the ages of fifteen and twenty. Since the beginning of the country's most recent civil war in October 1993, the seminary in the country's south had been a tranquil refuge for members of the two warring ethnic groups. The pastoral Hutu and more nomadic Tutsi have been locked in deadly genocidal war since 1972.

The seminarians themselves had made a special point of living in a Christian fraternity, where love of Christ was more important than ethnic origins. They had just completed an Easter season retreat before their massacre. Fr. Nicolas Niyungeko, rector of the Sanctuary of Buta in the Diocese of Bururi, wrote of the seminarians:

> At the end of the retreat, this class was enlivened by a new kind of spirit, which seemed to be a preparation for the holy death of these innocents. Full of rejoicing and joy, the word in their mouths was "God is good and we have met Him." They spoke of heaven as if they had just come from it, and of the priesthood as if they had just been ordained.... One realized that something very strong had happened in their heart, without knowing exactly what it was. From that day on, they prayed, they sang, they danced to church, happy to discover, as it were, the treasure of Heaven.

The following day, when the murderers surprised them in bed, the seminarians were ordered to separate into two groups, the

Hutus on one hand, the Tutsi on the other. They wanted to kill some of them, but the seminarians refused, preferring to die together. Their evil scheme having failed, the killers rushed on the children and slaughtered them with rifles and grenades. At that point some of the seminarians were heard singing psalms of praise and others were saying "Forgive them Lord, for they know not what they do." Others, instead of fighting or trying to run away, preferred helping their distressed brothers, knowing exactly what was going to happen to them.

Their death was like a soft and light path from their dormitory to another resting place, without pain, without noise, nor fear. They died like Martyrs of the Fraternity, thus honoring the Church of Burundi, where many sons and daughters were led astray by hatred and ethnic vengeance.[83]

Forty days after the massacre, the small seminary dedicated its church to Mary, Queen of Peace, and it has since, according to Fr. Niyungeko, "become a place of pilgrimage where Burundians come to pray for the reconciliation of their people, for peace, conversion, and hope for all. May their testimony of faith, unity, and fraternity send a message for humankind and their blood become a seed for peace in our country and the world."

Almighty God, you call your witnesses from every nation and reveal your glory in their lives. Make us thankful for the example of the Martyrs of the Christian Fraternity of Burundi, and strengthen us by their example, that we, like them, may be faithful in the service of your kingdom, through Jesus Christ our Lord. Amen.   — *Celebrating Common Prayer, 489*

THE MARTYRS OF UGANDA

1886

Uganda was a country of rolling hills and temperate climate, of intelligent, purposeful people, but with undercurrents of violence as well. In 1877 the first Church Missionary Society (CMS) missionaries arrived, representing the Church of England, followed two years later by the Roman Catholic White Fathers. The country (then called Buganda) was ruled by a powerful king, the Kabaka Mutesa, head of an elaborate political hierarchy. At first the Kabaka welcomed the missionaries, believing they would provide access to superior weaponry, but his initial interest soon waned, for their focus was on preaching the Gospel and founding schools.[84] One young Scottish engineer, Alexander Mackay, however, attracted a following for introducing wheeled transportation, printing presses, and water pumps, and the ruler grew nervous, fearing he might lose control of his people. His paranoid son and successor, Mwanga, was distrustful of the Christians and ordered the murder of Bishop James Hannington (see p. 95) and his companions, as they entered Uganda in 1885. In the following year four young pages of the royal household went on safari with Mackay. They were ordered back to the royal capital, where three of them had their arms cut off and were roasted alive, singing a Christian hymn as they died and as hundreds of persons watched.

As so often happens, the act of repression backfired. Hundreds of persons became interested in Christianity, and many sought baptism, sneaking in small groups to the missionary compounds by night. A Roman Catholic advisor and court favorite, Joseph Balikuddembe, was killed for protesting to the Kabaka about the murder of Bishop Hannington and the ruler's blatant sexual immorality with the young male pages.

Repressions reached their height in 1886. One day as he was returning from an unsuccessful hunt, the Kabaka found groups of pages intently reading and discussing the Bible. Enraged, he ordered the youths to abandon their newly found faith or die. Most chose death, and on June 3, thirty-three of them, Roman Catholic and Anglican, were bound together in dry reed matting and placed over a slowly burning fire. They died, like their predecessors and the children in the Book of Daniel, singing the Lord's praises. Even the executioner was forced to burn his own son to death.

Mwanga, an African Caligula, continued the executions, as brutal as any martyrdom ordered by the Roman emperors. More young men were brutally killed by being burned alive, dismembered, beheaded, speared to death, or ravaged by wild dogs. The twenty-two Catholics who were martyred at this time were canonized by Pope Paul in 1964. The Anglican Church commemorates the martyrdom of twenty-three others, but the combined totals of those who died for their faith probably exceeded these numbers. The increased violence brought further conversions, and soon the Christian faith was solidly established in Uganda, mostly the work of local African evangelists. Today Uganda is among the most Christian nations in Africa.

> *O God, by your providence the blood of the martyrs is the seed of the Church: Grant that we who remember before you the blessed martyrs of Uganda, may, like them, be steadfast in our faith in Jesus Christ, to whom they gave obedience, even to death, and by their sacrifice brought forth a plentiful harvest; through Jesus Christ our Lord, who lives and reigns with you and the Holy Spirit, one God, for ever and ever. Amen.*[85]

MANCHE MASEMOLA

South African Martyr, c. 1913–1928

❀❀❀❀❀❀❀❀

I shall be baptized with my own blood.
— Manche Masemola

London's Westminster Abbey is filled with statues of the famous, poets, prelates, and political leaders. Among them, since 1998, is the statue of a simple South African girl, Manche Masemola, who died for her faith at the hands of her non-Christian parents. Born around 1913 in the Transvaal, Manche grew up in a barren and unproductive land left to the African people by their colonizers after the original settlers had been driven from their own farms and pastures. A member of the Pedi ethnic group, she lived with her parents, two older brothers, a sister, and a cousin, working at home and not exposed to a school education. In 1919 an Anglican monk, Fr. Augustine Moeka of the Community of the Resurrection, established a mission in her part of the Transvaal, and Manche and her cousin Lucia attended services there. Soon they began to attend Christian instructional classes twice a week, and their enthusiasm for their new religion grew.[86]

This was a source of stress within the family, however, for her parents feared she would leave them and not marry the person they would select as her husband. Such arranged marriages were a source of wealth to the families who contracted them. Her parents beat her, and the constantly abused child told her sister and cousin she would die at their hands. "Manche's mother said she would force us to leave the church. She beat Manche every time she returned from church," the cousin recalled later. Relations worsened, and the mother hid the girl's clothes so she could not attend Christian instructional classes. On February 4, 1928, her parents led the teenager to a lonely place, where they killed her, burying her by a granite rock on a remote hillside. Her younger sister soon became ill and died, and was buried nearby. Their father planted some trees by the graves.

Small groups of Christians began to visit the gravesite beginning in 1935. In 1969 her mother was baptized, and in 1975 the Church of the Province of Southern Africa added the name of Manche Masemola to its list of heroic Christians marked for special commemoration.

140

Now each year, especially on the first weekend in August, large groups of pilgrims frequent the site where this illiterate but faithful victim of parental abuse is buried.

Over the door of historic Westminster Abbey, a structure dating to at least the fifteenth century, were ten empty niches, set among many sculptures of saints and allegorical figures like Mercy, Truth, Righteousness, and Peace. The abbey clergy decided to honor martyrs of the twentieth century, one of the most violent centuries in human history, by placing representative twentieth-century Christians in this prominent place. Two Africans, Manche Masemola and Archbishop Janani Luwum of Uganda, were selected, along with such heroic figures as Martin Luther King Jr., killed in the United States of America, Oscar Romero, Latin American martyr assassinated for his human rights activity, Dietrich Bonhoeffer of Germany, and Maximilian Kolbe of Poland, both of whom were executed for opposing Hitler. The statues were unveiled by the archbishop of Canterbury and church leaders from many parts of the world. The Rev. Anthony Harvey, subdean of Westminster, wrote, "During this most violent of centuries thousands of men and women have paid with their lives and their convictions. Those represented here have left their testimony to the ultimate cost of Christian witness and to its enduring significance."

> *The sparrow has found her a house*
> *and the swallow a nest where she may lay her young;*
> *by the side of your altars, O Lord of hosts,*
> *my King and God.*
>
> —Psalm 84:2

ST. MILTIADES
Pope and Martyr, Pontificate 311–314

Miltiades (also known as Melchiades) was the second of three African popes in the early church, the others being Victor I and Gelasius. Pope from 311 to 314, Miltiades, like his predecessor Victor I, was the leader of the Roman Catholic Church during a demanding time. An intense period of internal and external strife had just ended and the Roman emperor proclaimed an edict of toleration, ending the harsh period of persecution in the West. Extensive properties confiscated by the state were returned to the church, exiled Christians returned, prisoners were freed, and Christianity was awarded legal recognition, placing it on equal footing with the established pagan cults. Miltiades was among those Christians who had suffered death under the emperor Maximian, and thus was placed by the church on its roll of African martyrs.

God of all nations, who raised up from among the peoples of Africa saints and martyrs who were faithful even to death: grant that in the face of all hatred and fear your people may be ready to live or die constant in love for friend and foe alike; for the sake of Jesus Christ our Lord. Amen.
— Collect for the Saints and Martyrs of Africa,
Celebrating Common Prayer, 435

BERNARD MIZEKI

Catechist and Martyr, c. 1861–1906

When he was about twelve years old, Bernard Mizeki left his home in Mozambique for Cape Town, South Africa, where he stayed for ten years as a laborer. He worked for white settlers and commuted each day to his home in the slums. He enrolled in an Anglican night school for blacks and refused to drink alcohol, which was what many poor Africans used to assuage their sorrows. With his gift for languages, the young African soon learned English, high Dutch, French, and eight African languages. This led to work for him as a translator of the Bible into indigenous languages.

Soon he became a Christian. Mizeki was prepared for baptism in 1886 by members of the Society of St. John the Evangelist. He then became a lay catechist in Mashonaland, accompanying an English bishop inland to what is now Zimbabwe. Here he built a mission station near the residence of the paramount chief Mangwende. Mizeki set about his work with a routine of daily prayer, attention to his subsistence garden, and the study of local languages, while also getting to know villagers.

Next he opened a school and, with the chief's permission, moved the mission station to a nearby plateau near a grove of trees where the ancestral spirits of the Mashona were believed to dwell. The Nhowe station prospered from 1891 to 1896, and the number of converts grew. The young catechist had considerable respect for local religious beliefs, suggesting that aspects of the Shona Spirit religion with its monotheistic faith in the high god Mwari were compatible with Christian thought. However, he angered local religious leaders when he cut down trees in the sacred grove and carved crosses into others.

During the Mashona rebellion of 1896 Mizeki was warned to flee, since local African Christians were regarded as agents of European imperialism rather than as independent agents. Mizeki would not leave the Christian community for which he assumed responsibility and, on the night of June 18, was speared outside his hut. His wife and another person racing to find food and blankets to keep him alive saw a blinding white light and heard a rushing wind on the hillside where they had left him. On their return, the martyr's body had disappeared. The place of his death has become a site for Protestants and Catholics to worship, and each year on the anniversary of his death pilgrims come from many parts of South Africa to pray and to commemorate his life.

Almighty God, whose glory is commemorated in the life of Bernard Mizeki, we thank you for the ministry of your servant among the people of South Africa as missionary, catechist, and martyr. Through the example of his steadfast courage even in death, may your church be called to renewed faith in you, the Great Shepherd of all people. Amen.

ROBERT MOFFAT

South African Missionary, Bible Translator,
1795–1883

Go into London's Bible House and you will find a stained-glass window commemorating the great translators of the Scriptures into vernacular languages, Jerome, William Tyndale, Martin Luther, and Robert Moffat, who spent fifty-three years in South Africa and translated the entire Bible into Sechuana, the language of the populous Bechuana peoples.[87]

Like many leading missionaries to South Africa, Moffat was a Scotsman, the son of a peripatetic customs agent. There were seven Moffat children, and their mother did much for their education, spending winter evenings reading them exciting tales of missionaries in distant lands. In addition, she taught girls and boys both how to knit and sew, skills she maintained they all could use.

Moffat's fortunes took a turn for the better with the arrival of his wife-to-be in 1819. After their marriage in St. George's Church, Cape Town, they set out to the interior for work among the Bechuana. An observer of the period noted of Mrs. Moffat: "She was in fortitude the equal of her husband, for she had a most vivid imagination and much loneliness in which to exercise it, while her husband was away on pioneering work."

Life was not easy for Mrs. Moffat, and whatever success came Moffat's way is due in large measure to her work as well. She set out to make a home for them, using cow dung as flooring material because "it lays the dust better than anything, kills the fleas that would otherwise breed abundantly, and is a fine clear green." The family settled in Kuruman, a mission station five hundred miles northwest of Cape Town; their first child, Mary, was born there in 1821. Additionally, the Moffats adopted two Bushman orphans in 1822. Moffat had come upon a party of Bushmen digging a grave and, following local custom, were prepared to bury the two tiny children with their deceased mother so that they might care for her in the nether world. Moffat named the two survivors Dicky and Ann; for many years they were part of the Moffat family.

Gradually the mission station grew. Water was piped from a three-mile long conduit, feeding large gardens and groves of willows and poplars. The number of stone mission houses expanded; Kuruman became a stopping point for explorers, traders, hunters, and missionaries moving northward.

During one of his visits further to the interior in 1829 Moffat converted Mzilikazi, chief of the Matebele, to Christianity. Greeted by approximately eight hundred warriors in full dress, with another three hundred on the compound's outskirts, Moffat stayed with the leading regional chief, explaining the Gospel to him. He had come, not as a trader or a hunter, but as an emissary of God, creator of the universe and all its contents, and Christ, the Prince of Peace. Toward the end Mzilikazi laid his hand on his new friend in benediction.

Moffat's published accounts describe his travels and his work as a missionary, as in this 1829 description of a church service:

> Our number, including ourselves and a Griqua [a person of mixed ancestry], was twelve. It was an interesting, cheering and encouraging season to our souls; and we concluded the delightful exercises of the day by taking coffee together in the evening. Our feelings on that occasion were such as our pen would fail to describe. We were as those who dreamed, while we realized the promise on which our souls had often hung. "He that goeth forth weepeth, bearing previous seed, shall doubtless come again rejoicing, bringing his sheaves with him." The hour had arrived on which the whole energies of our souls had been intensely fixed, when we should see a church, however small.

> *Lord, here we have no abiding city, but seek that which is to come: guide and deliver us in all earthly changes and direct our ways toward the haven of salvation; through Jesus Christ our Lord. Amen.* — *Celebrating Common Prayer, 629*

MONICA

Mother of Augustine, d. 387

Not much is known about Monica, the mother of St. Augustine (see p. 34). She appears to have been a Berber Christian woman married to a local pagan North African Roman official in Tagaste (modern Souk Ahras, Algeria). Although she raised her son, he was absent from her for some of his important teenage years, especially from ages twelve to sixteen. When he went to study in Carthage, she joined him, representing her orthodox faith with its belief in miracles and veneration of martyr cults against her son's Manicheist beliefs. (Manicheism was a widespread heresy that treated Christ, the second person of the Trinity, as Light, through which the Father was made known to humanity. The Trinity's third person was Mani, sent into the world by the Light.)

Monica stayed with Augustine in Italy (383–387). She had tried to arrange an advantageous marriage for the young Roman functionary before he turned completely to religion. Increasingly, in the immediate years before her death, he began to share more and more of his religious thoughts with her and appreciated her counsel. "I am daily struck anew by your natural ability," he told her shortly before her death. Monica had other children as well. A daughter became head of a convent near the monastery Augustine founded. Her second son, Navigius, was with her at her death in Ostia, Italy, in 387 as she was waiting to return to North Africa.

Some critics have seen in Monica an interfering, in-your-face mother, which she may have been; others consider her a spiritual companion, a shrewd woman of faith who helped anchor her brilliant son. It is easy to attribute too much to Monica, but neither should too little be accorded to her, for she was an important, steadying influence on Africa's most original theological mind.

O Lord, you strengthened your servant Monica to persevere in her love, prayers, and tears for the conversion of her husband and of Augustine their son: Deepen our devotion, we pray, and use us in accordance with your will to bring others to acknowledge Jesus Christ as Savior and Lord. Amen.

—Collect for Monica, Mother of Augustine (adapted)[88]

ALICE MULENGA LENSHINA
Visionary, Evangelist, 1950s

🙞🙞🙞🙞🙞🙞🙞🙞🙞

"In the district of Chinsali in the village of Kasome in the country of Chief Nkulu a woman, Alice Mulenga Lenshina Lubusha, the wife of Petro Chintankwa, came back from the dead in September 1954." So began a 1955 report from an African Church of Scotland minister to his presbytery in what was then Northern Rhodesia, now Zimbabwe. The report refers to a remarkable Christian woman visionary and evangelist whose unequivocal message converted thousands of people in several countries to Christ.

Alice Mulenga Lenshina had entered the local Church of Scotland's instructional classes when at some point she fainted. (The minister interpreted this as her dying and rising again, and in a way that is what happened.) In any case, she returned to her village with evangelical fervor, proclaiming the good news, urging villagers to follow a strict moral code and to surrender their implements of traditional religion to the missionaries. Adultery, hatred, cursing, stealing, lies, and swearing should cease, she taught, and she wrote a new hymn that followers of her movement often sang: "A man who does not repent and believe in Jesus, he can never stand near the judgment throne of God." Visions came to her from God with some regularity, angels were divine messengers, and Lenshina preached to increasingly large followings about what God had told her. She began giving people seeds, which she blessed, to mix with their own seeds, and began baptizing people. Sometimes a thousand persons a week visited her.

By 1955 more than fifty thousand persons had made pilgrimages to her village. Lenshina lived in simple circumstances, in a small house, with an external kitchen, dovecot, and grain storage building, all surrounded by a fence. She not only baptized and preached in several countries but was also widely regarded as a counselor, and many people came to her with their personal problems.

Music was central to the church, and much of its belief was encapsulated in song. Singing processions were a feature of worship in the African townships. The most common form of music was a folk hymn, led by a cantor who sang a short phrase, which was then repeated with slight variations. One favorite hymn proclaimed:

You who love the land of darkness,
let us break through, be saved.
He will help us in everything,
he will take us out of evil,
when, when?

Come all near,
it is my Father,
he calls us.

Stand all in a line!
Those who stay behind should look at us, the brothers.
Our Father stretched his arm out.
You are blessed, you who have been given.
Now shout with joy, you blessed ones.

Gather all together for the Lord.
We shall be spread out far and wide in the beautiful country;
we shall always roll in the dust [the way a chief was greeted].
Hallelujah, always.

You, the mountain of refuge which stands in this world,
you, the highest mountain.
Those who fail to climb this mountain,
they shall be cut to pieces.
But you who have climbed the mountain,
rejoice, sing.
You are fortunate, you have found the refuge.[89]

VALLIAMMA MUNUSAMY

Teenage Martyr, South Africa,
c. 1897–1914

The photo of Valliamma Munusamy shows a serene yet defiant young woman, a beautiful face, with fine bones and careful attention to grooming, the sort of person most people would want to know. But this black and white photo, dating to about 1913, is not for a school year book or to be set on top of a parlor piano; it is a memorial to a teenage martyr.

The gravestone inscription in the Hindu section of South Africa's Braamfontein Cemetery says:

> In loving memory of our sister Valliamma Munusamy who died February 22nd 1914 aged 17 years of illness contracted in the Maritzburg gaol to which she was sent as a passive resister.

The young woman from South Africa's Tamil community was a follower of Mohandas Gandhi (see p. 88), who in 1906 organized a massive passive resistance campaign among that country's resident Indian community. The small but commercially oriented Tamil community suffered heavily.

Gandhi called the struggle Satyagraha, or "truth force," a carefully orchestrated program of nonviolent noncooperation with the authorities. Members were willing to suffer fines, imprisonment, and even death. The Indian community protested British laws that prevented them from holding real property and living outside segregated zones. The laws also severely limited their trading prospects, which was devastating to the largely commercial community.

Many Indian women joined the campaign in March 1913, triggered by a local British court decision refusing to recognize Hindu and Muslim marriages as legal. The court decree left Indian women not as wives but as concubines whose children were considered illegitimate and who had no inheritance rights. Valliamma's parents owned a Johannesburg fruit shop; she joined several hundred Indian women who encouraged Natal mine workers to strike. Arrested as vagabonds, the women were sentenced to hard labor. Valliamma, released from prison while suffering from a fatal fever, died on February 22, 1914.

Speaking at the rededication of Valliamma's grave on April 20, 1997, Indian High Commissioner Gopalkrishna Gandhi said:

> There is something wisp-like about you, Valliamma, that eludes us. No longer a child, not yet a woman, what made you decide to join the marchers, to become a revolutionary? The others were all much older, were they not? Mostly married women and men stung into action by the law that disrecognised Indian marriages. You were barely seventeen and unmarried. . . . You were South African, of South African earth, knowing only its sugar cane acres and its mines. But whatever your thoughts were, they were certainly about life, about living, about the future. Death could not have entered your mind. Certainly not your impending death. . . . You were given hard labor. You had been assigned to do laundry work. To have to live on food that was virtually inedible and then to wash clothes. That must have been hard.

Later, when Gandhi visited the dying young person and asked her if she repented going to jail, she said, "Repent? I am even now ready to go to jail again if I am arrested."[90]

> *Praise be to the High God of all peoples for children of courage, the frail and the powerless, who in various times and places have stood up for right, and borne the cost, even to the giving of their lives. They shall be called Children of God. Amen.*

MARC NIKKEL

Apostle to Sudan's Oppressed,
1950–2000

⊗⊗⊗⊗⊗⊗⊗⊗⊗

God of widows and orphans, the God of the weak, the suffering and dying,
heal Mark Nikkel.
— Prayer of Sudanese people, Kakuma refugee camp

Thousands of Sudanese knew him as *akon*, the "bull elephant," as he
made his way across the devastated country for almost twenty years.
Marc Nikkel was tall and quick, with merry, piercing eyes. A person
of many talents, he was a painter, peacemaker, and teacher, a one-
person seminary who taught hundreds of Sudanese to become pastors,
evangelists, and eventually bishops. At an Anglican missionary college
in Mundri, he painted murals that celebrated Sudan's rich heritage of
spirituality; in his teaching he drew on a rich tradition of indigenous
poetry, music, and the visual arts. He also translated works from local
languages into English.[91]

The Sudan has been wracked by warfare since 1968, and in February 1999 Nikkel helped unite more than two thousand feuding tribal
leaders for a peace conference. Eventually, four hundred of the Dinka
and Nuer signed a peace accord. Nikkel recorded the deliberations on
his laptop computer, from which he fashioned a spiritual journal, an
account of his interaction with the oppressed and oppressors. In 1987
he was abducted by the Sudanese People's Liberation Army and held
captive for two months. What would have been a bitter ordeal for
most persons was transformed into a time of quiet joy and compassion. Nikkel was used to a life of hard work, isolation, and physical
challenge. "He was compelled by a quiet passion that proved itself,
both in his time as hostage and during his long illness, to be fired by a
deep love of God and an unshakable confidence in the Resurrection,"
a colleague said of him. "Marc was an apostle to the oppressed and
persecuted church," another friend wrote of Nikkel. "He understood
his mission to Sudan through the eyes of Jesus. The theme of God's
liberation of the poor and oppressed was always heard in his messages." Shortly before his death he wrote a letter to the church in the
Sudan: "These days I find myself becoming physically weaker. As for

myself, I simply long for the Great Transition that will allow me to enter my new life in the fellowship of Christ and all who have gone before me."

Stricken by stomach cancer, Nikkel died at age fifty in California on September 3, 2000. Meanwhile, at the Kakuma refugee center, a camp for thousands of marginalized and dispossessed persons within a war zone in southern Sudan, women gathered each day in his cramped mud brick house, laying hands on his simple bed, while praying for his return. "God of widows and orphans, the God of the weak, the suffering, and dying, heal Marc Nikkel," they prayed. Shortly before his death, Nikkel visited the convention of the Protestant Episcopal Church in the United States, where he showed the audience the cross he wore, made by a Dinka artist who transformed metal from a weapon of war into a symbol of self-giving new life in the Risen Christ.

This song written by Sudanese children in exile in Ethiopia and translated by Marc Nikkel reflects the tragedy of war in that country:

> *We ask you, O Creator, who created us,*
> *Who has created us?*
> *Isn't it you who created us?*
> *We call upon you, God of all peoples:*
> *Who created us?*
> *You said that the land of Sudan*
> *will be devoured by birds, flapping their wings.*

> Refrain:
> *Look upon us, O Creator, who made us.*
> *God of all peoples, we are yearning for our land.*
> *Hear the prayer of our souls in the wilderness.*
> *Hear the prayer of our bones in the wilderness.*

> *Hear our prayer as we call out to you.*

> (Refrain)

> *Hear the cry of our hearts in the wilderness.*

> (Refrain)

CHRISTINAH MA (MOTHER) NKU

South African Healer, 1894–c. 1980

❀❀❀❀❀❀❀❀❀

Born into South Africa's Dutch Reformed Church in 1894, Christinah Nku experienced numerous visions as a young girl. Plagued with illness as a young woman, she was told by God she would not die. A decade later, she received a vision of a large church with twelve doors, and then in 1939 a vision to build it not far from Johannesburg. In her dreams, Christinah recalled the healing of the crippled bystander in John's Gospel, which led her to focus on the healing ministry in her own religious life.

Christinah and her husband, Lazarus, in 1924 had been baptized into the Apostolic Faith Mission, a large Transvaal indigenous church, but after a personal and doctrinal conflict with its leader, the young woman struck out on her own as a healer. She named her church the St. John Apostolic Faith Mission, and while it began as a Pentecostal church, her powers and interest in the healing ministry soon gave it a distinctive character. AFM became one of the largest indigenous churches in South Africa, attracting over fifty thousand members. Its founder was known as "a mother with a thousand teats" whose spiritual gifts fed millions. Although the church and its founder took no overt position on political issues, both Lazarus Nku and the couple's son, Johannes, who eventually assumed the senior male leadership position, were active in the African National Congress (ANC.)

An important feature of the Zionist-Apostolic Pentecostal churches was the place they accorded women as members and ministers. Most such churches had strong women's organizations that provided friendship, assistance, and a sense of feeling important in a lonely world. Excluded from power in the mainstream churches and marginalized by apartheid's cruelty and a male-dominated African society, at least two million women found these churches to be welcoming places. Female prophets were common, as were "lady bishops," as women leaders were sometimes called. Mother, or "Ma," Nku, as she was known, began her ministry in the Johannesburg slums, and crowds made their way each day to her two-room dwelling for prayer at 5:00 and 9:00 a.m., and at 3:00 and 7:00 p.m. Hundreds of persons reported being healed, and Christinah neither sought fame nor took money for her healing prayers. Eventually she agreed to accept a shilling for each person who came to her for healing, and from these offerings she was able to build seventy churches throughout South Africa. Schools and youth programs were added as well.

Much of the Apostolic Faith Mission service resembled the rite of other Pentecostal churches. Scripture readings, hymns, preaching, and offerings were part of the liturgy. People were encouraged to talk directly to God and to deliver their testimony and petitions, after which those in attendance knelt and loudly uttered their own prayers of the heart.

The use of water was a distinctive attribute of the church, and Christinah was given to praying over buckets and bottles of it for her adherents. The healing service began with persons drinking water that had been blessed; then the ministers, having washed in the holy water, laid hands on each person. Sometimes in smaller services, ritual bathing and the controlled use of enemas and vomiting were administered as part of the rites to a few participants.

The church created its own marching band, which attracted new members, for the lively sound and blue and white uniforms were show-stoppers on slum streets. Choirs added compelling music to the services and became ways of interacting with other churches through choir festivals and competitions. Like choirs in the black churches of segregated America, the African choral groups expressed solidarity and affirmed personal and corporate worth and dignity in an otherwise harsh and restricted world. A four-day annual choir festival was a galvanic event for the entire church. Members came from all over South Africa, sang and shared meals together, prayed, and were baptized.[92]

> *When Jesus saw him lying there and knew that he had been there a long time, he said to him, "Do you want to be made well?" The sick man answered him, "Sir, I have no one to put me into the pool when the water is stirred up; and while I am making my way, someone else steps down ahead of me." Jesus said to him, "Stand up, take up your mat and walk." At once the man was made well, and he took up his mat and walked.*
>
> —John 5:5–8

NTSIKANA

Xhona Christian Prophet,
c. 1780–c. 1821

By the end of the eighteenth century, a generation of indigenous South African Christian religious leaders was emerging. Among them was a chief's son, Ntsikana, a John Wesley–like figure, a tireless evangelist and prodigious hymn writer. Although exposed to European missionaries, he never identified with them. After receiving a vision in 1815, he sent one of his two wives away with a generous property settlement, broke with another Xhona prophet who stirred the people to revolt against the British, and preached river baptism, Sunday as a day of rest, and a life of prayer to the sovereign God.

Ntsikana organized twice-a-day prayer services in his compound and urged his people to pray unceasingly to the sovereign God. His people called themselves the "Poll-headed," cattle without horns, pacifists living amid war-like neighbors. Ntsikana's religious views, arrived at on his own, were conventionally Christian. Transmission of the faith often took place without direct European influence. "I am sent by God, but am only like a candle," he said. "I have not added anything to myself." Hastings has said of Ntsikana, "He was never baptized, never knew a European language, and never went through any course of missionary catechesis, but his subsequent influence as prophet, poet, and pacifist has been incomparable. In a unique way Ntsikana represents a genuinely new birth of Christian insight within African society and culture."[93]

Four of his hymns have become staples in the South African Christian repertoire, including *Ulin guba inkulu siambata tina:*

> He who is our mantle of comfort,
> the giver of life, ancient on high,
> He is the Creator of the heavens,
> and the ever-burning stars:
> God is mighty in the heavens
> and whirls the stars around in the sky.
> We call on him in his dwelling place
> that he may be our mighty leader,

for he maketh the blind to see;
we adore him as the only good,
for he alone is a sure defense.[94]

Toward the end of his life Ntsikana, whom people called "the man with the milk-bag of heaven," told his followers to settle at the nearby mission. In his last address to his people he said,

I am going home to my Father. Do not, after I die, go back to live by the customs of the Xhosa. I want you to go to Buleneli [Brownlee, the missionary] at Gwali. Have nothing to do with the feasts [traditional observances] but keep a firm hold on the word of God. Always stick together. . . . Should a rope be thrown round your neck, or a spear pierce your body, or [should you] be beaten with sticks, or struck with stones, don't give way. Keep it and stick to it and to each other.

To my two sons I say, Kobe, you will be my backbone, and Dukwana, you will be my walking-stick. Do not allow the children to return to the red clay [covering oneself with red clay was a traditional religious practice].[95]

ORIGEN

North African Teacher and Church Father,
c. 184–254

⁂⁂⁂⁂⁂⁂⁂⁂⁂⁂

The principal theological voice of the early Greek church, Origen was probably born in Alexandria and died in Tyre. At the time Origen wrote and taught, Alexandria was the cultural and intellectual center of the Roman empire, its fervor and urbanity enhanced by North African, Greek, Roman, and Jewish figures who settled there.

He was called Adamantius, or man of iron or diamond, and studied with his father, who may have been a student of Clement of Alexandria. In 202 Origen's father was decapitated; the young man wished to die a martyr's death as well, but this did not happen. Like many young Christian intellectuals, he opened a school, hoping to support his six brothers and sisters with his earnings, but gradually he was drawn to an ascetic life, mutilated himself, and devoted himself to the study of the Scriptures and doctrine. A rich convert supported him with secretarial help, and Origen traveled along well-established routes to Rome, Jerusalem, and Arabia. Imprisoned and tortured in the Roman persecutions of 250, he was finally set free but, in broken health, soon died.[96]

Bible commentaries dominate his surviving writings. Origen was less concerned with history and context than he was with seeing all Scripture pointing to Christ the Son of God as redeemer of fallen humanity. For Origen, all Old Testament prophecy, characters, and events point to Christ, the church, and the sacraments. After his ordination to the priesthood Origen became increasingly interested in Christian mysticism; he prefigured later mystics like St. John of the Cross and Teresa of Avila with his explanations of the Ascent of the Mount or, drawing on the Canticle of Canticles, suggesting similarities between the human body and the church. Like other early figures of the North African church, Origen devoted considerable energy to combating heresies.

O Jesus, my feet are dirty. Come even as a slave to me, pour water into your bowl, come and wash my feet. In asking such a thing I know I am overbold, but I dread what was threatened

*when you said to me, "If I do not wash your feet I have no
fellowship with you." Wash my feet then, because I long for
your companionship. And yet, what am I asking? It is well for
Peter to ask you to wash his feet; that was all that was needed for
him to be clean in every part. With me it is different; though you
wash me now, I shall still stand in need of that other washing,
the cleansing you promised when you said, "There is a baptism
I must needs be baptized with."*   —Origen[97]

ST. PACHOMIUS

Founder of Coptic Monasticism,
292–346

Born of pagan parents in Upper Egypt, this most important of the early Coptic saints came in contact with a local Christian community that befriended him while he was a conscript in the Roman army in 312. When he was taken prisoner, they brought him food and provided support and friendship, and in turn Pachomius became a Christian and devoted his life to helping others.[98]

After he had completed his army service, Pachomius settled in a small community, was baptized, and began a life of regular prayer, fasting, and almsgiving. Eventually he organized a monastic *koinonia* (community) based on mutual service and sharing among members. The idea caught hold, and by the time of Pachomius's death in 346, it had grown to more than five thousand monks in nine monasteries and two convents of nuns. This idea of a carefully organized Christian community praying together several times a day and then going about individual or group tasks was in sharp contrast to the equally popular practice of monks becoming hermits and living alone in desert places.

The monastic communities (including the convents run by the sister of Pachomius) were based on a constantly evolving rule, which the founder extracted from New Testament teachings of Jesus. It contained a heavy teaching component, and the superior of a monastery, the house master, or another monk were expected to lead Bible study several times a week, on feast days, and at the annual gathering of monks near the year's end. The rule also included total obedience to superiors and common ownership of all property.

The goal was to organize a large group of unruly people into an efficient, effective praying and working community, and to do this Pachomius borrowed on the Roman military forms of organization he had been exposed to as a youth. He thus shaped the new Christian community into an economically and spiritually viable organization of several thousand members in an agriculturally unproductive region filled with hostile peoples.

160

Seven archangels stand glorifying the Almighty and serving the hidden mystery.

Michael the first, Gabriel the second, and Raphael the third, symbol of the Trinity.

Surael, Sakakael, Saratael, and Ananael. These are the shining ones, the great and pure ones, who pray to God for humankind.

The cherubim, the seraphim, the thrones, dominions, powers, and the four living creatures bearing the chariot of God.

The twenty-four elders in the Church of the Firstborn praise him without ceasing, crying out and saying:

Holy is God; heal the sick.
Holy is the Almighty; give rest to the departed.
Holy is the immortal; bless thine inheritance.
May thy mercy and thy peace be a stronghold unto thy people.

Holy, holy, holy, Lord of hosts.
Heaven and earth are full of thy glory.
Intercede for us, O angels our guardians,
and all heavenly hosts,
that our sins may be forgiven.

— A Coptic Orthodox Prayer to the Archangels[99]

ALAN PATON

Writer, 1903–1988

❀❀❀❀❀❀❀❀❀❀

There is a lovely road that runs from Ixopo into the hills. These hills are grass-covered and rolling, and they are lovely beyond any singing of it. The road climbs seven miles into them, to Carisbrooke; and from there, if there is no mist, you look down on one of the fairest valleys of Africa.[100]

These are the opening words of *Cry, the Beloved Country,* perhaps the most famous novel ever written about Africa. Alan Paton, a Christian author, prison reformer, and liberal politician wrote the work in 1948. It soon was translated into over twenty world languages and was made into a film and a play, calling further attention to South Africa's racial inequities.

Paton was born in the British colony of Natal in South Africa on January 11, 1903. As a child he was exposed to the Bible and the great classics of English fiction. Paton became a high school teacher and in 1935 was named principal of the Diepkloof Reformatory for nearly seven hundred young black offenders, where he gained a reputation as a progressive reformer. For example, each evening the young offenders were locked up, twenty to a room, with one bucket for water and another bucket for urination and defecation. "The stench was unspeakable," he wrote. Paton arranged for the cells to be unlocked at night, allowing the young men to use the lavatories. This produced not only greater trust in them, but a sharp decline in typhoid fever, which until then had caused many deaths.

Paton was a founder of the Liberal Party in 1953 and became its president. Harassed by the government for his opposition to apartheid, he and his party were banned in 1968 and Paton's passport was confiscated. If he gained the government's ire, antiapartheid activists found his gentle Christian-liberal solutions too weak, and Paton was left to pursue a lonely middle road with only a modest number of followers. Always an idealist, he recalled the resolve of his university days "that life must be used in the service of a cause greater than oneself."

It was during a 1947 study tour of prisons in Europe and the United States that Paton began work on *Cry, the Beloved Country*. In the novel, the elder Jarvis, whose son is killed by a young black, emerges from his world of white separateness. Meanwhile, the old African pastor, Stephen Kumalo, whose son is the murderer, also emerges from his own isolation and takes steps to prevent other youths from following a course similar to his son's. Informing Paton's work is an irenic world "where the wolf lies down with the lamb and they do not hurt or destroy in all that holy mountain." It is the vision of John of Patmos of a world "where there shall be no more death, neither sorrow, nor crying."

While he was teaching at Ixopo, an earthly paradise with "a prodigal endowment of hills and valleys and rivers and streams," Paton joined the Anglican Church of the Province of South Africa. His works were published to international acclaim. *Too Late the Phalarope* (1953) explored the exploitative relationship of a white police officer with a young black girl after introduction of a law specifically prohibiting sexual relations between races. Short story collections like *Tales from a Troubled Land* (1961) and his autobiographical works, *Toward the Mountain* (1980) and *Journey Continued: An Autobiography* (1988), contained similar themes. Paton died on April 12, 1988, at home, near Durban, South Africa.

A note of sadness pervades his work, as in this passage for which his best-known book is named:

> *Cry, the beloved country, for the unborn child that is the inheritor of our fear. Let him not love the earth too deeply. Let him not laugh too gladly when the water runs through his fingers, nor stand too silent when the setting sun makes red the veld with fire. Let him not be too moved when the birds of his land are singing, nor give too much of his heart to a mountain or a valley. For fear will rob him of all if he gives too much.*[101]

FRANZ PFANNER

Monk, Missionary to South Africa,
1825–1909

The journey from the Austrian Tyrol to Marianhill in Natal was a long one for the Roman Catholic Trappist monk Fr. Franz Pfanner. It was not until he was fifty-five years old that he set foot in South Africa. Previously, he had been a diocesan priest and an Austrian army chaplain. Pfanner always maintained a strong interest in missions and hoped to found one in Turkey, which proved too difficult, but he did build an abbey in Bosnia in 1879.[102] In that year, he heard a Roman Catholic missionary bishop appeal for priests for South Africa, a call Pfanner heeded. After several years experimenting, he established a farm near Pinetown, Natal, where the monastery of Marianhill was eventually built with its procathedral, schools, farms, and vocational training programs. Pfanner also founded the Sisters of the Precious Blood to work with young African women, and soon their numbers totaled three hundred. Mostly the daughters of German farmers, the "Red Sisters" dressed in red skirts, black capes, and white blouses and veils. The Zulu called them "Amakosazana," or "princesses."

It is hard to be a contemplative Trappist monk and an action-oriented working priest at the same time, and this was Pfanner's dilemma. He went to Africa as a contemplative, but soon the farmer's son was into the fray. "Nobody has to work more than I do," he said, recalling his own father's words. While Boers and Protestant missionaries often left the work to Africans, Pfanner said, "No missionary, be he priest or superior, should despise manual work. He has to be a literal imitator of Jesus who first worked before he preached." Pagans, Protestants, and Catholics were welcomed with no doctrinal tests in the schools he founded, and Pfanner was an early opponent of apartheid. Pfanner was suspended from his order when his European superiors concluded that his life was the reverse of the traditional *ora and labora* (pray and work) pattern of monastic life, representing *labora and ora* (work and pray) instead. In 1893, after thirteen years' intense work, he retired to a mission station at Emmaus, where he remained until his death in 1909. The main mission's activities grew, and by the time of Pfanner's death 55 priests, 223 lay brothers, and 326 nuns were at work in 42 mission stations.

> *Nations will come to your light,*
> *and kings to your dawning brightness.*
> *Arise, shine out, for your light has come;*
> *the glory of the Lord is rising upon you.*
> *Above you the Holy One appears,*
> *and above you God's glory appears.*
> —Isaiah 60:1–3

JOHN PHILIP

Missionary in South Africa,
1775–1851

❁❁❁❁❁❁❁❁

There can be no religion in such a country as this without civilization....It
can have no permanent abode among us, if that civilization does not shoot
up into regular and good government.   —John Philip

He was a contradictory character, warm yet stubborn, a person of
deep faith yet unyielding in his treatment of opponents, a reader of
the Bible while a dabbler in politics, and a staunch opponent of slavery who exasperated friends and enemies alike. John Philip was a
beefy, strong-voiced Scotsman who spent thirty years in Cape Town
as pastor of a major church and a vociferous advocate for an increased
English presence as a buffer against Afrikaner expansion.[103]

The son of a poor Scottish weaver, Philip benefited from his parents' passion for education, and at an early age he rose to become
manager of a mill in Dundee, but left the job because he could not
accept the policy of hiring children to work long hours for scant wages
in appalling conditions. After studying for the Congregational ministry, he spent fourteen years as minister of an Aberdeen church. Then
on February 26, 1819, he went to Cape Town for the London Missionary Society. Philip was accompanied by his wife, Jane, who, for
thirty-eight years, kept mission and family finances, raised a family
of seven children, and was a welcoming hostess to a steady stream
of visiting missionaries and local parishioners. While a deeply religious person herself, in 1836 she wrote her traveling husband, "Pray
remember I am still flesh and not all spirit." Joan was also adept at
restraining her husband, who was given to excessive generosity.

When he first arrived in Cape Town, the new pastor was welcomed
with open arms by the resident settler community. He also encouraged
an influx of French, American, German, and Scottish missionaries,
built local schools, and trained pastors and evangelists. But his brand
of evangelism was not content to rest with personal conversion and
salvation; society must be redeemed as well; the city must become
a holy city, the home of all God's children living in harmony and
prosperity. He urged a more equitable administration of justice in

166

the colony and became an outspoken voice for a free press. His advocacy of racial equality influenced later Cape Colony constitution writers, who created a short-lived experiment in which both Africans and whites could vote as British subjects, until the Cape Colony was absorbed into the wider Union in 1910.

Two things may be said about Philip's vision. First, it required the support of a strong British political-military presence to succeed, and such a British presence was never forthcoming in South Africa. Second, it enraged those who did not agree with it, principally resident British traders and Afrikaners. Additionally, Philip advocated a separate zone for colored people, not to exclude them from life in the colony, but to protect their property and persons from the steadily intruding Afrikaners. Later generations would find Philip's efforts well-intentioned but inadequate, but he was a product of his times and his intentions, given their context, were revolutionary.

The politically active pastor was responsible for two colonial governors being removed; his unyielding advocacy for Africans resulted in increasing animosity from resident whites. The settler colonists were out to get the pastor, a relatively easy target because of his outspokenness. He lost a libel suit brought by a local official who denied Philip's charges that he had abused his authority in opposing the Hottentots. Philip's supporters in England paid the £1,100 judgment, an exceedingly heavy levy.

His final years were not easy ones. Philip's oldest son, a promising missionary, died in a tragic drowning accident in 1845, as did a grandson; his beloved wife was carried away by death two years later, and Philip, by then in his seventies, retired to a mission station. Even in death, he was a controversial figure. A South African prime minister of the mid-twentieth century, urging missionaries not to be like the outspoken Anglican monk Fr. Trevor Huddleston (see p. 102), admonished them "not to do a Philip." But Huddleston and Philip, in different centuries, were prophetic figures that offered South Africans a word of hope not often heard in the churches of that land.

> *The sound of violence*
> *shall be heard no longer in your land,*
> *or ruin and devastation within your borders.*
> *You will call your walls Salvation,*
> *And your gates Praise.*
>
> —Isaiah 60:18

ALBIE SACHS

Jewish South African Human Rights Activist,
Supreme Court Justice, b. 1935

❊❊❊❊❊❊❊❊❊

> We are not somnambulists meandering vacuously through life, but human
> beings incandescent with purpose. — Albie Sachs

He would resist being called a saint or hero. "That's the name of a
sandwich in New Jersey," Albie Sachs remarked. Sachs is impossible
to fit into any traditional religious category and studiously avoids any
effort to categorize his views.[104] If not a saint in traditional terms, his
life mirrors those godly virtues of consistency of belief and practice
associated with sainthood. Not quite a martyr, he is someone who
suffered great physical and mental abuse for his beliefs. He would
deny being a holy person, but he is clearly a proud and faithful defender of just causes. A Jew who was brought up in a moral home,
Sachs did not engage in traditional Jewish practices and synagogue
worship. His right arm was blown off from a car bomb planted by
South African security services. Presently he is a justice of the Constitutional Court of South Africa, renowned for his legal acumen and
his interest in human rights and gender issues.

Albert Louis (Albie) Sachs was born in Johannesburg on January 30, 1935. His father was a trade unionist, his mother a typist
for the South African Communist Party, which Albie later joined and
then left. After graduating from local institutions of higher education,
he became an attorney, specializing in civil rights cases, until he was
twice arrested and held without trial by the dreaded South African
Security Police. The detention process crushed Sachs, a verb he frequently employs. "The sleep deprivation and the fact that I made a
statement even though I managed to contain it," is one of his bitterest
memories. "It was a terrible humiliation. When I went to England I
was hoping that love and marriage and companionship would restore
my morale. But it doesn't work that way. You can't get your courage
back through another person."

While in exile in Great Britain beginning in 1966, Sachs completed
a doctoral degree and taught at the University of Southampton law
faculty and later in Maputo, Mozambique. In 1988 Sachs was nearly

killed by a car bomb planted by the South African Security Police. He returned to England until 1992, when he returned to South Africa as a leader of the African Nationalist Party (ANC) in constitutional negotiations.

Religious motives weave their way throughout his discourse. The only book he was permitted to read while in solitary confinement was the Bible. "I'd never read the Bible as a book before, I'd read bits and pieces here and there. Now I read it from page one all the way through the Old Testament and I read the Gospels. I found the passages in the Prophets very beautiful, and there were some wonderful passages in the Song of Songs. And as a story it was immensely powerful and strong." Sachs saw the New Testament as "internationalist in outlook," recognizing "neither Jew nor Gentile, neither man nor woman." The idea of loving your enemy "was something that I found appealed to me as a person," as did the Sermon on the Mount.

"The real question for me was over the matter of belief. What seemed to emerge is that people can have a religiosity of character, personality, and relationship without formally identifying with any particular faith, and I'm not uncomfortable with that at all. Someone said to me, 'You don't speak about faith, you live faith.' I was pleased to have dialogue with a believer, someone who had views of the world I can't share, some of which I find a little bit odd, but that doesn't matter."

How did Sachs approach being named to the South African Constitutional Court? "My main personal preoccupation related to a small but worrying matter of conscience: how should I take the oath? Should I affirm or swear to God? Two of my colleagues affirmed; the others lifted their right hands, and swore the words "So help me God" in Tswana, Xhosa, Zulu, Afrikaans, and English. If I affirmed, I would not raise my arm, which if I swore the oath in the name of the deity, I would." Despite his reservations, Sachs had insisted on the new constitution containing the words of a hymn of sacrifice and hope, "Nkosi Sikelel' iAfrika" — God watch over Africa. Finally, Sachs raised the stump of a right arm under his judicial robe and declared, 'So help me God.' "

Discussing the issue of forgiveness, Sachs recalled an encounter with an Afrikaner who asked, "*Verksoon my*" (Forgive me). He pondered the issue and thought, "Don't request it from the one white person whose trauma you know about. Ask it of the million persons of color who had no choice, whose oppression was enduring, all-encompassing, much deeper than mine, and who are still forced to exist in unlivable conditions." Later he reflected, "I regretted that I had not simply put my arm around him and given him a big hug of acknowledgment and acceptance."

> *No more will the sun give you daylight,*
> *nor moonlight shine upon you;*
> *but the Lord will be your everlasting light,*
> *your God will be your splendor.*
>
> *For you shall be called the city of God,*
> *the dwelling of the Holy One of Israel.*
> —Isaiah 60:19, 14

ALBERT SCHWEITZER

Missionary, Medical Doctor, Humanitarian,
1875–1965

The great Alsatian-German missionary, musician, humanitarian, and Nobel Peace Prize winner (1952) is an enigmatic figure. Albert Schweitzer spent almost fifty years in Africa, most of it deep in the rain forests of the Gabon Republic where, at Lambaréné, he built a hospital on the Ogowe River. Although Schweitzer's views about Africans puzzle the modern reader, to keep the matter in perspective we need to recall that few Europeans showed a more enlightened view, and Schweitzer did tireless good work in an isolated place for almost a half century.

In 1913 he obtained his third doctorate, adding medicine to philosophy and theology, and with his nurse-wife, Hélène Bresslau, he set out under sponsorship of the Paris Missionary Society for the rain forests of French Equatorial Africa not far north of the Equator. His "call" to Gabon was simple. Several years earlier he had mechanically opened a missionary publication asking that some of those "on whom the Master's eyes already rested" present themselves for work in the understaffed Gabon mission. "The article finished, I quietly began my work. My search was over," he recalled. There he stayed until his death over a half century later, except for several lengthy trips to Europe and internment as a French prisoner of war during World War I. Schweitzer attracted a stream of medical doctors and nurses to aid him in his jungle hospital, often as short-term volunteer specialists who would perform operations under demanding conditions.

Throughout his life the missionary continued to write and give interviews on wide-ranging biblical, philosophical, and civic topics. Schweitzer always kept one foot in Africa, the other in Europe. He once remarked, "I have always been torn. When I was in Europe, I had the desire and sense of duty to get back to try to allay the misery of those people whom I knew and loved. Yet when I'm here I can't say I don't miss the things Europe offers."

Schweitzer's perspective as medical doctor and Christian is reflected in this passage from *On the Edge of the Primeval Forest* (1920):

When the poor, moaning creature comes [with a strangulated hernia], I lay my hand on his forehead and say to him: "Don't be afraid! In an hour's time you shall be put to sleep, and when you wake you won't feel any more pain." Very soon he is given an injection; the doctor's wife is called to the hospital, and with Joseph's help, makes everything ready for the operation. When that is to begin she administers the anaesthetic, and Joseph, in a long pair of rubber gloves, acts as an assistant.

The operation is finished, and in the hardly lighted dormitory I watch for the sick man's awakening. Scarcely has he recovered consciousness when he stares about him and ejaculates again and again: "I've no more pain! I've no more pain!" ... His hand feels for mine and will not let go. Then I begin to tell him and the others who are in the room that it is the Lord Jesus who has told the doctor and his wife to come to the Ogowe, and that white people in Europe give them the money to live here and cure the sick Negroes. Then I have to answer questions as to who these white people are, where they live, and how they know that the natives suffer so much from sickness. The African sun is shining through the coffee bushes into the dark shed, but we black and white sit side by side and feel that we know by experience the meaning of the words: "And all ye are brethren" (Matt. 23:8). Would that my generous friends in Europe could come out here and live through one such hour![105]

O, heavenly Father, protect and bless all things that have breath; guard them from all evil, and let them sleep in peace.
                         — A Childhood Prayer of Albert Schweitzer[106]

LÉOPOLD SÉDAR SENGHOR

Senegalese Poet-President,
b. 1906

A leading African twentieth-century political-cultural figure, Léopold Sédar Senghor was born into a Senegalese Catholic family. His father, Basile Diogoye, was a wealthy grower of ground nuts, a Catholic in a largely Muslim region south of Dakar. After attending a mission school run by the Holy Spirit Fathers at N'Gasobil, Senghor moved on to Dakar's prestigious College Libermann, named for François Libermann, 1802–1852, founder of the Holy Spirit Fathers (see p. 125). Later Senghor acknowledged that Libermann's ideas had aided him, especially the missionary's challenge to priests and sisters, "Faites-vous nègres avec les nègres, afin de les gagner a Jésus-Christ." ("Make yourself black with the blacks to win them for Jesus Christ.")

In a preface to a study on Libermann's life and thought, Senghor cited his appeal to Europeans not to judge Africans by European standards, but to come among them as servants, to demonstrate that all people are equal before God. When God chose to have his son, Jesus, be born of Jewish parents, Libermann argued, Jesus joined a colonized people, the Jews then under Roman domination.

Senghor wrote, "All human civilizations are equal.... That is why one should not judge the Negro-Africans with the racial prejudices of white Europe. That is why one must become 'Negroes' with the Negroes, in judging their civilization from inside, in its coherence, more specifically, in adapting to its history and geography. The second idea is not to make a value judgment, but a practical counsel to let the Negro-Africans live, not only today on the earth, but tomorrow in the land of the Saints, in heaven."[107]

The young Senghor received a classical education in France and in 1933 became the first black African to gain an "aggregation" from the Sorbonne. He also earned a doctorate there, after which he taught French, Greek, and Latin classics in two French lycées. A prisoner of war from 1940 to 1942, he wrote some of his most memorable poetry during this time. Following the war, he was a co-founder of the cultural journal *Présence Africaine*. Georges Pompidou, later president of France, was a classmate of Senghor's and a political ally.

Politics were important to Senghor, and in 1946 he was elected to the French Constituent Assembly and later to French parliamentary bodies. Elected Senegal's first president in 1960, he retained that post until 1980, smoothly turning over the office to a successor. As chief of state, was he frequently cited as a spokesperson for the Third World, especially on developmental issues. In 1966 Senghor organized the first World Festival of Negro Arts in Dakar, and during the 1940s and 1950s he published extensively as a leading francophone poet and essayist. In 1983 he became the first black member of the Académie Française.

Senghor was not explicitly a Christian or Catholic poet in the way some contemporary French poets were, but his beliefs infused his writing, as in his powerful "Elegy for Martin Luther King" and a short series of poems called "Prayer for Peace."

> *Lord Jesus, at the end of this book, which I offer You*
> *As a ciborium of sufferings*
> *At the beginning of the Great Year, in the sunlight*
> *Of Your peace on the snowy roofs of Paris*
> *— Yet I know that my brothers' blood will once more redden*
> *The yellow Orient on the shores of the Pacific*
> *Ravaged by storms and hatred*
> *I know that this blood is the spring libation*
> *The Great Tax Collectors have used for seventy years*
> *To fatten the Empire's lands*
> *Lord, at the foot of this cross — and it is no longer You*
> *Tree of sorrow but, above the Old and New Worlds,*
> *Crucified Africa,*
> *And her right arm stretches over my land*
> *And her left side shades America*
> *And her heart is precious Haiti, Haiti who dared*
> *Proclaim Man before the Tyrant*
> *At the feet of my Africa, crucified for four hundred years*
> *And still breathing*
> *Let me recite to You, Lord, her prayer of peace and pardon.*

—Prayer for Peace (I of V) to Georges and Claude Pompidou[108]

SHAMIMA SHAIKH

South African Muslim and Cancer Victim,
1960–1998

Shamima Shaikh, a leading South African Muslim voice for gender equality, died of cancer in early 1998. She left a husband and two sons, ages nine and seven. As a courteous but determined advocate, she was a thorn in the side of conservative Islamic clerics who sought to enforce new Sharia laws in independent South Africa that would create a religious apartheid rivaling the political apartheid from which the country was just emerging. A former editor of a progressive Muslim monthly, Shamima also chaired the Muslim Community Broadcasting Trust, which ran a Johannesburg Muslim community radio station. Once during Ramadan, the Muslim month of fasting, she led a group of women into Johannesburg's Twenty-Third Street Mosque to pray in a secluded space upstairs. (There is a debate within Islam about whether women are allowed in mosques.) On the twenty-seventh night of the fast, a time of heightened spiritual importance, Shamima and the women arrived to find their space occupied and a tent erected outside for them. With determination they reentered their prayer space. On another occasion, Shamima and a friend, denied entry to the mosque, stood outside in the pouring rain and said their prayers. Eventually she and several female and male co-religionists started an "alternative" Muslim congregation with gender equality as a norm. For this and her other activities Shamima was given the sobriquet "that mad Shaikh woman."

In the midst of her active life, Shamima was stricken with cancer. Forsaking the rigors of chemotherapy, she resorted to traditional homeopathic treatments. Despite her deteriorating condition, she lectured on "The Koran and Women" in Durban three weeks before her death.

A prominent South African Muslim leader and writer, Farid Esack (see p. 78), a friend of Shamima's, reflected on her death, drawing on a verse from the Koran: "Do not say about those who are slain in the path of God that they are dead; nay they are alive." Dr. Esack noted that a woman led the funeral prayers at the deceased's home, and her husband presided over prayers at the mosque, despite the presence of several senior clerics. Many women entered the main part of the mosque. He wrote:

Do we always have to make a fuss about the presence of women? Do we always have to panic when they enter "our" sacred space?

So we can deal with women, but we need to reduce them to half human beings in order to feel less threatened before doing so. (In some ways, I am reminded of the way most Muslim communities deal with gay people. They are welcome as flamboyant camp singers at weddings on the Indo-Pak subcontinent, hairdressers for the bride, handy to come and do the washing and ironing. All of these are acceptable at a social level and passed over in silence at a theological level, as long as they are very clearly effeminate, obviously "funny" and "know their place." Heaven forbid that they try to be just "ordinary" and "normal" and visit our homes or befriend us like any other human being. It's then that the roof caves in.)[109]

The author concluded:

Shamima, we do not have to pledge that we will pick up the battles where you left off. About that you have no doubt. We can pledge to try to do so with the gentleness and love which you fought them.

What a life! What a way of passing on! What a death!

"If this be madness, God," her husband, Na'eem, prayed at her funeral service, "Give us all the courage to be mad."

Amin.[110]

SIMON OF CYRENE

c. 33

As they went out, they came upon a man from Cyrene named Simon; they compelled this man to carry his cross. —Matthew 27:32

No one knows why he was in Jerusalem that day or much about him, except that of all the bystanders at Jesus' crucifixion, he was picked from the crowd to carry Jesus' cross. His name was Simon of Cyrene. He may have been a Jew who had come to Jerusalem for Passover from Cyrene, a major Roman coastal town in what is now Libya. Possibly he was a follower of Jesus or a curious bystander. Whatever the reason — maybe it was pure chance — he became a participant in a great historical drama, the crucifixion of Christ. As such, he symbolizes the relationship of Africa and Christ in a deep and mysterious way. At a moment of great physical pain and mental stress, an African aided Jesus. And always Christ is there to bear the suffering of the poor, the marginalized, and the victims of injustice, those waiting on the Way of the Cross in Africa and elsewhere.

Simon of Cyrene, traveler to Jerusalem, bystander who carried Christ's cross and felt its weight, grant that those who are called to be cross-bearers may find their blood-drenched journey the way to life eternal through Jesus, the Savior of the world, our wounded and despised brother. Amen.

MARY SLESSOR ("MA")

Missionary in Calabar, 1848–1915

An indomitable Scottish Presbyterian who described herself as "wee and thin and not very strong," Mary Slessor lasted over forty years in the malaria-ridden Calabar region of Nigeria, where she was especially active in promoting the dignity of African women.

Born on December 2, 1848, near Aberdeen, the second of seven children, Mary's mother was a deeply religious woman, her father a drunken shoemaker. She was just twenty-eight years of age, with red hair and bright blue eyes, when in 1876 she arrived in Nigeria as a missionary for the United Presbyterian Church. The slave trade had been abolished, but local society had been disrupted by it and by the influx of commerce. Britain had seized Lagos in 1861 and was gradually extending its presence to the interior. Issues that Mary confronted as a young missionary included widespread human sacrifice at the death of a village elder, who, it was believed, required servants and retainers to accompany him in the next world, and the lack of education or any status for women.

Mary soon learned the Elfik language and showed an intense interest in local people and their customs. (Local people spoke of her as "Ma," or "Mother of All the People.") She lived simply, close to the people, in native housing. The greatest dangers she faced came from the disease-ridden climate. Malaria was rampant, as was smallpox and numerous undiagnosed tropical fevers. She set about establishing hospitals, dispensaries, and schools and through a constant flow of letters badgered colonial governors and mission headquarters for the means to expand her activities. "Why should I fear?" she asked. "I am on a Royal Mission. I am in the service of the King of kings."

Sometimes she went on preaching trips. Local members of her mission team went ahead, beating drums, and when a crowd had gathered under a shade tree, she preached in the local language, sometimes dwelling on a single verse of Scripture, for example, "Very truly, I tell you, anyone who hears my word and believes him who sent me has eternal life, and does not come under judgment, but has passed from death to life"(John 5:24).

Saving the lives of twins was an important part of her ministry. According to local custom, twins were an ill omen, and the babies were killed or left outside villages for ants or leopards to devour. The father was thought to be possessed by an evil spirit, the mother guilty of a grievous sin, and one of the children supposedly was a monster. Mary preached against this custom, and several twins lived with her until she could place them with receptive local families. There were also numerous accounts of her confronting local leaders who attempted to have wives killed at the death of a chief to accompany him to the next world. Similarly, she spoke against ordeals by poison in which, if a local chief believed witchcraft had been worked against him, he would order suspects to drink a poisonous drink to ascertain their guilt or innocence.

On the issue of infanticide and twin murder, she observed:

> Though chiefs and subjects alike, less than two years ago, re-
> fused to hear of the saving of twins, we have already their
> promise...in the persons of two baby girls aged six and five
> months respectively, who have already won the hearts of some of
> our neighbors and the love of all school children. Seven women
> have literally touched them, and all the people, including the
> most practical of the chiefs, come to the house to hold their
> palavers in full view of where the children are being nursed. One
> chief, who with fierce gesticulations some years ago protested
> that we must draw the line at twins, and that they should never
> be brought to light in his lifetime, brought one of his children
> who was very ill, two months ago, and laid it on our knee
> alongside the twin already there, saying with a sob in his voice,
> "There! They are all yours, living or dying, they are all yours.
> Do what you like with mine."[111]

The debilitating climate took its toll, and on January 13, 1915, the sixty-seven-year-old missionary died after a severe bout of fever. Until life's end she retained her optimistic spirit. "The time of the singing of birds is where Christ is," she said, and "Never talk about the *cold* hand of death. It is the hand of Christ....Life is so grand and eternity is so real."

Lord, the task is impossible for me, but not for Thee. Lead the way and I will follow. — Mary Slessor

TIYO SOGA

First Black Presbyterian Minister
Ordained for South Africa, 1829–1871

He was always frail and died at age forty-two, but Tiyo Soga, the first black minister ordained for the Presbyterian Church in South Africa, achieved distinction as both a church-builder and a scholar. He was born in Gwali in the Eastern Cape in 1829. His father was reputedly the first Xhosa to use a plough with oxen and to employ running water to irrigate his crops, thus allowing him to sell produce to the nearby British garrison. Soga's mother was a Christian and refused to let her son be circumcised, which left the youth open to the cat-calls of his peers, for it meant, according to them, that he had not completed the steps to make him a man.[112]

Soga was the product of a mission education, and in 1846 when the Rev. William Govan, head of the Lovedale school, decided to return to Scotland, he personally paid for the African youth's passage. It was a traumatic parting from his homeland, and Soga's mother said, "My son belongs to God.... He is as much in God's care in Scotland as he is here with me." Arriving in Glasgow, Tiyo enrolled at the Normal School of Glasgow, was baptized in 1848, and returned to the Eastern Cape, where he worked as a pastor and translator for the next twenty-two years.

Although he passed all the college courses prescribed for ministerial training in Glasgow and was licensed as a minister of the United Presbyterian Church in 1856, Soga was designated as an "ordained Caffre missionary" ("Caffre," or "Kaffir," refers to black Africans and is sometimes a term of derision). Then Soga married a Scottish woman in 1857 in Glasgow. When Janet Burnside Soga appeared on her husband's arm, neither Africans nor Europeans reacted well. Some thought Soga was trying to look like "a black Englishman." During their fifteen-year marriage the couple raised seven children, including a son with a crippled leg. This required several trips to England by Mrs. Soga, who also returned there for the birth of each of her children. She was described as "a most honorable, thrifty, frugal, and devoted woman who marched heroically and faithfully by her husband's side through all the checkered scenes of his short life."

Soga hoped that his sons would be educated in Scotland, as he had been. He told them, "For your sakes, never appear ashamed that your father was a "Kaffir" and that you inherit some African blood. It is every whit as good and as pure as that which flows in the veins of my fairer brethren.... You will ever cherish the memory of your mother as that of an upright, conscientious, thrifty Christian Scots woman. You will ever be thankful for your connection by this tie with the white race." After his death, Janet Soga and her four youngest children were returned to Scotland by the mission authorities.

The young minister held several mission pastorates, opening stations in isolated locales, but his frail health inhibited him from full-time field work. He is remembered for his skilled work as a writer and translator. Soga's written journal, the earliest such document by a black South African, is an important historical source. Many of the hymns he wrote were included in the Lovedale Press hymnal of 1873. On November 21, 1866, he noted, "Quarter past nine o'clock, finished, through the goodness of Almighty God, the translation of the first part of *The Pilgrim's Progress,* my fingers aching with writing." He was working on a new translation of the Bible in Xhona at the time of his death from tuberculosis in 1871. Two of his sons continued his church work. One, John Henderson Soga, completed the translation of *Pilgrim's Progress,* a second, Allan Kirkland Soga, became a local newspaper editor and participant in a political movement that was a precursor of the African National Congress (ANC).

Almighty God, who called your servant Tiyo Soga to be a minister and translator of your Gospel in South Africa and endowed him with the gift of bringing your saving Word to peoples in their own language: Reveal to us your presence in your wider church, that through prayer and the study of Scriptures, people everywhere may be gathered as one great flock under One Shepherd. Amen.

BLESSED CYPRIAN IWENE TANSI

Priest and Monk, Southern Nigeria,
1903–1964

಄಄಄಄಄಄಄಄಄

If you are going to be a Christian you might as well live entirely for God.
— Blessed Cyprian Iwene Tansi

As an active parish priest and later as a Trappist monk, Blessed
Cyprian Iwene ("let human malice not kill me") Tansi was an African
Roman Catholic religious, beatified by Pope John Paul II in Nigeria
in 1998.

Born of Igbo parents in southern Nigeria in 1903, Cyprian attended
mission schools, graduated from St. Paul's Seminary in Igbariam, and
was ordained a priest in 1937, the first indigenous priest of the Aguleri
region. Traveling by foot or bicycle between several Nigerian villages,
from 1937 to 1950 he was an active parish priest. He systematically
visited the homes of the poor, the lame, and the blind. (He was blind
in one eye.) Creating marriage preparation centers for young women
was an important activity for the young priest. Separate courses were
established for women already married in traditional ceremonies and
those about to be married in the church. When he was baptized a
Christian, Cyprian shocked his non-Christian parents by destroying
the personal idol given each Igbo male child at birth.[113]

In 1950, following the call of a missionary bishop seeking to establish a contemplative order in Africa, he entered the Trappist Abbey
of Mount St. Bernard in Leicestershire, England, where he stayed for
thirteen years. The transition from Nigeria to England was difficult.
The cold took its toll on his health, and English monks had difficulty
understanding an African colleague. But Fr. Cyprian was determined
to stay the course. "If you are going to be a Christian," he once said,
"you might as well live entirely for God."

Returning to Nigeria in 1963 in the midst of a civil war, he was
transferred to a newly established monastery near Bamenda, Cameroon, and named novice master. The African monk died the following
year of an aortic aneurysm after returning to England for medical
treatment. Eventually his body was returned to the priest's cemetery
at Onitsha Cathedral, where he had been ordained fifty-one years ear-

lier. On March 22, 1998, Pope John Paul II traveled to Onitsha to beatify Fr. Cyprian.

Although he left no systematic body of writings, from scattered notes and oral recollections it is possible to reconstruct some of his observations.

From a 1959 letter to his houseboy:

> Yourself and your wife should keep always before your eyes that fact that you are creatures, God's own creation. As a man's handiwork belongs to him, so do we all belong to God, and should accordingly have no other will but his. He is a Father, a very kind Father indeed. All His plans are for the good of His children. We may not often see how they are. That does not matter. Leave yourself in His hands, not for a year, not for two years, but as long as you live on earth. If you confide in Him fully and sincerely He will take special care of you.

A recollection of Augustine Chendo:

> He taught us to say: "O my God, I am a piece of cloth bought for your clothes. You are the tailor and weaver. Make us clothes therefore in the style and fashion to suit you."

A recollection of Stephen Eme:

> God will give you double what you give him.

Mount St. Bernard retreat notes:

> The first steps of a small child are full of hope. They are often a rush toward Mother's arms. The little one has a sense of awful loneliness and suddenly thinks it will move, hoping that Mother's arms will catch it; then a dance, dart, a tumble, what a study in Hope.

Letter to Augustine Chendo, 1959:

> Prayer is the best weapon for obtaining favors from God. Pray, pray often, pray with all your heart, pray to God, pray to our Blessed Mother. Mass is the most powerful of all prayers.

Retreat notes:

> One of the sure signs of fervor and progress in the religious life is joy and contentment. When we are satisfied with God and

with His way of dealing with us, it reflects on the countenance. The face is aglow with joy.[114]

Merciful Redeemer, who by the life and teaching of Blessed Cyprian Tansi, as parish priest and monastic, raised up a faithful witness to your saving word among the people of Africa, grant that through his steadfast fidelity and life of prayer your people may find their way to you, the God who already waits for each of us and knows each of your children by name. Amen.

TERTULLIAN

North African Christian Teacher,
c. 160–220

Let us drop the name "prison" and call it a place of seclusion. Though
the body is confined, though the flesh is detained, there is nothing that
is not open to the spirit. In spirit wander about, in spirit take a walk,
setting before yourself not shady promenades and long porticos but that
path which leads to God. — Tertullian in *To the Martyrs*

Cyril, Clement, Augustine, Origen, Tertullian — it is an impressive list
of African theologians and leaders who helped give shape and defini-
tion to the Christian church in its early years. Tertullian emerged as
the most articulate of the group in the third century. Born in Carthage,
the son of a Roman military officer, Tertullian was a well-educated
Roman lawyer before converting to Christianity in his thirties and
turning his career to arguing the case for the new religion then spreading throughout the empire. Tertullian was probably not a priest,
unlike the other early church leaders; most likely he was married,
and certainly he was someone who burned the candle at both ends.
Debauchery and licentious behavior were hallmarks of his young life.
And even when he got his act together, Tertullian was a difficult case,
variously described as schizoid or paranoid in temperament. Loud,
often violent, and intolerant, he was a killer debater with any opponent. Alternatively, Tertullian was a person of intense prayer, extreme
asceticism, and a brilliant, prolific writer, interlarding dazzling commentaries on the Scriptures with remarks like those referring to one
writer as "a rat from Pontus who gnaws away at the Gospels" and
another as "a first-class chatterbox and a liar."

Tertullian counseled women on their dress, urging them to avoid
vanity and "the radiance of precious stones with which necklaces
are decorated in different colors, the bracelets of gold which they
wrap around their arms, ... and that black powder which they use to
enhance the beauty of their eyes." Such vanity, Tertullian had it, came
directly from woman's perfidy in the Garden of Evil: "The sentence
of God on this sex of yours lives on even in our times, and so it is
necessary that the guilt should live on, also. You are the one who
opened the door to the Devil, you are the one who first plucked the

185

fruit of the forbidden tree, you are the one who first deserted the divine law.... All too easily you destroyed the image of God, man. Because of your desert, that is, death, even the Son of God had to die. And you still think of putting adornments over the skins of animals that cover you?"

Tertullian is well known for his third-century sound bytes, the most famous being "The blood of the martyrs is the seed of the church," which some people mistakenly believe comes from the Bible.

Tertullian was concerned with the plight of the martyrs, a constant issue when the Roman empire was at its height and feared the claims of the growing Christian bands. Using the lawyer's logic and passion, Tertullian argued that the Romans denied due process of law to the Christians. Charges of disloyalty to the empire or secret atrocities and rites were ridiculous, he argued. Instead, the Christians were solid, contributing members of society and should be treated as such. In his discourse *To the Martyrs* he wrote:

> The prison now offers to the Christian what the desert once gave to the Prophets. Our Lord Himself quite often spent time in solitude to pray there more freely, to be there away from the world. In fact, it was in a secluded place that He manifested His glory to His disciples. Let us drop the name "prison," and call it a place of seclusion. Though the body is confined, though the flesh is detained, there is nothing that is not open to the spirit. In spirit wander about, in spirit take a walk, setting before yourself not shady promenades and long porticos but that path which leads to God. As often as you walk that path, you will not be in prison. The leg does not feel the fetter when the spirit is in heaven. The spirit carries about the whole man and carries him wherever he wishes. And where your heart is, there will your treasure be also. There, then, let our heart be where we would have our treasure.[115]

Prayer is the wall of faith, our shield and weapon against the foe who studies us from all sides. Hence, let us never set forth unarmed. Let us be mindful of our guard-duty by day and our vigil by night. Beneath the arms of prayer let us guard the standard of our general, and let us pray as we await the bugle call of the angel.   —Tertullian, "On Prayer"[116]

DESMOND TUTU

Archbishop, Nobel Prize Laureate,
b. 1931

※※※※※※※※※

I hold to the view that this is a moral universe. Goodness matters as it did
forever in the past. It will continue to do so. Truth matters. Corruption
matters. We have seen why some of the financial institutions ... have gone
under. It is basically, ultimately that they have flouted ethical rules.
— Desmond Tutu, World Economic Forum,
Davos, Switzerland, January 1998

The voice is what you remember most about being in Desmond Tutu's
presence. Then the eyes, then the gestures, the perfectly enunciated
English delivered with the African storyteller's lilt. "I only have one
sermon," he told me once. "It is God's love" (pronouncing "God"
with a short "o," as in "Gott"). And carefully savored phrases like "In
the full ... ness of time" or "the bubbliness of life." And the retelling
of biblical stories that have both black and white audiences laughing,
anticipating — what will God say next, how will Adam or Mary reply
in this cosmic dialogue?

The archbishop, possibly wearing a Greek fisherman's cap, bursts
into a room, leaving a whirl wherever he has been, although a bout
with cancer has slowed his gait. Desmond became seriously interested
in the church when Trevor Huddleston (see p. 102), an Anglican monk,
doffed his hat to Mrs. Tutu, a cook in a hospital for the blind. And
when young Desmond was confined to a hospital bed, the Community
of the Resurrection monk visited him, not once, but several times. If
this a lanky, deeply spiritual personage could pay attention to him,
maybe the church was worth looking at seriously, the African youth
reasoned. (The first of Tutu's four children was named "Trevor.")

"I was not doing anything special," Huddleston told me years later,
when he was in residence at London's St. James' Piccadilly church, but
a friendship was struck up. Tutu became interested in the priesthood
and was ordained in 1960. After study and teaching in England and
in South Africa, in 1975 he was elected dean of St. Mary's Cathedral
in Johannesburg and then bishop of Lesotho and general secretary
of the South African Council of Churches. The Nobel Peace Prize
laureate became bishop of Johannesburg in 1985 and archbishop of

the Province of South Africa in 1986. Following South Africa's independence in 1994, Tutu was given the difficult task of chairing the country's Truth and Reconciliation Commission.

The archbishop's rise to African and international prominence came during the final decades of South African apartheid. Nelson Mandela was in prison, the color bar and pass laws were ubiquitous, educational and job opportunities for Africans were minimal, hope was a scarce commodity. Tutu was a firm, clear, unyielding opponent of apartheid.[117]

Discussing the work of the Truth and Reconciliation Commission, Tutu pointed out that its particular format was unique to the South African situation. Local people could have tried other solutions, but this formula was forced on South Africa "because of the realities of the situation: No one won. The apartheid government didn't win, the liberation movements didn't win." The compromise was: "In exchange for truth, you will get amnesty. In exchange for telling us everything you know about what you want to ask amnesty for, you will get freedom. Of course, if you don't, the judicial process, we hope, will take its course."

Tutu gave an example of the reconciliation process at work:

A white woman is a victim of a hand-grenade attack by one of the liberation movements. A lot of her friends are killed. And she ends up having to have open-heart surgery. She comes to the Truth and Reconciliation Commission to tell her story. And she says, "You know, when I came out of hospital, my children had to bathe me, had to clothe me, had to feed me. And I can't walk through the security checkpoint at the airport — I've still got shrapnel inside me...." Do you know what she said...of this experience that left her in this condition?... "It has enriched my life." She says, "I'd like to meet the perpetrator, I'd like to meet him in a spirit of forgiveness. I would like to forgive him." Which is extraordinary. But then,...can you believe it? — she goes on to say, "I hope he forgives me."[118]

> *Goodness is stronger than evil;*
> *Love is stronger than hate;*
> *Light is stronger than darkness;*
> *Life is stronger than death;*
> *Victory is ours through Him who loves us.*
> —Desmond Tutu[119]

HENRY VENN

Missionary Statesman,
1796–1893

His bust in the crypt of St. Paul's Cathedral, London, shows a strong face, squared jaw, and steady eyes — a decisive, determined person. That was Henry Venn, honorary clerical secretary of the Church Missionary Society for thirty years. The cautious, careful Venn engineered the election of West Africa's first native Anglican bishop and hammered out the missionary policy, radical for its time, of self-governing, self-supporting, self-propagating churches, which contributed to the independence of African churches long before most mission groups were willing to relinquish control.[120]

Venn was a fourth-generation English clergyman. His father was a leader of the Clapham Sect, the antislavery group named for the village outside London where they met and from which the Church Missionary Society (CMS) evolved. The twelve or so Clapham Sect members believed that God had given them much (most were from positions of social prominence and wealth) and that they should be God's agents to redeem the world through good works, such as educating the heathen. Theirs was not a highly complicated theology; it basically turned the Gospel into practical programs. Their action arm was the Church Mission Society, founded, in their words, "upon church principles, not high church principles," which distinguished the CMS from another missionary group, the Society for the Propagation of Christian Knowledge (SPCK) allied with the Anglo-Catholic wing of the Church of England.

Most of his revolutionary ideas did not originate with Venn, who stayed with the CMS from 1841 to 1871. He was an intensely practical, results-oriented administrator, aware of what others were saying missions needed. It was in this context that the concepts of mission churches as self-governing, self-supporting, and self-propagating unfolded in contradistinction to the generally accepted mission slogan of imperialism: "commerce, civilization, and Christianity."

Venn never linked Christianity with civilization, just the opposite. "The principle that men must be civilized in order to embrace

Christianity is untenable; for civilization, though favorable to the development of Christianity, so far from being essential for its initiation is, on the contrary, the consequence, not the forerunner of the Gospel."[121] Self-governing was necessary, he believed, because it was both a biblical concept, as seen in, for example, the governance of the early church in Antioch, and because Britain could not continue to send streams of missionaries abroad. Between 1825 and 1834 twenty-six missionaries had been sent to the Niger region of West Africa, of whom eighteen had died. Self-financing was required to keep the local churches from becoming dependent on the mother church and because donations to mission were not always easy to come by.

Venn believed that if the church was to catch hold in indigenous societies it would require local leadership, people who could interpret the Christian Gospel in a local context. At the same time, Venn was aware of the opposition African Bishop Samuel Ajayi Crowther faced (see p. 64). White clergy would not serve under a black bishop, and "native agency under European superintendence" was the watchword of most white Victorian mission sponsors. He carefully carved out an episcopate for Crowther that did not interfere with the established white missionaries' turf, but even so the resident British community of traders and government officials complained. Crowther, a person of deep humility, was replaced by a white bishop with two black assistants, a solution satisfactory to no one. It was not until after World War II that Nigerians would have their own episcopal leadership. Meanwhile, many Nigerians formed their own independent churches that mirrored the colonial churches from which they had been rejected or marginalized. Venn's ideas were ahead of his time and helped pave the way for later African nationalism and the independence of African churches.

> *Alleluia! Christ has procláimed his Gospel in all lands.*
> *O come, let us worship. Alleluia!*
> —Preparation, Feast of Missionaries

VICTOR I

Pope and Saint,
Pontificate c. 189–199

Victor I was the first of the early church's three African popes. During his ten-year pontificate (c. 189–199), he played a significant role in tilting the Roman Catholic Church's emphasis toward support of its Latin, Western element, at the expense of ties with the Eastern church. The dispute centered over which calendar would be accepted to determine the date of Easter for the entire church, a dispute that later divided the church in England from its Celtic counterpart as well, producing a lasting separation in both cases. Victor stopped short of excommunicating those who opposed him; he could afford to be conciliatory, since his position was fully accepted by the Western church. He was also an early, strong proponent of using Latin as the main language for church services and documents. During his reign he interceded with the powerful imperial household, providing them with a list of Christians sentenced to work in the mines of Sardinia, persons who were later freed through the intervention of the emperor Commodus's Christian common-law wife.

O God, whose glory the redeemed in heaven eternally praise, grant that we who rejoice in the memory of Victor I may be brought to praise you, the giver of life everlasting, through Jesus Christ our Lord. Amen.

VICTOR OF VITA

North African Bishop, Church Historian,
fifth century

❈❈❈❈❈❈❈❈❈

By the fifth century, the persecution of Christians was well under way by Vandal invaders from the north, extending to both sides of the Mediterranean. Rome was sacked in 455, and in the small North African province of Byzacene, Victor of Vita, a fifth-century bishop, chronicled the invasions and tortures inflicted by the Vandal leader Hunneric (477–484). Drawing on his own eyewitness accounts and earlier reports, Victor also described the heroic courage and resistance of the new Christian communities. In one instance, he noted the tendency of martyrs to joyfully sing hymns and psalms as they were being led to their death and the cruelty of invaders who required that they be buried in silence, for singing was the one final means of expression of their faith left to them.

Grant, O heavenly Father, that we who with joy commemorate the life of Victor of Vita, bishop and historian of the persecuted church in North Africa, may at length be found worthy, with all the redeemed, to worship you in that heavenly Jerusalem where dwell the blessed dead of all ages, with Jesus Christ our Lord, our mediator and advocate. Amen.

KIMPA VITA (DONA BEATRIZ)

1684–1706

❀❀❀❀❀❀❀❀

The early eighteenth century was a time of political fragmentation and cultural disarray in the Kongo, which included parts of present-day Angola. Civil wars were numerous, food shortages widespread in wartime, and political disorder rampant. In such a setting one of Africa's first Christian female prophets arose, precursor of hundreds of such figures who would be a feature of Christianity on that continent in later centuries. Her name was Kimpa Vita, or Dona Beatriz, as she was known by her baptismal name.

Kimpa Vita, descendent of a noble family, received her call in 1704 while she was gravely ill and near the point of death. A figure wearing a Capuchin habit appeared to her in a vision. He said he was St. Anthony, a patron saint of Portugal and Kongo, sent by God through her to preach to the people, hasten the restoration of the kingdom, and usher in a happy time when the Kongo would have its own saints, just as the Europeans did.

Between 1704 and 1706, the time of her revelation and her martyrdom, this prophetic figure moved about the lower Kongo region, preaching and attracting an immense following. She upset local rulers and the Italian missionaries. The prophet's theology was anything but orthodox, for she claimed St. Anthony was a second God who wanted to restore the Kongo Kingdom. Moreover, she was in the habit of dying each Friday, in imitation of the passion of Christ, going to heaven "to dine with God and plead the cause of the Negroes, especially the restoration of the Kongo," in one missionary account, then being "born again on Saturday." Arguing that both the king and the missionaries lacked the will to restore the fallen kingdom, she said missionaries did not want the Kongo to have black saints and that through her now the Kongolese could have their own saints. Kongolese parroted mission prayers and teachings, she preached, adding it was more important to go beneath the surface of the words and actions, since intention is what really counted.

As her following grew dramatically, Kimpa Vita soon was regarded as a saint by local people. Believing she had healing powers, especially to cure infertility, they sought her prayers and asked her to touch articles of their clothing or possessions. "Little Anthonys," as her followers were known, spread throughout the Kongo. Panicked by her success and enraged by her teachings, which they profoundly misunderstood, the Capuchins, to whom she originally appealed as a co-religionist, set out to destroy her, aided by the weak and indecisive Kongolese local ruler Pedro IV. She was arrested and she and her consort, Barro, were sentenced to be burned to death. Her self-confidence had been badly shaken when she became pregnant. How could she preach a godly life when she was visibly unchaste herself? It was not a forgiving age, and, believing her sins made her worthy of death, she said, "I lost the virtue by reason of my sins, which have reduced me to the state in which I now find myself."[122]

The couple were burned to death in a public square on July 2, 1706. Before that happened, the couple were ordered to sit on the bare ground near the place where they would be executed. In the presence of a large crowd, Dom Bernardo, a Portuguese missionary and the chief judge, excoriated Dona Beatriz and Barro for heresy, seized her child from her, and pronounced the sentence of death by fire. A mob moved forward and began to beat the couple, now bound tightly by ropes. Both were badly bruised and bloodied by the time they were thrown on the flaming pyre. On the following morning, some of the crowd returned, searched for their remaining bones, and burned them.[123]

The movement which Kimpa Vita founded lived on, and after her death, Pedro IV used it to unify the fragmented kingdom. Peasants incorporated her ideas into their own folk beliefs, and some reappeared in messianic cults. Two centuries later, it could be said that another popular preacher, Simon Kimbangu (see p. 111), followed in the tradition of Kimpa Vita, who became the subject of popular literary works. By her own reckoning and within the framework of traditional African belief systems, Kimpa Vita was not a heretic, but represented a perfectly explicable stream of Christianity, albeit one different from the imported Portuguese version that officially prevailed. Her confrontation was that of a woman of faith, destroyed by her own people and the missionaries, all acting in the name of Christ.

> *"Salve" you say and you do not know why. "Salve" you recite and you do not know why. . . . God wants the intention, it is the intention God takes. Marriage serves nothing, it is the intention God takes. Baptism serves nothing, it is the intention God takes.*

Confession serves nothing, it is the intention God takes. Prayer serves nothing, it is the intention God wants. Good works serve nothing, it is the intention God wants ... St. Anthony is the merciful one. St Anthony is our remedy. St. Anthony is the restorer of the kingdom of Kongo. ... St. Anthony is the door to Heaven.
— Translation of the "Salve Antoniana,"
Kongolese adaptation of the "Salve Regina"
by Kimpa Vita[124]

JOHN WHITE

Missionary to the Mashona People of South Africa, 1866–1933

> Five goats were in residence when I retired, and these, an evangelist, four carriers, and myself slept together in this awful place! I was glad when dawn came. But should I grumble, when the Son of Man had nowhere to lay his head?
> — John White

Born in 1866 in England's Lake District, the eldest of seven children, John White received only a smattering of formal education. As a youth, White had a conversion experience and sought to become a Methodist missionary.[125]

In those days a chartered company that controlled the region's economic life and administered justice ruled much of what is now Zimbabwe. White became an early exponent of equity and fairness for Africans, and this brought him sustained criticism from the settler community. Newspaper cartoons pictured him as a *kaffirboetie,* or friend of local peoples. White had many friends in the English community in Salisbury and was a great admirer of the British system of justice, but he was also an early exponent of the brotherhood of all peoples. In 1896 the Mashonaland Rebellion broke out, and the Mashona were fearful of being annihilated by the British. White told them, to the consternation of British authorities, "I will sleep each night amongst you outside the laager, so that if they come to kill you, they will kill me also."

Life was not easy for White. During one raid he witnessed local insurgents kill both an African evangelist and a wounded white missionary the African was carrying to safety. Later White spent Christmas Day in a wagon stuck in the mud in the middle of a small flooded lake. In another instance, he had been traveling all day and into the evening when the party was given a small hut by a local chief to spend the night. "Five goats were in residence when I retired, and these, an evangelist, four carriers, and myself slept together in this awful place! I was glad when dawn came. But should I grumble, when the Son of Man had nowhere to lay his head?"

Once while traveling, he bent down to treat the injured foot of a carrier and, reaching behind him for a knife, instead grasped a deadly snake, which he instantly threw to the ground. His dog attacked the snake, was bitten by it, and soon its head and neck were swollen to double their normal size.

From his work as a Methodist leader in the Southern Rhodesia district, White developed a three-part strategy: (1) the Gospels must be translated into the Shona language, (2) the heart of the mission effort must come from local evangelists, and (3) the Christian message must be integrated into the social life of Africans. To this end, he established the Waddilove Institution, a teachers training college. And in 1894, with the assistance of James Chiremba Chihota, his wagon-driver and interpreter, he began translating St. Mark's Gospel. A packing-case formed his table, a soap-box his seat, and a fruit-tin his writing pad.

As he grew older, White's heath declined, and he transferred to Bulawayo. Racial tensions between Africans and Europeans were acute in the growing city, and White's steadfast insistence on racial justice for people who were voiceless and voteless brought him charges of being a political meddler. White would have identified with the sentiments in the "Black Christ," a poem by his friend A. S. Cripps:

> *To me, as one born out of his due time*
> *To me, as one not much to reckon in,*
> *He hath revealed Himself, not as to Paul,*
> *Christ throned and crowned,*
> *But marred, despised, rejected,*
> *The Divine Outcast of a terrible land,*
> *The Black Christ, with parched lips and empty hand.*[126]

SALIM WILSON,

The Black Evangelist of the North,
d. 1946

Conventional wisdom has it that white missionaries came from abroad to Africa, but Salim Wilson was an African who went the other way and exercised a long and effective ministry in the North of England. Born in the mid-nineteenth century, Salim, whose original name was "Hatashil" (The Continuer), was the son of a Dinka Sudanese chief. He was sold into slavery but freed by Anglican missionaries. He became a servant in their compound and later converted to Christianity.[127] After initially becoming an evangelist in Africa, he spent the next sixty years serving numerous small English churches, where he was remembered as a lively preacher and compassionate pastor.

For Salim, acceptance of Christianity came as "a gradual awakening — the breaking in of the spiritual light." Although Salim published three books, including his *Life Story* in 1889, knowledge of this remarkable person is spotty. In 1887, after working with the YMCA and the *British Women's Temperance Journal,* Salim returned to the Sudan with Graham Wilmot Brooke, a British missionary, with whom he soon had deep differences of interpretation. Although both prayed together, they clearly saw Africa from different perspectives. Brooke kept a map of Africa with one part marked under Islamic influence, another for European commercial interests, and a third zone, including the Sudan, where Brooke sought to combat "Mohamedanism." Declining an opportunity to bring Christianity to the country's receptive south, which was not Islamic, Brooke sought instead a frontal confrontation with well-organized Muslims in the north.

Returning to England in 1888, Salim attended a missionary college and spoke at numerous Church Missionary Society (CMS) "missionary exhibitions." Gradually he drifted away from Anglicanism and settled in Yorkshire, where he earned a living as a Methodist evangelist.

In 1913 Salim married his landlady, a widow, Mrs. Eliza Alice Holden. A congregation of over eight hundred persons filled the chapel, and a further crowd of mostly women gathered outside the building where they were married. The event was filmed and reported on in the *Grimsby Telegraph* and other papers. There were headlines like "Black Prince Marries White Woman," and both provincial curiosity and acceptance were displayed toward Wilson. When the Wilberforce Centenary was held in 1933, he was a center of attention. The *Hull Times* opined, "Once a Branded Slave.... Scunthorpe Man Sold for Calico." Much in demand as a preacher, he constantly displayed affection for children. "It was like a blessing," one parishioner recalled. When he placed his hand on their head, "You could fairly feel the goodness and gentleness." Years later, at the time of his death, people remembered Salim's warmth, gentleness, and sense of fun.

His last years were not easy. Crippled with arthritis, his wife required expensive treatments. Salim cared for her until her death in 1941. Old, near blind, and in failing health, he died in a charity hospital on January 26, 1946. The town paper called him "one of the best-loved figures in the town." His estate of five hundred pounds was left to the daughter of a missionary friend, but she predeceased him, so it passed to his kinsmen in Sudan. Salim Wilson's life was living evidence that missionary outreach is a two-way street.

> *Spread, O spread, thou mighty word,*
> *Spread the kingdom of the Lord,*
> *Wheresoe'er his breath has given*
> *Life to beings meant for heaven.*
> *Word of life, most pure and strong,*
> *Lo, for thee the nations long;*
> *Spread, till from its dreary night*
> *All the world awakes to light!*[128]

ZENO OF VERONA
Bishop and Saint, d. c. 371

Not much is known about this early African saint. Zeno probably came from North Africa, although we cannot be sure. Head of the important diocese of Verona, this fourth-century bishop cited several African authors in his sermons and writings. He thus exemplified the brisk intellectual exchange that characterized the early Mediterranean church, one in which a North African presence was a key ingredient.

Almost ninety of his sermons survive; they show a concerned pastor with a strong interest in the sacramental life, especially baptism and the Paschal mystery of Christ's death and resurrection. No abstract theologian, Zeno also insisted that his people feed the poor and extend hospitality to strangers. A statue of him remains in the Basilica of St. Zeno Major in Verona, where he was called "the saint who smiles."

Almighty God, you call your witnesses from every age and nation, and reveal your glory in their lives. We thank you for the example of Zeno of Verona, who knew your church in Africa and Europe. Grant that through his example, your followers everywhere may know each other more fully, and so proclaim your kingdom to all parts of the world. This we ask in the name of Christ, whose Gospel was proclaimed to people everywhere. Amen.

AFRICAN DIARY

The following excerpts are from the author's diary of a trip to Africa in 1987.

October 3, 1987. "What is the highest priority in your diocese?" I asked the bishop of Zimbabwe. "To pray for rain," he replied without hesitation, adding, "We have had a drought for six years. Our people are farmers and cattle raisers and now their stocks have dwindled and they have little to eat. Every day we pray for rain, and so do the traditional rain makers," he added humorously. The bishop and his wife were on their way to make Sunday afternoon hospital calls. A gentle, reserved man, he was a good listener whose low-voiced pastoral responses were hard to hear above the hotel lobby's noises. An exodus of British clergy in recent years, including the closing of two large installations of the Community of the Resurrection, an Anglican monastic order, left the diocese with depleted clergy numbers. Trying to start a clergy training center, the bishop recruited part-time faculty from among the diocesan clergy. Not many young persons have been attracted to the ministry because talented persons can find much better paying jobs with the government or private sector. There is almost nothing for young people to do, no discussion groups, no sports equipment, no excursions. The bishop had a carefully worked out proposal to turn a desolate rural area into productive farming land, but there were no takers within the international community. At great cost, the church had built wire fences around the land to keep out marauding cattle. A companion diocese built a tool shed. Next comes electrification, which is costly. And tools. And seed. And animals. All that is needed to start a farm was only a dream at this point.

The cathedral faced Cecil Square, the heart of downtown Harare. A brownstone building finished in the 1950s, it could easily hold a thousand persons. Usual British ecclesiastical furnishings were combined with tastefully designed African elements, including an African Stations of the Cross. A massive Christus figure, depicting hope and suffering, hung over the altar, the work of a crippled African sculptor from a village 150 kilometers distant. On each side of the freestanding altar were six-foot carved wooden candleholders with African scenes from the four Gospels. All around the walls were well-scrubbed brass memorial plaques of an earlier era, tributes to the dead of two world wars, to victims of numerous "native" uprisings and a few airplane wrecks, and to Africans who fought in the European wars.

October 7. I visited with the archbishop of Central Africa in his office, an unpretentious single-story cinderblock building on the outskirts of Gaborone, Botswana's capital. Behind a simple metal desk is a small bookshelf, and over it is hung his episcopal credential, with three royal seals. He said his own diocese was small and poor, and shortly after being elected its bishop, he was elected archbishop of five countries, an area that includes conservative Malawi, socialist Zambia, moderate Botswana, Marxist Tanzania, and unpredictable Zimbabwe. The archbishop spends much time "getting a bench of ten bishops, many of them new, to work together. It is a new experience for us all." His own diocese is only twenty years old, although an Anglican presence in this part of Africa goes back over a century. Upgrading the skills of his twenty clergy and establishing active lay leadership are high priorities. Most expatriate clergy have left and many of the more talented local clergy have taken better-paying secular jobs. Although the Bible and *Book of Common Prayer* have been translated into the two principal local languages, "we need Bible teaching material to make the Bible come alive to local congregations. We also need to train our clergy in church administration and to deal with church councils. A strong interest exists in prayer and meditation, which would come naturally to Africans, and there is a growing interest in the healing ministry as well.

"We need to focus our efforts on the day-to-day, the here-and-now. I always begin prayers with a recollection of what happened that day to individual persons. That is where we find reconciliation and grace. Recently I spoke to four hundred young people in Zambia. I said to them, 'People say you are the church of tomorrow, but that is wrong. You are the church of today.' We must do more for our young people. Islam is an attraction for some of them. Recently, in South Africa I saw bumper stickers: 'Islam for Africa, Africa for Islam' and 'I Love Islam.' I do not think the attraction of Islam, or even more important, the rampant spread of Pentecostalism, will prove enduring, but we must be able to offer programs to our young people." We said a prayer together; I remember the cadence of his voice and the depth of his faith. Walking away from the cathedral, I passed two basketball hoops with nets but no backboards and wondered how a youth program could be launched with so few resources.

Next day I attended a 6:15 a.m. Eucharist in the Cathedral of

Christ Our Savior. A handful of us gathered in the chapel off the circular main building. An African priest celebrated. The dean, from Britain, read the lessons; two Anglican nuns, the dean's wife, the archbishop, two African clergy, and I were the congregation. A modern icon of the Virgin and Child was on one wall; the rising sun sent a shaft of light across a wooden African Christ on the far wall. The service was simple, ending with the Africa prayer (see p. 104). Psalm 137 was read — about how can we sing the Lord's song in a strange land — and I thought of it not only as a psalm of Zion written in captivity, but as a psalm of special meaning for patriots during the American Revolution and for those who struggle for freedom in South Africa.

One of the intercessory prayers said:

Father, you provide for all your children, grant good rain for
    our crops.
You were rich yet for our sake you became poor; move those
    who have wealth to share generously with those who
    are poor.
You who were unjustly condemned by Pontius Pilate, strengthen
    our brothers who are suffering injustice and persecution.
You lived as an exile in Egypt; be with all migrant workers and
    protect their families.

October 9. On the flight from Gaborone I sat next to a Methodist pastor who will retire next year. His savings have allowed him to buy a parcel of land two hundred kilometers from the city; land near the capital is expensive. In exchange for part-time work with the local church, its pastor — a former carpenter — will help his colleague build a house as soon as the retiring minister raises the money for wood and tin. He squeezed my hand and we said a prayer as the small plane bumped down the runway. "Many blessings" he said, as the pilot gave the two piston engines a final revving up.

It was early morning, the overnight flights from Europe had arrived, and we were tired as we went through the long passport control line at Johannesburg airport. My wife, Charlotte, had headed for the local flights desk to confirm our onward booking when our driver came running up. "Here's Bishop Tutu," he said excitedly. There, in the next line, was the well-known profile, in dark suit, episcopal purple shirt, and Greek fisherman's hat. We set a time to meet in Cape Town.

October 15. The Vortreekers Monument is a squarish Babylonian-style structure set on top of a hill overlooking Pretoria. Built of brown stone, each of its four corners is guarded by the statue of a gun-holding pioneer looking out at the points of a compass. Inside is a vast, dark, cold chamber, at the center of which is a large marble cenotaph. An "eternal flame," a replica of a pioneer's oil lamp, has been burning since 1938.

Around the main hall were large sculpted panels from Boer history. Wagons were the unifying element, surrounded by sturdy men and valiant women, teapots hanging from axles, campfire scenes, women making candles, while being watched by children and dogs. The wagons would be drawn up around the campfire and the settlers would fend off attacks by Mantabele and Zulu. Scenes of massacres, treachery, agreements made and broken, and finally the building of Pretoria as the biblical "city on a hill" are depicted in carved stone. A white guide earnestly recounted to a busload of Afrikaner school children the meaning of the panels and the racist folk myth they perpetrated. There was, of course, an African side to these events, but it was never presented. Not since seeing the ruins of Darius the Great in Persia or Lenin's tomb, have I experienced such a comparable sight. The Persian ruins, like this monument, depict raw power. Like Lenin's tomb, it was the symbol of a culture, an attempt to codify the history and mythology of a people.

October 16. St. Paul's, Rondebosch, is in a Cape Town suburb. A largely white middle-class parish, it has some black and colored members who attend loyally, even after being evicted from homes that were once not far from the parish.

Twenty persons will be baptized or confirmed by Archbishop Tutu, and I asked our taxi driver, who had been awake for twenty-four hours and who lived in his taxi, to wait for us. He slept, with the radio crackling in case he could catch another fare. After an hour of the service had elapsed and only one of the seven hymns had been sung, I slipped out and told the driver to sleep on, it would be a long morning.

As the Gospel was chanted, Bishop Tutu held his pastoral staff with two hands, head bowed. His sermon text was from John 6, the feeding of the five thousand, delivered with a strong storyteller's voice. Desmond used no tricks or gimmicks, letting the intensity of the message and the authority of his voice predominate, making me think of Phillip Brookes's statement about preaching representing the personality of the preacher. A few days later, when we talked about his technique as a preacher he was puzzled that anyone would ask such a question. I asked, "what in your formation as a preacher makes you tell the Gospel stories in such a striking way? Does your training as a teacher have something to do with it?" "I've never thought about it," he said.

The seven-hundred-person congregation was intently focused on the sermon. Last Sunday, the archbishop was scheduled to preach on South African radio's regular Sunday morning religious broadcast. Earlier in the week, the government, after decades of religious broadcasting, instituted a new regulation: sermons would have to be prerecorded, supposedly to assure broadcast quality but in reality to censor any adverse political comments. Of course the archbishop refused.

This Sunday's sermon retold the story of people waiting by the Sea of Galilee to be fed. "God wants us to be his partners," he said, recounting the ancient narrative and noting that a boy producing a fish allowed God to act. "He waited on the crowd to be his partner." Tutu reviewed other examples of God's interaction with persons, with Moses who led his "frail, puny, often unreliable people" from slavery in Egypt; with Jeremiah who said, "I'm too young, I can't do it really," when called to be a prophet. "He sent an archangel to a young lass in Nazareth and instead of her saying, 'I'm a decent girl, try next door,' she said 'Behold the handmaiden of the Lord' and the universe breathed a cosmic sigh of relief."

He drew an occasional laugh from the seriously attentive congregation with phrases like "the naked would not be given a Kadushi suit from heaven" or "the hungry fed with samosas." "The bread is the bread of our soil, the wine the joy, the bubbliness of life."

"God doesn't want your possessions; his claims on us are totalitarian." (Complete silence. Here comes the political message, some people thought.) But it was all New Testament. "He wants all of you or me as we are, so he can make you into what he wants you to be." (A heavy-set white plain-clothes police officer in reflecting blue polyester suit and buzz haircut sat next to a rear pillar, writing furiously.)

The story was told, and before anyone was ready came the summary. "Will you be my agent of transfiguration, so there will be caring, concern, laughter, and joy, at school, at play, yes, in this land where there is injustice and separation. God says, 'Be my partner to bring about unity, compassion, and laughter.'" Bishop Tutu then disappeared from the pulpit as quickly as he had entered, and there was a deep silence while people reflected on a strong sermon, well delivered.

The moment's beauty turned quickly to pandemonium. The organist, in the choir loft at the rear of the church, with back to the altar and guided only by an ill-adjusted small ceramic mirror circled with painted roses, had prepared a loud and ambitious program for the modest instrument. The hymn came like rolling thunder as the procession moved toward the baptismal font; the rector gestured like a football referee, his swooping arms flapping at puzzled children and their sponsors. None of this was visible to the musician who by now was adding a descant as black, colored, and white children and their sponsors were led by a smiling archbishop toward the baptismal font. Meanwhile, a determined curate in white alb and heavy shoes sped down a side aisle for some forgotten ecclesiastical fixture.

Intercessory prayers were for "the strengthening of our faith; the peace of the world, especially between Iran and Iraq, and in Southern Africa. For those who work for justice and an end to civil war in our land. Detainees and their families. For the end of injustice and the establishment of a true base for negotiations toward a just constitution for the land. Those doing military service and all conscientious objectors. Doctors and nurses and the staff of hospitals."

The bishop was celebrant, again in the same strong, sure, flowing voice. The congregation took a stab at singing "Nkosi Sikelel' iAfrika," one verse of "God Bless Africa" in English and Zulu. "Very good," Tutu said, and gave the blessing in Zulu. At the end of the service he greeted each parishioner at the door. It was one of eleven pastoral visits he scheduled that month, including another three-hour confirmation service that evening.

October 24. We were awakened by the call to prayer of the muezzin in a nearby mosque in one of the city's last colored sections. Our hotel is within walking distance of St. George's Anglican Cathedral in downtown Cape Town. Twelve of us gathered for the early morning Eucharist, black, colored, and white, and I thought of how fragile were our prayers, yet how they represent the fiber, sinews, and veins of all our activity in a Hindu, Muslim, and Christian community.

The choral evensong planned for the next Sunday evening would do credit to an English cathedral. The choir will sing Mozart's *D Minor Requiem.* The church leaflet reads like one from an English parish, except for the note that it will be Prisoners' Sunday. "Today we remember all political prisoners and detainees. There will be a retiring collection after services today for the work of the Dependents' Conference," and "Dependents' Conference needs volunteers to offer hospitality, mainly weekend drives, teas, etc., to visiting parents/relations of detainees. If you feel you can help with this ministry call the church."

The Braaivleis *of the Lamb*

Just around the bend from our hotel stood a massive stone building; over the door was carved a gentle lamb, like those seen in the South African countryside, and a cross. The Dutch Reformed Church was meeting in synod at its headquarters. Since it was early evening, the proceedings stopped for a *braaivleis,* the Afrikaners' word for barbecue. The smell of charred sausages and meats wafted from the compound where a large gathering of gray- and tan-suited men with shortly cropped hair were enjoying one another's company.

Press reports from the synod were cryptic, and the South African press is self-censoring, but a cursory glance suggested that the issues being debated peaked in many other countries a quarter-century ago. A story in the *Citizen* (October 22, 1987) reported "Synod Probes Oriental Influences," saying the group discussed "the onslaught of Oriental religion and culture on South African Christians, but decided it was still possible for Christians to glorify God by using yoga and karate as a method of exercise and thus keeping their bodies healthy and fit. Members of the church were requested to acquaint themselves with the religious views of prospective coaches of these activities before they start working with them."

A synod group urged that the state of emergency be lifted, discriminatory legislation be abolished, and human rights be honored in South Africa's proposed constitution. The proposal was returned to committee for further study. A heated debate broke out between delegates over the meaning of the word "peace" in a report on the responsibility of the church to work for peace. The church document said structural injustice is a major cause of political unrest and violence in South Africa; increased government restrictions on protest only exacerbate bitterness and tension. "The search to find an answer for violence and revolution has grown proportionally as the scope for peaceful protest has become smaller," it concluded.

The storm had lifted from the Cape of Good Hope and an iridescent sea spread out before us. We followed the winding road from Devil's Table south. "That's Robben Island," our driver said. Not far out at sea was a small, almost flat island a few acres in size. A trail of smoke rose from what may have been the kitchen. Hundreds of political detainees are kept there, and still more at Pollsmoor prison on the mainland.

Under a state of emergency, the government can seize anyone, hold them for as long as it wants to, and tell no one, nor is it required to charge detainees before the courts. A newspaper report described a South African academic who spent ten years on the island for sabotage and then was held under a banning order until 1979. Invited by Yale University to pursue work on post-apartheid language policy, he was denied a passport, his fifth turndown in twenty months.

A letter to a local newspaper from a "concerned Anglican" complained that Bishop Tutu was overseas speaking on grand issues while people suffer, as from the recent devastating floods in Durban. In fact, the bishop had sent 10,000 rand, approximately $5,000, from his meager relief funds. On the day I saw him he was scrambling about with representatives of other churches to find money, food, and shelter for fourteen squatter families who had been forcibly removed from a "white" or "gray" area after bulldozers destroyed their frail tin-and-packing-wood shacks.

A press report said, "The Squatters, upset by the demolitions and concerned about their future, were sitting on top of their dumped furniture amid clouds of swirling dust. Mrs. Sarah Low (Shack 13) said her six-month-old baby Michael was asleep inside with her blind father, Mr. Jacobus Damans, 69, when the men started tearing down the house." From the municipality's viewpoint, it was a simple case of seventeen crowded, numbered shacks with over a hundred persons in them. When the armed security guards and bulldozers finished their work, only eight shacks remained.

I thought of the American embassy wife who joined the protesters when another part of Cape Town, District Six, was being bulldozed out of existence in 1970. With a small group of Christians from the slums, she stood against the fierce Atlantic wind and the destroyers and responded with the only gesture they could make, singing "O God, Our Help in Ages Past." I think of them every time I hear it sung.

Religious programming starts and ends the day on South African radio, and there are meditations and reflections before or after newscasts, sometimes with excellent choirs, at others with insipid stringed instrumental music. Most of the messages are inspirational mush, uplifting anecdotes revived from the Second World War, tales of adversity overcome, and personal mountains climbed. The state radio in such a controlled society does not allow religious commentators to reflect openly on political and social issues, although one preacher did slip in an allusion to "the local scene."

October 25. The long, winding street led up the hills to Bishops-court, Cape Town's most exclusive residential district, and to a vast, sprawling estate with red and gold miters on each side of the large white gateposts. It is the office and residence of the archbishop of the Province of Cape Town and Metropolitan of South Africa, the Most Reverend Desmond M. Tutu, as it was of his white predecessors for over a century.

"Where is your spouse?" asked the archbishop as he raced in the door in sparkling white cassock and purple sash. "Excuse me, we have a crisis. More black squatter families have been evicted by the government from what was described as a white area," and the archbishop and his staff were trying to come to their aid.

We entered the dark, rectangular, high-ceilinged library for tea. The room was lined with oil portraits of archbishops of the past century and with faded titles of Anglican theological books dating to the 1920s. A busy secretary occupied a corner of the room; two clerks with word processors filled the entryway. Looking out from the library was a vast, well-maintained formal garden and behind it the awesome view of Table Rock, the geological formation that dominates the Cape.

An elegant, elderly South African lady who lived next door told me of garden parties she had known in the past at Bishopscourt. "Cucumber sandwiches and Pimm's Cup?" I asked. "Strawberries and cream and Roses' tea deliciously weak," she replied.

One of the British ladies asked if I could take a picture of her with the bishop. A one-armed African laborer who had come to see the bishop joined us for tea, as did drivers who had been waiting outside. The bishop's assistant, Matt Esau, was making arrangements for a school bus full of black children to use the residence's swimming pool.

Just then a delegation of the Women of Achievement chapter from Hollywood, California, entered confidently through the dark, well-polished doors and formed a semicircle in the middle of the room. "Excuse me, I must greet my guests," said the bishop, moving out to chat with each person.

Tea was pumped from a mechanism we saw all over South Africa, a large plastic cylinder resembling a fire extinguisher, and Matt passed me a "Boston cake," which he said originated in America. "Keep praying for us, we are not doing badly," the archbishop said in his general greeting to the large group. (An open tea is held once a week.) He then started to leave, but the British lady who asked me to take her picture with him told him she had cancer and asked him to pray with her, which he did in Zulu.

I asked him to sign my New Testament, and while I was doing so, said, "Would there be any value in getting a small group of people, Dutch Reformed and Anglican, black and white, together in a quiet place, a desert place, for a few days to talk about reconciliation, the Passion Gospels, or Christ's vision of the Kingdom, or the Atonement as a way of bringing people together?" His expressive face registered curiosity and skepticism as I talked. "It would only work if it wasn't endless academic discussion," he said and was gone.

London, November 8. A cold, dreary morning and I picked my way around empty metal beer barrels and plastic bags of last night's garbage and headed from the Oxford and Cambridge University Club to St. James's, Piccadilly, for the early morning Eucharist. The Christopher Wren church, where William Temple had once been rector and William Blake a communicant, was filled with the soft early morning autumn light. Ten of us gathered in the cold side chapel, when Trevor Huddleston, who, as a Community of the Resurrection monk in South Africa, had been responsible for Desmond Tutu's interest in ministry, entered briskly from the dark sacristy. As a youth, Tutu was hospitalized with tuberculosis and Huddleston visited him frequently, from which a life-long friendship developed.

The Anglican monk, later archbishop of the Province of the Indian Ocean, led the service with dignity and clarity and few gestures. His gaunt frame, high cheekbones, and long hands were recognizable from news photos and book covers. The previous day he had addressed a London political rally of seventy thousand persons, but this morning he was deeply into liturgical language, pronouncing each word with the accumulation of decades of thoughtful reflection.

After the service I said, "Your book *Naught for Your Comfort* is responsible for my interest in the church in Africa. I read it when it came out in 1956 and several times since." I told him I had just seen Bishop Tutu. "I'm godfather to one of his children," he responded. "Desmond went to our mission school as a child and wanted to be a doctor. Then he came down with tuberculosis for two years and continued his school work in a different direction. He always was a brilliant student." I asked him to write the "God Bless Africa" prayer on a card, and we shook hands; his grip was frail but sure, his eyes keen. Then he disappeared quickly into one of the many large doors leading into the church building.

AFRICAN PRAYERS, PROVERBS, AND WISE SAYINGS

Africa's rich prayer life covers almost two millennia and includes Christian, Muslim, and indigenous expression. Many of the prayers deserve a place in world anthologies of worship. The following selection is an introduction to the depth and variety of African prayer life. Also included are African proverbs and wise sayings that, while not specifically prayer forms, contain insights into human nature and religion.

PERSONAL PRAYERS

A Morning Prayer (Boran, Kenya)

O God, you have let me pass the night in peace,
let me pass the day in peace.
Wherever I may go upon my way
which you made peaceable for me,
O God, lead my steps.
When I have spoken, keep lies away from me.
When I am hungry, keep me from murmuring.
When I am satisfied, keep me from pride.
Calling upon you, I pass the day,
O Lord, who has no Lord.[129]

A Morning Prayer: O Sun, as You Rise in the East (Abaluyia, Kenya)

O sun, as you rise in the east through God's leadership, wash away all evils of which I have thought throughout the night. Bless me, so that my enemies will not kill me and my family; guide me through hard work. O God, give me mercy upon our children who are suffering; bring riches today as the sun rises; bring all fortunes to me today.[130]

Morning Prayer of a Bushman (South Africa)

Father-Creator, Provider-from-of-old, Ancient-of-days, fresh-born from the womb of night are we. In the first dawning of

211

the new day draw we nigh unto thee. Forlorn are the eyes till
they've seen the Chief.[131]

Evening Prayer: The Sun Has Disappeared (Ghana)

The sun has disappeared.
I have switched off the light,
and my wife and children are asleep.
The animals in the forest are full of fear,
and so are the people on their mats.
They prefer the day with your sun to the night.
But I still know that your moon is there,
and your eyes and also your hands.
This day again
you led us wonderfully.
Everybody went to his mat satisfied and full.
Renew us during our sleep,
that in the morning
we may come afresh to our daily jobs.
Be with our brothers far away in Asia
who may be getting up now. Amen.[132]

A Hungry Man's Prayer (Baralong, South Africa)

God of our fathers, I lie down without food,
I lie down hungry,
Although others have eaten and lie down full.
Even if it be but a polecat, or a little rock rabbit,
Give me and I shall be grateful!
I cry to God, Father of my ancestors.[133]

A Ghanaian Truck Driver's Prayer

"Jesus Is Mine" (West African truck motto)
Lord,
the motor under me is running hot.
Lord,
there are twenty-eight people
and lots of luggage in the truck.
Underneath are my bad tires.
The brakes are unreliable.
Unfortunately I have no money,
and parts are difficult to get.
Lord, I did not overload the truck.

Lord,
"Jesus is mine"
is written on the vehicle,
for without him I would not drive a single mile.
The people in the back are relying on me.
They trust me because they see the words:
"Jesus is mine."
Lord,
I trust you!
First comes the straight road
with little danger,
I can keep my eyes on the women,
children, and chickens in the village.
But soon the road begins to turn,
it goes up and down,
it jumps and dances,
this death-road to Kumasi.
Tractors carrying mahogany trunks drive
as if there were no right or left.
Lord,
Kumasi is the temptation
to take more people than we should.
Let's overcome it!
The road to Accra is another problem.
Truck drivers try to beat the record,
although the road is poor
and has many holes
and there are many curves
before we come to the hills.
And finally to Akwasim.
Passing large churches in every village,
I am reminded of you, and in reverence
I take off my hat.
Now downhill in second gear.[134]

A Prayer for God's Protection (Nandi, Kenya)

O God, turn your ear to hear me. Protect my children and my
cattle, and even if you are weary, please be patient and listen to
my prayer. Under the dark cloak of night, the splendor of your
world sleeps on, invisible to us. And when your sun moves across
the sky each day, I continue to pray to you. May the spirits of

our departed ancestors, who can still exercise their influence on us, keep guard over us, from their places beyond the earth.[135]

Litany for a Sick Child (Aro, Sierra Leone)

Mother: O spirits of the past, this little one I hold is my child: she is your child also, therefore be gracious unto her.

Women (chanting): She has come into a world of trouble; sickness is in the world, and cold and pain: the pain you knew; the sickness with which you were familiar.

Mother: Let her sleep in peace, for there is healing in sleep: let none among you be angry with me or with my child.

Women: Let her grow; let her become strong; let her become full-grown; then will she offer such a sacrifice to you that will delight your hearts.[136]

Nuer Prayer for a Sick Person

In this prayer, a cow is offered as a means of expiation to God to cure a sick person, and a goat and a wild cucumber are added as well. The person who prays also asks what the village has done to cause such sickness.

Oh, God, let the man recover, let him become well, that he may have strength again. God, what is this? Leave the sick one with us, let him recover. Return to thine own body. Take thy cow, for she was ordered for the deliverance of souls. It is thee thyself who said thus. Take the cow that she may deliver the soul of the sick one. It is thou who created us, it is the cow that delivers souls. Here is the goat, and the wild cucumber. Let him recover! In what have we wronged? Give us the soul of the sick one. Thou art our father. Why shall we suffer from sickness all days? Give us the soul, we pray thee, our great-grandfather.

Prayer for a Woman in Labor (Nuer)

In this prayer a man, believing it is God's will for women to be child-bearers, asks what can be done for a barren woman "that she may create descendents."

God, what is it? Why can the woman not bear? It is thou who has ordered the woman to bear children, that she may create descendents, that the man's family may be preserved.

PRAYERS ABOUT DEATH

Commemoration of the Faithful Departed
(Mende, Sierra Leone)

O good and innocent dead: hear us, you guiding, all-knowing ancestors, you are neither blind nor deaf to this life we live: you did yourselves once share it. Help us therefore for the sake of our devotion, and for our good.[137]

Two Mensa Laments for the Departed

Of ancient Arabian descent, the Mensa, a Cushite people, live in northern Ethiopia. The two laments that follow are for a dead man and a youth. The first compares the deceased to a strong boulder and a rope that holds the country together. The geographical names represent regions of the country. In the second elegiac, the half-grown boy is compared to a young camel "of the dancing age."

I.

From the top of Haygat
Came down a heavy thunder.
Segli and Sabara
And Karer were settled.
He is a boulder, he leads Amhara,
He, having laid many traps,
The sword-hilt shone brightly,
Set with its jewels.
The sky from one end to the other,
He was the rope that held the land together.

II.

Truly, you mourners, say something for him.
About the breaking of the young camel, you mourners.
The young, the young one, the young.
The young, the young one, the young.
The young, young camel of the dancing age.
The boy of the resting place in the field.
And of dancing and of music.
He whose scarf hung down to the ground.
He whose sense of honor was high.
His ball and his stick.
He was at the age of the wooden spear.
Say to him *aulele*, you mourners.

And a bridegroom of sorrow.
A shoulder draws a cover over him.
We saw N _____, son of N _____, being broken.
May his foe be broken. But he himself, broken we saw him.[138]

Let us Behave gently (Yoruba, Nigeria)

Let us behave gently,
that we may die peacefully;
that our children may stretch out their hands
upon us in burial.[139]

An Islamic Meditation on Death

Hear the meaning when I speak to you:
Life resembles a lamp-flame in the wind;
It cannot be stopped when it goes out;
One moment one sees it; then it has gone out.

Or it resembles a roaring fire,
In a clearing, in the bushes;
There descends a cloudful of rain in the woods,
And it is extinguished; you could not blow life into it again.[140]

Two Reflections on Death (Beti, Cameroon)

The Beti people, a rain forest Bantu-speaking society in central Cameroon, believed misfortunes such as crop failures, sickness, and death were caused because ancestors were unhappy with the conduct of their living successors. Diviners determined the specific cause of a misfortune, and a council of villagers then met and offered sacrifices to propitiate the ancestors.

Death, having taken my father, also took my mother
And I went out on the roads, crying:
"Is it I that have brought death?"
Death, having taken my mother, also took my brother,
Death, having taken my brother, also took my husband's father,
Death, having taken my husband's father, also took my father's
    father
And I went out on the roads, crying:
"Is it I that have brought death to earth?"

Death was no stranger to the rain forest. Average life expectancy was under forty years, infant mortality was high. The Beti, like many

African societies, faced death with dignity and stoicism. This child's song against an inconsequential burial is not far-fetched, since funeral rites were usually limited to tribal elders.

> Do not bury me in a dunghill,
> For there people pour anything,
> Leave anything,
> Throw anything.
> Do not bury me in the courtyard,
> For there anyone can walk,
> And anyone can sit.
> Do not bury me under the footpath,
> Where anyone can pass.
> Do not bury me in the forest,
> Where there is too much noise,
> Where people cut anything,
> Where they hack trees down.
> Bury me among the raffia grass
> For there the frogs will cry,
> The frogs will cry a lot...
> My mother, do not cry![141]

PRAYERS FOR THE NATURAL WORLD

A Fire Blessing (Masi, Tanzania)

> Thank you, Father, for your free gift of fire.
> Because it is through fire that you draw near to us every day.
> It is with fire that you constantly bless us.
> Our Father, bless this fire today.
> With your power enter into it.
> Make this fire a worthy thing.
> A thing that carries your blessing.
> Let it become a reminder of your love.
> A reminder of life without end.
> Make the life of these people to be baptized like this fire.
> A thing that shines for the sake of people.
> A thing that shines for your sake.
> Father, heed this sweet-smelling smoke.
> Make their life also sweet smelling.
> A thing sweet smelling that rises to God.
> A holy thing. A thing fitting for you.[142]

God the Creator (Dinka, Sudan)

In the time when God created all things,
he created the sun.
And the sun is born and dies and comes again.
He created the moon,
And the moon is born and dies and comes again.
He created the stars,
And the stars are born and die and come again.
He created man.
And man is born and dies and comes not again.[143]

God and Satan, the Tree, the Twig, and the Bird (Nigerian)

God in heaven, you have helped my life to grow like a tree. Now
something has happened. Satan, like a bird, has carried in one
twig of his own choosing after another. Before I knew it he had
built a dwelling place and was living in it. Tonight, my father, I
am throwing out both the bird and the nest.[144]

God has Turned His Back on Us (Dinka, Sudan)

God has turned his back on us;
the words of men have made him angry.
And yet he will turn round again.
God has turned his back on us.
We are the children of our Maker
and are not afraid that he will kill us.[145]

Harvest Prayer (Betammaribe [Somba], Benin)

The time of harvest is over;
you have given us good crops;
we are going into the bush.
Now I call on you,
so that no evil falls on us
and our feet do not step on anything bad,
and that nothing bad touches us:
you guaranteed these things
and have kept your promise.
May the animals in the bush come to meet us;
let them come within our circle.
Let our arrows not miss them;
Let our arrows kill them.
Let the arrows not kill any of us.

You who have given us such a good harvest,
continue to walk before us
as you have been doing for our grandparents.[146]

Nuer Prayer before Taking Cattle across a River to New Pasturage

Possession of cattle was a traditional Nuer sign of wealth and each year the cattle were driven to pasturage across a river. In this prayer, a traditional religious figure prays for safe passage of the cattle and also offers a sacrifice to the river or river god.

Oh, God, it is thou who said I should ... bewitch the crocodile. The cattle have no more grass. Let the cattle go across the river that they may gaze on yonder shore. Oh God, it is thou who created the cow, that man might be nourished by her, let them swim safely across. (*Invocation to the spirit presiding over the river*) Let the cattle go safely across, all of them; let them reach the shore safely; let no one be touched by the crocodile. We are making a bargain. (*A ram is driven into the river as a sacrifice, after which the cattle cross the stream.*)[147]

Pharaoh's Hymn to the Sun

This ancient Egyptian hymn to the Sun, Ikhanton, fourteenth century B.C., bears many similarities to later Jewish and Christian religious canticles, an awareness of a cosmic creator who intervenes in human life, an omnipotent force present in all aspects of the universe, and a compassionate God as well.

Creator of the germ in woman,
Maker of seed in man,
Giving life to the son in the body of his mother,
Soothing him that he may not weep,
Nurse (even) in the womb,
Giver of breath to animate every one that he maketh!
When he cometh forth from the womb ...
On the day of his birth,
Thou openest his mouth in speech,
Thou suppliest his necessities.
When the fledgling in the egg chirps in the shell
Thou givest him breath therein to preserve him alive....
He goeth about upon his two feet
When he hath come forth therefrom.

How manifold are thy works!
They are hidden from before us
O sole God, whose power no other possesseth.
Thou didst create the earth according to thy heart.[148]

At the planting of seeds (East African planting prayer)

Seed we bring
Lord, to thee, wilt thou bless them, O Lord!
Gardens we bring
Lord, to thee, wilt thou bless them, O Lord!
Hoes we bring
Lord, to thee, wilt thou bless them, O Lord!
Knives we bring
Lord, to thee, wilt thou bless them, O Lord!
Hands we bring
Lord, to thee, wilt thou bless them, O Lord!
Ourselves we bring
Lord, to thee, wilt thou bless them, O Lord![149]

A Pygmy Prayer

In the beginning was God,
Today is God,
Tomorrow will be God.
Who can make an image of God?
He has no body.
He is the word which comes out of your mouth.
That word! It is no more,
It is past, and still it lives!
So is God.[150]

Sacrifice for Rain (Guir, Sudan)

We make this sacrifice in order to have rain.
If thou hearest our prayer, grant us rain.
Thou art our Father; everyone is here to ask rain of thee.
We are wrong-doers.
If one of us sheds blood, we will not have rain.
Thou art our Father. Grant us rain.
The earth is dry, our families are ruined.
Thou art our Father. Grant us rain.[151]

A SOUTH AFRICAN NATIONAL SERVICE OF THANKSGIVING PRAYER (May 1994)

O God our loving Eternal Parent, we praise you with a great shout of joy! Your ruling power has proved victorious! For centuries our land seemed too dark for sunrise, too bloody for healing, too sick for recovery, too hateful for reconciliation. But you have brought us into the daylight of liberation; you have healed us with new hope; you have stirred us to believe our nation can be reborn; we see the eyes of our sisters and brothers shining with resolve to build a new South Africa. Accept our prayers of praise and thanksgiving.

We thank you for our grandmothers and grandfathers who taught us to believe in liberation. We thank you for those great names to all our country now: Luthuli, Sobukwe, Biko, Visser, Joseph, Ngoyi, Hani, Tambo, and a thousand others. Many are named with our own names, treasured in our hearts, honored in our memories. Many rest in graves in other lands so that South African love embraces the world. We remember those thousands of people overseas who gave themselves in solidarity that our nation might be changed.

For all of these we thank and praise you. We thank you that democracy has come, and for the wonder of a government of national unity. We thank you for the commitment among all people to seek justice and peace, homes and jobs, education and health, reconciliation and reconstruction. We thank you that because apartheid has gone we can turn from the days of destruction to the work of reconstruction together. For our rich variety, our rich vision and our rich land, we thank you.

We thank you for the spiritual power which gives us new birth. You have given us the courage to change our minds, to open our hearts to those we despised, and to discover we can disagree without being enemies. We are not winners and losers, but citizens who push and pull together to move the nation forward. We thank you for the Good News that you will always be with us, and we will always overcome: that love will conquer hatred; that tolerance will conquer antagonism; that cooperation will conquer conflict; that your Holy Spirit can empower our spirits; through Jesus Christ our Lord.[152]

NKOSI SIKELEL' IAFRIKA, GOD BLESS AFRICA
(written 1897)

"Nkosi Sikelel' iAfrika," God Bless Africa, is often called the African National Anthem. Enoch Sontonga, a prolific Methodist composer and teacher at a Johannesburg mission school, composed the work in 1897. Soon it became a popular church hymn and a political anthem, and singing it in the pre-independence era was an act of defiance against South Africa's racist government. In 1994 the independent country's president, Nelson Mandela, decreed that both it and *Die Stem*, the "Call of South Africa," would be the country's national anthems, and in 1996 both pieces were combined in shortened form as the national anthem. What follows is the original version of "Nkosi Sikelel' iAfrika" in the Lovedale English translation. Reflecting South Africa's multiple language and ethnic groups, different verses are sung in Xhosa, Sotho, Zulu, Afrikaans, and English.

Lord, bless Africa;
May her horn rise up high;
Hear Thou our prayers and bless us.

Chorus

Descend, O Spirit,
Descend, O Holy Spirit.
Bless our chiefs
May they remember their Creator.
Fear him and revere Him,
That He may bless them.

Bless the public men,
Bless also all the youth
That they may carry the land with patience
And that Thou mayst bless them.

Bless the wives
And also all young women;
Lift up all the young girls
And bless them.

Bless the ministers
of all the churches of this land;
Endue them with Thy Spirit
And bless them.

Bless agriculture and stock raising
Banish all famine and diseases;
Fill the land with good health
And bless it.

Bless our efforts
Of union and self-uplift
Of education and mutual understanding
And bless them.

Lord, bless Africa
Blot out all its wickedness
And its transgressions and sins,
And bless it.[153]

OUR LADY OF AFRICA
(Ethiopian Orthodox)

O my Lady, the holy Virgin Mary, thou hast been likened to many things, yet there is nothing which compares with thee. Neither heaven can match thee, nor the earth equal as much as the measure of thy womb. For thou didst confine the Unconfinable, and carry him whom none has power to sustain.

The Cherubim are but thy Son's chariot bearers, and even the Seraphim bow down in homage at the throne of thy Firstborn. How sublime is the honor of thy royal estate.

And now I cry unto thy Son, O Virgin, saying:

O Lord, remember thy descent from the heights of Heaven and thine indwelling within the womb of the Holy Virgin.

Remember how thou wast laid in a manger, wrapped in swaddling clothes, in a stable.

O Lord remembering all this, do not disregard thy sinful servant. Help me with thy deliverance and cover me with the shield of thy salvation for the sake of Mary thy Mother; for the sake of her breasts which suckled thee and her lips which kissed thee; for the sake of her hands which touched thee and her arms which embraced thee; for the sake of her spirit and flesh which thou didst take from her to be part of thyself.

The Virgin's womb is greater than the mystical chariot of light, loftier than the heights of the firmament, more sublime than the distances of space, more glorious than the Seraphim and Cherubim.

The Virgin's womb was the gateway to Heaven, which without being opened, became the way in and the way out of the Son of Righteousness. The Virgin's womb was the ark and dwelling-place of the Lord God Adonay.

And now let us praise God, saying: Glory to thee; glory to him who sent thee; and glory to the Holy Spirit who is co-equal with thee.

Honor to her who bore thee; homage to her who gave birth to thee; devotion to thy mother; and holiness to her who tended thee.[154]

A XHONA PRAISE-POEM
TO GOD THE CREATOR

Ntsikana (c. 1780–c. 1821) was a Xhosa chief's son who wrote several Christian hymns and praise-poems, including "Ulo Tixo omkulu, ngosezulwini" (He is the Great God, Who is in heaven). It lists the praise-names of God, and its mood is solemn, plaintive, and moving, evoking among its South African audiences the sort of response "A Mighty Fortress Is Our God" might among German Lutherans.

He is the Great God, Who is in heaven;
Thou art Thou, Shield of truth.
Thou art Thou, Stronghold of truth.
Thou art Thou, Thicket of truth.
Thou art Thou who dwellest in the highest.
He, Who created life (below), created (life) above.
That Creator who created, created heaven,
This maker of the stars, and the Pleiades.
A star flashing forth, it was telling us.
The Maker of the blind, does he not make them of purpose?
The trumpet sounded, it is calling us.
As for his chase, He hunteth for souls.
He, Who amalgamates flocks rejecting each other.
He the Leader, Who has led us
Thou art the great Mantle for us to put on
Those hands of Thine, they are wounded.
Thy blood, why is it streaming?
Thy blood, it was shed for us.
This great price, have we called for it?
This home of Thine, have we called for it?[155]

AFRICAN PROVERBS AND WISE SAYINGS

African cultures are rich in proverbs and wise sayings, and much of the collective wisdom of peoples, including their religious sentiments and observations about human nature, are conveyed through such sayings, as well as through animal stories, riddles, and folk narratives.

Proverbs

It is not his deserts that a man gets but his destiny. (Fulani)

No matter how far the town, there is another beyond it. (Fulani)

He who rides the horse of greed at a gallop will pull it up at the door of shame. (Fulani)

If death encircles the mortar, it wants not the mortar but the pounder. (Fulani)

Alive he was insufficient, dead he is missed. (Fulani)

It is when one is in trouble that he remembers God. (Hausa)

A stone in the water does not comprehend how parched the hill is. (Hausa)

The man with one eye thanks God only after he has seen a blind man. (Hausa)

Bowing to a dwarf will not prevent you from standing erect again. (Hausa)

Faults are like a hill: You stand on your own and talk about those of other people. (Hausa)

A conscientious man will repay every good deed done for him except the digging of his grave. (Hausa)

It is the fool who proclaims, "The insults are not meant for me but for my colleague." (Ashanti)

If you swear an oath alone in a pit, still it leaks out. (Ashanti)

"I Will Do It Later On" is a brother to "I Didn't Do It." (Ashanti)

It is because of man that the blacksmith makes weapons. (Ashanti)

If you do not allow a friend to get a nine, you yourself will never get a ten. (Ashanti)

Even though you may be taller than your father you still are not his equal. (Ashanti)

The slave is naturally the guilty party. (Ashanti)

If one wants to catch a large fish he must give something to the stream. (Dahomean)

Mawu [the creator] sent sickness into the world but also sent medicine to cure. (Dahomean)

When one is at sea he does not quarrel with the boatman. (Dahomean)[156]

Wise Sayings

A big goat does not sneeze without reason.

A fig tree found on the way is enough to keep you from starving.

A full stomach does not last overnight.

A house that is built by God will be completed.

A lion does not eat its own cubs.

A stick that is far away cannot kill a snake.

An African should not be made to suffer the loss of an arm from a gunshot in Europe.

An elephant never fails to carry its tusk.

Do not desire a woman with beautiful breasts — if you have no money.

God exercises vengeance in silence.

God is sharper than a razor.

God knows the things of tomorrow.

God saves the afflicted according to His will.

He who eats alone, dies alone.

He who has diarrhea knows the direction of the door without being told.

If God dishes you rice in a basket, do not wish to eat soup.

If the calf sucks too greedily, it tears away the mother's udder.

If you want to speak to God, tell it to the wind.

Never mind that your nose is ugly, as long as you can breathe through it.

One fly causes the whole carcass of a cow to rot.

People get fed up even with honey.

Sleep killed the lion.

The cock in drinking water raises its head to God in thankfulness.

The earth is the mother of all.

The leopard that visits you is the one that kills you.

The poor man's main tool is his tongue with which he defends himself.

The strength of the crocodile is the water.

"Though I am not edible," says the vulture, "yet I nurse my eggs in the branches of a high tree because man cannot be trusted."

Two male hippos do not stay in the same pond.

We are born from the womb of our mother; we are buried in the womb of the earth.

We do not see God, we only see His works.

You can trust neither the rainy season sky nor babies' bottoms.[157]

NOTES

✸✸✸✸✸✸✸✸✸

1. Lowell Mason, "From Greenland's Icy Mountains," Hymn 254, *The Hymnal of the Protestant Episcopal Church in the United States, 1940* (New York: Church Pension Fund, 1943).

2. Jacques Thobie, "Le bilan coloniale in 1914," in *Histoire de la France coloniale, 1914–1990*, ed. Jacques Thobie, Gilbert Meynier, Catherine Coquery-Vidrovitch, and Charles-Robert Ageron (Paris: Armand Colin, 1990), 45–47.

3. Roland Oliver, "By Word of Mouth: How Africans Themselves Propagated the Gospel Message before the Missionaries Came" (London: TLS, September 29, 2000), 3.

4. "Western Theological Models No Longer Dominate," *enlist@epicom.org*, October 16, 2000.

5. Walter L. Williams, *Black Americans and the Evangelization of Africa, 1877–1900* (Madison: University of Wisconsin Press, 1982), 187.

6. Four recent survey works on the history of Christianity in Africa are John Bauer, *2000 Years of Christianity in Africa: An African Church History*, 2d ed. (Boston: Daughters of St. Paul, 1998); Adrian Hastings, *The Church in Africa, 1450–1950* (Oxford: Clarendon Press, 1996); Elizabeth Isichei, *A History of Christianity in Africa: From Antiquity to the Present* (Grand Rapids: Eerdmans, 1995); and Bengt Sundkler and Christopher Steed, *A History of the Church in Africa* (New York: Cambridge University Press, 2000).

7. A White Father explained the reason: if a priest went alone he would be tempted by alcohol or women, if two went together they would quarrel, if three were assigned, a leader would emerge and a team would form.

8. Diana L. Eck, *Encountering God: A Spiritual Journey from Bozeman to Banaras* (Boston: Beacon Press, 1993), 94.

9. Quoted in Jacques Dupuis, *Toward a Christian Theology of Religious Pluralism* (Maryknoll, N.Y.: Orbis Books, 1997), 288.

10. Andrew F. Walls, *The Missionary Movement in Christian History: Studies in the Transmission of Faith* (Maryknoll, N.Y.: Orbis Books, 2000), 15. For those who would examine the question of pluralist-vs.-exclusivist positions in detail, two thoughtful works are Diana L. Eck, *Encountering God: A Spiritual Journey from Bozeman to Banaras*, and Jacques Dupuis, *Toward a Christian Theology of Religious Pluralism*, which brought the seventy-four-year-old Jesuit scholar the opprobrium of Cardinal Ratzinger and the Roman Curia and gave his book instant notoriety. An effort to bring the world's religions together for common discussion and action without attempting to unify their theological positions is the effort of Bishop William E. Swing of United Religions, 1055 Taylor Street, San Francisco, CA 94108.

11. Frederick William Faber, "There's a Wideness in God's Mercy," hymn 469, *Prayer Book and Hymnal, 1982, According to the Use of the Episcopal*

Church (New York: Church Hymnal Corporation, 1986). See Eck, *Encountering God*, 186.

12. Adrian Hastings, *The Church in Africa, 1450–1950* (Oxford: Clarendon Press, 1996), 79–85.

13. Ibid., 83.

14. Rex Niven, *Nine Great Africans* (London: G. Bell and Sons, 1964).

15. USPG: Africa & Asia, vol. 2, 1902, in Raymond Eveleigh, "Roland Allen: Prophet of Non-Stipendiary Ministry," *www.revray.co.uk/ministry/nsm.html*.

16. Sermon note for September 29, 1935, Rhodes House collection, in Hubert J. B. Allen, *Roland Allen: Pioneer, Priest, and Prophet* (Cincinnati: Forward Movement Publications, 1995), 155.

17. James Wellard, *Desert Pilgrimage* (London: Hutchinson of London, 1970), 77. See also Douglas Burton-Christie, *The Word in the Desert* (New York: Oxford University Press, 1993).

18. Ibid., 81.

19. Beverley B. Mack and Jean Boyd, *One Woman's Jihad: Nana Asma'u, Scholar and Scribe* (Bloomington: Indiana University Press, 2000), 122.

20. *Prayer Book and Hymnal* (New York: Church Hymnal Corporation, 1986), 864.

21. *Celebrating Common Prayer* (London: Mowbray, 1994), 445.

22. Desmond Tutu, *An African Prayerbook* (London: Hodder & Stoughton, 1996), 10.

23. Garry Wills, *Saint Augustine* (New York: A Lipper/Viking Book, 1999), 115–116.

24. Tutu, *An African Prayerbook*, 135–136.

25. Quoted in Wills, *Saint Augustine*, 24–25.

26. "Significant Steps in the Life of Mother Josephine Bakhita," *www.nbccongress.org/facts/josephine.htm*.

27. Donald Woods, *Biko* (New York: Henry Holt and Company, 1987), 116–117.

28. Quoted in Lamin Sanneh, *Abolitionists Abroad: American Blacks and the Making of Modern West Africa* (Cambridge: Harvard University Press, 1999), 211.

29. "Eugéne Casalis," in Horton Davies, *Great South African Christians* (New York: Oxford University Press, Geoffrey Cumberlege, 1951), 57–66.

30. "Mother Cecile," in Davies, *Great South African Christians*, 160–168.

31. Isichei, *A History of Christianity in Africa*, 249.

32. G. Shepperson and T. Price, *Independent African: John Chilembwe and the Origins, Setting and Significance of the Nyasaland Native Rising of 1915* (Edinburgh: Edinburgh University Press, 1958), 234–235.

33. Hastings, *The Church in Africa*, 489.

34. Henry Chadwick, *Early Christian Thought and the Classical Tradition: Studies in Justin, Clement, and Origin* (New York: Oxford University Press, 1966).

35. "François Colliard," in Davies, *Great South African Christians*, 120–133.

36. A. G. Mondini, *Africa or Death: A Biography of Bishop Daniel Comboni, Founder of the Missionary Societies of the Verona Fathers and the Verona Sisters* (Boston: St. Paul Editions, 1964).

37. "Ernest Creux and Paul Berthoud," in Davies, *Great South African Christians*, 151–159.

38. Lamin Sanneh, "The CMS and the African Transformation: Samuel Ajayi Crowther and the Opening of Nigeria," in *The Church Mission Society and World Christianity, 1799–1999*, ed. Kevin Ward and Brian Stanley (Grand Rapids: Eerdmans, 2000), 173–197.

39. Quoted in Walter L. Williams, *Black Americans and the Evangelization of Africa, 1977–1900* (Madison: University of Wisconsin Press, 1982), 11.

40. Ibid.

41. "Christ for the World We Sing," hymn 537, in *Prayer Book and Hymnal, 1982*.

42. "St. Cyril of Alexandria," *Catholic Encyclopedia*, vol. 4, 1908, online edition 1999 by Kevin Knight, *www.newadvent.org/cathen/04592b.htm*.

43. Helen Waddell, *The Desert Fathers* (London: Constable & Co., 1994).

44. Quoted in Wellard, *Desert Pilgrimage,* 106.

45. Ibid., 54.

46. Sanneh, *Abolitionists Abroad,* 24–31.

47. Olaudah Equiano, *The Interesting Narrative of the Life of Olaudah Equiano, Written by Himself,* ed. Robert J. Allison (Boston: Bedford Books, 1995), 1–23.

48. "The Life of Olaudah Equiano," *www.bl.uk/collections/africa/equiano.html*

49. Farid Esack, *On Being a Muslim: Finding a Religious Path in the World Today* (Oxford: Oneworld, 1999), 25–27.

50. *The Koran,* trans. J. M. Rodwell (North Clarendon, Vt.: Everyman, 2000), 27.

51. "Church History Documents: The Martyrdom of Perpetua and Felicitas," *www.churchhistory.net/documents/perpetua.html*.

52. Gonville ffrench-Beytagh, *Encountering Darkness* (New York: Seabury Press, 1973), p. 41.

53. Ibid., 144, 276.

54. Charles de Foucauld, *Letters from the Desert*, trans. Barbara Lucas (London: Burns & Oates, 1977), 143–144. See also Robert Ellsberg, "Charles de Foucauld," in Susan Bergman, ed., *Martyrs* (Maryknoll, N.Y.: Orbis Books, 1998).

55. Quoted in *Charles de Foucauld,* writings selected with an introduction by Robert Ellsberg (Maryknoll, N.Y.: Orbis Books, 1999), 89.

56. Ellsberg, "Charles de Foucauld," in Bergman, *Martyrs,* 297.

57. Eric Itzkin, *Gandhi's Johannesburg: Birthplace of Satyagraha* (Johannesburg, South Africa: Witwatersrand University Press, 2000), 1.

58. "Robert Gray," in Davies, *Great South African Christians,* 53.

59. J. R. H. Moorman, *History of the Church in England*, 3d ed. (Harrisburg, Pa.: Morehouse Publishers, 1994), 404.

60. *The Proper for the Lesser Feasts and Fasts*, 3d ed. (New York: Church Hymnal Corporation, 1980), 361.

61. "Commemorating the Death of Imam Abdullah Haron," *www.islam.org .za/claremont/29September2000.htm*.

62. David A. Shank (abridged by Jocelyn Murray), *The Prophet Harris: The "Black Elijah" of West Africa* (Leiden: E. J. Brill, 1994), 227.

63. Sheila S. Walker, "The Message as the Medium: The Harrist Churches of the Ivory Coast and Ghana," in *African Christianity: Patterns of Religious Continuity*, ed. George Bond, Walton Johnson, and Sheila S. Walker (New York: Academic Press, a Subsidiary of Harcourt Brace Jovanovich, Publishers, 1979), 9–63.

64. Desmond Tutu, "An Appreciation of the Rt. Revd. Trevor Huddleston," in *Trevor Huddleston: Essays on His Life and Work*, ed. Deborah Duncan Honor (New York: Oxford University Press, 1988), 2.

65. "U.S. Priest Killed in Kenya," *Christian Century*, September 13, 2000.

66. "Khama Boikano," in Davies, *Great South African Christians*, 101–111.

67. Wyatt MacGaffey, *Modern Kongo Prophets: Religion in a Plural Society* (Bloomington: Indiana University Press, 1983), 1.

68. Quoted in Elizabeth Isichei, *A History of Christianity in Africa*, 200.

69. Anne Luck, *African Saint: The Story of Apolo Kivebulaya* (London: SCM Press, 1963).

70. Ibid., 137.

71. *www.wbaptist.com/fsi/kerux/990829–sermon.htm*.

72. Hastings, *The Church in Africa*, 572.

73. Ibid., 573.

74. Ligon Duncan, "Early African Apologists, 3–5," *www.fpcjackson.org/ resources/church-history/earlyafrapolog.htm*.

75. Jeremy Murray-Brown, *Faith and the Flag: The Opening of Africa* (London: George Allen & Unwin, 1977).

76. Quoted in Hastings, *The Church in Africa*, 296.

77. John Bauer, *Two Thousand Years of Christianity in Africa: An African Church History* (Nairobi, Kenya: Pauline Publications Africa, 1998), 136–141.

78. Quoted in Bengt Sundkler and Christopher Steed, *The History of the Church in Africa* (New York: Cambridge University Press, 2000), 456.

79. "A Vocation to Save Life," *Christian Century*, March 14, 2001, 5.

80. Albert Luthuli, *Let My People Go* (London: Collins, 1962, reissued 1982).

81. Quoted in Robert Ellsberg, *All Saints: Daily Reflections on Saints, Prophets, and Witnesses for Our Time* (New York: Crossroad, 1997), 311.

82. Mary Craig, *Six Modern Martyrs* (New York: Crossroad, 1984).

83. Nicholas Niyungeko, "What's New in Burundi!" e-mail from Servane Ronin-Vermauwt to Frederick Quinn, January 10, 2001.

84. Ibid.

85. *The Proper for the Lesser Feasts and Fasts*, 237.

86. Andrew Chandler, ed., *The Terrible Alternative* (London: Cassell, 1998).

87. "Robert Moffat of Kuruman," in Davies, *Great South African Christians,* 19–30.

88. *The Proper for the Lesser Feasts and Fasts,* 213.

89. John V. Taylor and Dorthea A. Lehmann, *Christians of the Copperbelt* (London: SCM Press, 1961), 257–258.

90. Itzkin, *Gandhi's Johannesburg,* 33–36, 82–85.

91. Jerry Hames, "Marc Nikkel: 'Apostle' to Sudan's Oppressed," *Episcopal Life,* October 20, 2000, 3.

92. Linda E. Thomas, "Christinah Nku: A Woman at the Center of Healing Her Nation," in *Embracing the Spirit,* ed. Emilie M. Townes (Maryknoll, N.Y.: Orbis Books, 1997), 65.

93. Hastings, *The Church in Africa,* 218.

94. Quoted in ibid., 220.

95. Quoted in ibid.

96. Henry Chadwick, *Early Christian Thought and the Classical Tradition: Studies in Justin, Clement, and Origin* (New York: Oxford University Press, 1966).

97. Tutu, *An African Prayerbook,* 42.

98. Saint Pachomius in *The Coptic Encyclopedia,* ed. Aziz S. Atiya (New York: Macmillan Publishing Company, 1991), 6:1859–1863.

99. Tutu, *An African Prayerbook,* 14–15.

100. Alan Paton, *Cry, the Beloved Country* (Harmondsworth, Middlesex: Penguin Books, 1958), 7.

101. Ibid., 72.

102. "Francis Pfanner," in Davies, *Great South African Christians,* 85–92.

103. Andrew Ross, *John Philip (1775–1851): Missions, Race and Politics in South Africa* (Aberdeen: Aberdeen University Press, 1986).

104. Interview with the author, American University Law School, Washington, D.C., March 3, 2000. See also Albie Sachs, *The Soft Vengeance of an African Freedom Fighter* (Berkeley: University of California Press, 2000).

105. Albert Schweitzer, "On the Edge of the Primeval Forest," *www.pcisys.net/~jnf.*

106. "Memoirs of Childhood and Youth," trans. C. T. Campion, *www.pcisys.net/~jnf/prayer.html.*

107. Paul Coulon and Paule Brasseur, *Libermann, 1802–1852: Une pensée et une mystique missionnaires,* preface by Léopold Sédar Senghor (Paris: Éditions du Cerf, 1988), 9–11.

108. *web.uflib.ufl.edu/cm/africana/senghor.htm.* See also Melvin Dixon, trans., *The Collected Poetry of Léopold Sédar Senghor* (Charlottesville: University of Virginia Press, 1991).

109. Farid Esack, *On Being a Muslim: Finding a Religious Path in the World Today* (Oxford: Oneworld, 1999), 136.

110. Ibid.

111. W. P. Livingstone, *Mary Slessor of Calabar* (New York: Doubleday Doren, [1920]), 299.

112. D. Williams, *Umfundisi: A Biography of Tiyo Soga, 1829–1871* (Lovedale, South Africa: Lovedale Press, 1978).

113. Elisabeth Isichei, *Entirely for God: The Life of Michael Iwene Tansi,* Cistercian Studies 43 (Kalamazoo, Mich.: Cistercian Publications, 1980 and 2000).

114. Father Chidi Denis Isizoh, "Web Page on Blessed Cyprian Tansi," *www.afrikaworld.net/tansi4.htm.*

115. "Tertullian," *http://listserv.american.edu/catholic/church/fathers/ tertullian/tertullian.html*

116. Ibid.

117. Michelle Landis, "Desmond Tutu," *www.wagingpeace.org/hero/ desmond-tutu.html.*

118. Desmond Tutu, "Reconciliation in Port-Apartheid South Africa: Experiences of the Truth Commission," *www.virginia.edu/nobel/transcript/tutu.html.*

119. Tutu, *An African Prayerbook,* 80.

120. C. Peter Williams, *The Ideal of the Self-Governing Church* (New York: E. J. Brill, 1990).

121. Quoted in Wilbert R. Shenk, *Henry Venn: Missionary Statesman* (Maryknoll, N.Y.: Orbis Books, 1983), 26.

122. John K. Thornton, *The Kongolese Saint Anthony: Dona Beatriz Kimpa Vita and the Antonian Movement, 1684–1706* (New York: Cambridge University Press, 1998), 177.

123. Ibid., 177–184.

124. Ibid., 216.

125. "John White," in Davies, *Great South African Christians,* 169–180.

126. Ibid., 179.

127. Douglas H. Johnson, "Salim Wilson: The Black Evangelist of the North," *Journal of Religion in Africa* 21, no. 1 (1991): 26–41.

128. "Spread, O Spread, Thou Mighty Word," hymn 530, *Prayer Book and Hymnal, 1982.*

129. Tutu, *An African Prayerbook,* 121.

130. Ibid., 120.

131. Quoted in George Appleton, ed., *The Oxford Book of Prayer* (New York: Oxford University Press, 1985), 350.

132. Tutu, *An African Prayerbook,* 122–123.

133. Appleton, *The Oxford Book of Prayer,* 350.

134. Tutu, *An African Prayerbook,* 134.

135. Ibid., 72–73.

136. Quoted in Appleton, *The Oxford Book of Prayer,* 349–350.

137. Tutu, *An African Prayerbook,* 126.

138. Harold Courlander, *A Treasury of African Folklore* (New York: Crown, 1975), 568.

139. Tutu, *An African Prayerbook,* 134.

140. Quoted in Kenneth W. Harrow, "Islamic Literature in Africa," *The History of Islam in Africa,* ed. Nehemia Levtzion and Randall L. Pouwels (Athens, Ohio: Ohio University Press, 2000), 526.

141. Collected by the author while doing field work in Yaounde, Cameroon, 1967.

142. Tutu, *An African Prayerbook*, 129–130.

143. Quoted in Appleton, *The Oxford Book of Prayer*, 348.

144. Tutu, *An African Prayerbook*, 44.

145. Ibid., 44.

146. Ibid., 131.

147. Courlander, *A Treasury of African Folklore*, 520.

148. Tutu, *An African Prayerbook*, 19–20.

149. Quoted in Appleton, *The Oxford Book of Prayer*, 172–173.

150. Tutu, *An African Prayerbook*, 8.

151. Quoted in Appleton, *The Oxford Book of Prayer*, 348.

152. Tutu, *An African Prayerbook*, 64–65.

153. "Nkosi Sikelel' iAfrika," South Africa's National Anthem, *www.polity .org.za/misc/nkosi.html*.

154. Tutu, *An African Prayerbook*, 17–19.

155. Quoted in Bengt Sundkler and Christopher Steed, *A History of the Church in Africa* (New York: Cambridge University Press, 2000), 348.

156. Courlander, *A Treasury of African Folklore*, 37–38, 66–67, 183.

157. John S. Mbiti, *Introduction to African Religion*, 2d ed. (Oxford: Heinemann Educational Publishers, 1991), 208–212.